EXECUTIVE SKILLS AND WRITING INSTRUCTION

THE EXECUTIVE SKILLS FOR EDUCATORS SERIES

Kelly B. Cartwright, *Series Editor*

Helping students become active, self-regulated learners and thinkers is key to their academic and life success. This series gives K–12 educators innovative tools to understand and promote the development of executive skills—the brain-based capacities that enable students to coordinate and direct their thoughts, feelings, and behaviors toward desired goals. Practical and accessible, books in the series address multiple dimensions of teaching and learning, behavior, and emotional well-being in today's diverse classrooms. Volumes present clear strategies for lesson planning, instruction, and intervention, complete with engaging vignettes and reproducible/downloadable materials to facilitate implementation.

Executive Skills and Reading Comprehension, Second Edition:
A Guide for Educators
Kelly B. Cartwright

Executive Skills and Writing Instruction:
Developing Self-Regulated, Thinking Writers
Leslie E. Laud

Executive Skills and Writing Instruction

Developing Self-Regulated, Thinking Writers

LESLIE E. LAUD

Series Editor's Note by Kelly B. Cartwright

THE GUILFORD PRESS
New York London

A Division of Guilford Publications, Inc.
www.guilford.com

Printed in the United States of America

This book is printed on acid-free paper.

For product and safety concerns within the EU, please contact *GPSR@taylorandfrancis.com,* Taylor & Francis Verlag GmbH, Kaufingerstraße 24, 80331 München, Germany.

Last digit is print number: 9 8 7 6 5 4 3 2

Library of Congress Cataloging-in-Publication Data is available from the publisher.

ISBN 978-1-4625-5894-0 (paperback) — ISBN 978-1-4625-5895-7 (hardcover)

For my mother

Series Editor's Note

I am so grateful to Leslie Laud for writing this book! As educators, we hope to develop in our students the kinds of self-regulated management of reading and writing processes that enable our students to comprehend and compose in ever-growing ways. Research explicitly points to ways executive skills—those mental self-management skills that enable us to recruit and coordinate our thoughts, feelings, and behaviors to achieve goals—contribute to strong literacy outcomes.

That's why I wrote and revised *Executive Skills and Reading Comprehension: A Guide for Educators* (now in its second edition). Yet, until Leslie wrote this book, we had no such guide for how these important thinking skills show up in—and can be developed in—our students' writing. Not only does Leslie pull back the curtain to help us visualize how to equip students to be amazing, self-regulated writers, but she also models these skills herself in the writing of this book, from planning to revision.

I believe Leslie's readers will find incredible supports in these pages for their journeys as writing educators. In Chapter 8, Leslie writes that "writing becomes about creating possibilities and making the world better." She has made our world better in writing this book.

KELLY B. CARTWRIGHT, PhD
University of North Carolina at Charlotte

About the Author

Leslie E. Laud, EdD, is Director at thinkSRSD, an educational consulting group that focuses on evidence-based writing instruction. She has served as Adjunct Professor at Bank Street College of Education and Columbia University, and as Research Partner at the Written Expression Language and Literacy Collaborative. Dr. Laud has worked as a principal, as a teacher in special education and general education settings, and as a literacy specialist. She has served as a Principal Investigator on federally funded research grants and has published empirical studies on writing instruction in peer-reviewed journals. She regularly speaks at conferences nationally and internationally, and consults to state departments of education, districts, and schools on how to implement evidence-based practices for teaching writing. Dr. Laud is passionate about implementation science, translational research, and human-centered design approaches that make it easier for educators to use practices found to succeed.

Acknowledgments

About 15 years into my career, I never imagined I'd discover a new way to teach writing that would change the trajectory of the next 20 years and bring me (and my students!) so much more joy. Nor did I imagine I would then carry this over to new teachers and students at scale. Back in the late 1980s, when I studied at Columbia University, Dr. Lyn Corno taught courses on cognition and early self-regulated learning, as a pioneer in this area. She had us read the initial articles that Dr. Carol Sue Englert, Dr. Karen Harris, and others were publishing at the time, sparking my lifelong passion. I then began testing out this line of instruction in my classroom. Doing so helped me to bridge the gap between the theoretical and controlled-studies research I had learned in graduate school to practice in my own teaching. I then spent two decades teaching this approach myself and helping teachers learn it, carefully augmenting and adapting evidence-based practices to maintain core fidelity to the key underlying mechanisms that made them effective, but in ways that made them a lighter lift with higher impact. As a speech and language pathologist, Dr. Charles Haynes then helped me fill in the key language subcomponents and develop a larger vision around how language learning works. Dr. Melissa Feller taught me word boxes, a vital strategy for helping students write better. Together, the integration of these linguistic approaches enabled us to bring evidence-based practices for teaching writing to schools, but also in ways that sustain in their settings over time.

I'm grateful to the academics, coaches, and school leaders, and most especially to the teachers, who offered extensive, detailed feedback that enable us to continue iterating and improving. I also express gratitude to the esteemed researchers and practitioners who shared materials and feedback on drafts of this book, particularly Dr.

Linnea Ehri, Dr. Virginia Berninger, Nathaniel Hansford, and Jennifer Newman. A special thanks to my colleagues at thinkSRSD for holding down the fort so well during the many days that I disappeared to write this book. I am also grateful to my children for taking part in countless writing lessons, and my family for supporting me in finding the time to write this book. Many thanks to my editor at The Guilford Press, Craig Thomas, for encouragement, for pushing my thinking and clarity with his own deep expertise in the subject matter, and for making the book-writing process uplifting and delightful—as well as to the full production team at Guilford. I'm also particularly indebted to Dr. Kelly Cartwright for choosing me for this project, believing in me, inspiring my best work, meticulously reviewing the precision of research citations and subtle points throughout this book, and sharing her wisdom all along. Dr. Cartwright went far above and beyond as a series editor, showing her commitment to getting this right for the benefit, ultimately, of children.

Contents

Purchasers of this book can download and print copies of the reproducible appendices at *www.guilford.com/laud-forms* for personal use or use with students (see copyright page for details).

CHAPTER 1

Executive Skills

What They Are, and Why They Matter in Learning to Write

One of the goals of education is not simply to fill students with facts and information but to help them learn how to learn.

—ZARETTA HAMMOND

This book invites you to enter through two red, double doors and tour a school where explicit writing instruction works to build all levels of literacy—laying a foundation for students to use writing to discover what they think, share their messages, and, ultimately, *learn how to learn*. This includes learning *how to think*, as writing not only makes thinking visible but also offers a pathway to sharpen it. Our tour is based on examples from real schools that have successfully made the leap to implement evidence-based practices for teaching writing, now commonly termed the *science of writing*. This science of writing is grounded in the core principles of cognitive science, which focuses on how students learn, and is receiving growing attention (Swain, 2024). This book takes the next step to *cognitive science applied*—how real teachers apply these principles in granular and replicable ways that you can easily carry to your classroom tomorrow.

Back to our tour. After the teachers in our school learned and began using these principles in ways aligned with what research shows works, they saw remarkable gains in writing. These gains carried over to support English language arts (ELA) proficiency growth on their state assessments, with similar results seen in nearly 100 schools also using the thinkSRSD approach presented in this book (Hansford et al., 2024). Students compose daily across all disciplines, using writing as a tool to raise content learning (Graham et al., 2020) along with all the underlying levels of literacy, language, and reasoning. Yet—and perhaps this is the most inspiring fact—these students *self-regulate* as well, meaning that they can now independently take themselves through using the writing process.

From the first moment students pick up a pencil through when they craft advanced essays, writing raises all areas of literacy. Whether it is a kindergartener who labors to sound out words they want to write or a high school student who puts in the effort to explain a connection across two texts they read, writing builds skills all the way from the alphabetic principle (letters represent sounds) through advanced critical analysis (Quitadamo & Kurtz, 2007; Rowe et al., 2024). Despite its immense power, writing is one of the hardest areas to teach. Seventy-six percent of the students in our nation do not write proficiently (National Center on Education Statistics, 2011). We all see this statistic reflected in the students in our classrooms. This may be the reason you are reading this book.

Writing programs often focus on teaching isolated skills such as grammar, sentences, or paragraph organization rather than the bigger goal of self-regulation. This goal enables students not only to become skilled faster but also to take the bull by the horns and write on their own far more quickly. As you visit classrooms throughout this book, you learn how you can deliver this kind of instruction "from soup to nuts." More importantly, you have behind-the-scenes access into how these students now think while writing. Then, the curtain is drawn back to reveal how—and why—the instruction that got them there works. The most well-supported practices for teaching writing enable students to harness the power of executive skills and learn to self-regulate. This focus is spotlighted and brought to center stage throughout this book.

The Hidden Key: Supporting Executive Skills

Executive Skills Defined

Executive skills may be one of the most neglected—and yet critical—puzzle pieces that should drive how we think about writing instruction. These include three core *lower-order* skills: working memory (holding and juggling information), inhibition (holding back automatic responses), and cognitive flexibility (adapting, shifting focus and attention), along with the *higher-order* executive skills they support such as planning, organizing, self-monitoring, and developing social understanding (Diamond, 2013; Ruffini et al., 2024).

More broadly, the term *executive skills* refers to the top-down mental, or cognitive, processes students use to self-regulate their thoughts, actions, and feelings in ways intended to help them meet their goals (Doebel, 2020; Friedman & Miyake, 2017; McCloskey, Perkins, & Van Divner, 2009; Zhou et al., 2012. They are, essentially, what put us in charge of directing our own lives. Students can be taught to self-direct these processes starting as young as preschool and then continue learning these skills all through the highest levels of education (Diamond, 2013). Decades of empirical research show that supporting executive skills leads to better writing (Graham et al., 2012, 2016, 2019; Santangelo & Graham, 2016; Wanzek et al., 2017). Yet this research is not yet widely applied in schools (Graham, 2019).

Hiding Beneath the Surface

Looking inside our school, we see pencils moving or students keyboarding. When we stoop down and look at the students' notebooks, we see conventions such as spelling, punctuation, outlines, and drafts. Skimming what they draft, we can judge whether students seem to understand the material they're taught, if they can reason well, and if their intended meanings are clear. Less visible though, and critically important, is how these students are mentally *recruiting* and coordinating their executive skills (Kim & Graham, 2022), even in the earliest grades (Purinak et al., 2019).

> The term *recruit* implies that students actively make an effort to call up and enlist specific executive skills, such as consciously planning or working to sustain their attention.

Recruiting these hidden skills is a necessary gateway to learning to write (Kim & Graham, 2022; Ruffini et al., 2024). Better supporting these skills offers a rapid and easy way to strengthen writing skill acquisition and independence. When we teach in ways that do not recognize their importance, students with the greatest needs are the canaries in the coal mine who suffer the most (Altemeier et al., 2008; Diamond, 2013). The good news is that executive skills are not a fixed trait or something that is just happening. They can be taught and can improve. Let's take a virtual field trip to go see how, as our tour begins.

Let's Tour Our School for Examples of Self-Regulated Writing

Starting off our tour on floor one, in the kindergarten–grade 1 wing, we see students learning about the life cycle of butterflies. Their teacher has just shown a 2-minute video and read aloud a short informational book. As they shared what they learned, their teacher scribed a "fact list" on the whiteboard. This included drawn images, key words, and short phrases about the topic. While watching and contributing, students take notes on their clipboards, jotting down line images or single words. In these early grades, this work is done collaboratively, with the teacher closely guiding and supporting students' efforts for some time.

Students now make their way to their desks to tackle explaining this process to their future readers. When they take out their writing folders, they see their personalized goal sheets, which, for many, remind them to add more details when they write. Earlier in the year, these students might have shown task avoidance. Some might have asked to go to the restroom or gotten sidetracked and began playing with erasers. However, after several weeks of instruction, they settle right in and know what to do.

They first write encouraging self-talk such as "I've got this!" or a smiley face. They look over their drawings and notes from earlier. They might look at the opening-sentence stems in their writing folders, also posted on the wall, such as "I know about ____________" or "These are facts about ____________." Some begin to work independently. Some work with a buddy, and some go to the teacher's table for support as they work. They continue to the next sentence, using the letters they know in their attempts to sound out and spell the words they want to write. Since they practiced writing past tense verbs in their daily sentence exercises earlier in the day, correct grammar flows. They break down the words they want to write into syllables, then into individual sounds that they have been explicitly taught to identify. When they reach the end of a line, they remember to "sweep it back," subvocalizing this while writing, as they have now seen their teacher model many times.

Heading up two flights of stairs, we find the upper-grade classrooms. In a similar way, students are learning rich content about ancient Athens and Sparta while tackling a unit on Greek mythology. Likewise, students have watched a short 2-minute video about daily life in ancient Greece, read an introductory knowledge-building passage about this time period, and then read another, more complex passage that presented the advantages of each community. Students jotted notes as they read, then created an organizer on paper to prepare them to argue which community they would rather live in.

Before they begin writing, they had already argued about their position in small groups, using notes from their organizer to make and defend their point. As peers responded, they adjusted and revised their organizer notes. They now take out their writer's notebook and see the personalized goals they had all set after self- and peer scoring their last piece of writing the prior week. One recalls his grammar goal to use a less passive voice and try out artful use of participles to make his writing clearer and more stylish. He also sees his list of sentence stems that include: "By using (name a literary device such as mentoring or imagery) ___________, the author achieves the effect of ___________" (Levine, 2019). He remembers noticing this in a peer-written essay and wanting to try it out himself. Another remembers his goal is to not get discouraged as he writes. He reminds himself to "Stay the course; you've got this!"

As they begin writing, each student is checking off their organizer and referencing the materials they had read to find or adjust quotes in the process. Yet, just a few weeks before, when asked to write in response to texts, most quickly read the texts once, picked up a pen, and began free writing their essay with no plan or organizer. Their essays were filled with facts but were not organized well. Some points were off topic, and students may have included little analysis of the quotes they chose. Several students did not understand the prompt and so did not answer the question with a relevant response. Now, they know how to get themselves motivated to begin and they use strategic thinking processes as they take themselves through the phases of the writing process expertly.

Adding Executive Skills Instruction to the Mix

The lessons you just observed showcase what happens when teachers prioritize supporting executive skills. These teachers taught similar language lessons, such as effective word choice and sentence composing, in previous years, but this year was different. They added instruction and scaffolds to help students better manage their executive skills while writing. In response, students stopped passively believing that writing is something you are either good at or not and realized that they can all write far better if they use strategies and positive self-talk to get started, stay on track, and work to meet their goals.

Without direct instruction and support, less proficient writers do not recruit their executive skills (Costa et al., 2022) and may work even harder than their peers but not see the same rewards. Perhaps most importantly, the biggest difference teachers see now beyond just better overall writing is tangible confidence and even joy felt in the room. Writing has become liberating—the favorite time of day for students and teachers.

Writing Broken Down

Let's look now at the writing skills these students mastered. Broadly, as shown in Figure 1.1, writing can be broken out into five main areas. From pencil to Pulitzer, the following skills come into play. Each layer should be considered when assessing writing and targeting instruction (Truckenmiller, Cho, & Troia, 2022; Valentine & Truckenmiller, 2025).

Content/Reasoning

Developing writers initially engage in simple knowledge telling (Scardamalia & Bereiter, 1987) by listing ideas in sentences without connecting them, making inferences, or showing how they relate. This causes the writing to feel surface and disjointed. As they mature, they move ahead to knowledge transformation where their executive skills help them to better plan, revise, reason, and generate novel insights (Mason & Brady, 2022).

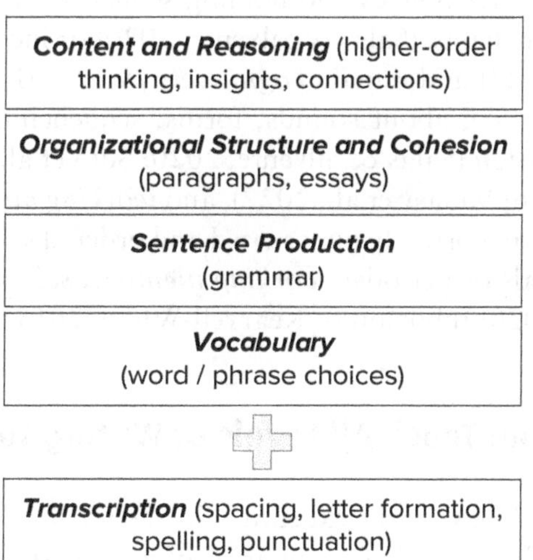

FIGURE 1.1. Five main areas of writing.

Organizational Structure and Cohesion

Students also need to organize their ideas into an introduction, related body sections, and a conclusion. Arranging ideas into logical groups and sequencing them draws on higher-order executive functions such as *organization*. This book discusses the three broad organizational text types—informative, argument/opinion, and narrative—while acknowledging subtypes within all.

Sentence Production

To produce sentences, students must take a preverbal idea and come up with labels, or words, for their ideas and use grammatical elements correctly to string the words together. For example, to write "I saw a cat walk by," students might first generate a label such as "cat," then add "I, saw, walk," and finally add the preposition "by" to complete the thought. They quickly arrange the words, move them around, and monitor whether the words make sense in *cognitively flexible* ways. To do this, they draw on *verbal working memory* (Olive, 2011), *planning*, and *inhibition* (Drijbooms et al., 2017).

Vocabulary or Word Choice

Next up is vocabulary. *Central executive skills tied to verbal fluency* impact how quickly students can call up words. This word retrieval fluency supports vocabulary diversity when writing, essentially varying word choices (Bourke, 2003).

Transcription

Transcription is the physical act of putting words on paper or keyboarding. More than just hand strength or motor control, transcription taps *working memory*, which aids students in pulling up letter images and holding sequences in mind. They must also *inhibit* (block out) other shapes (Salas & Silvente, 2020) or incorrect hand movements (Oshchepkova et al., 2023) and remain *cognitively flexible* (Lê et al., 2021; Stievano et al., 2016) while thinking about sounds, forms, sequencing, and ideas. Likewise, spelling taps into *inhibition* (Salas & Silvente, 2020; Soto et al., 2021), *cognitive flexibility* (Lubin et al., 2016; Vadasy et al., 2022), and *working memory* (Berninger et al., 2010). Turning words into correctly punctuated and ordered sentences draws on *visual attention* (noting capitals or periods), *working memory, self-monitoring,* and *inhibition* (Cordeiro et al., 2020; Ibbotson & Kearvell-White, 2015; Puranik et al., 2019).

Integrate Instruction: Teach All Levels of Writing Together

Before moving on to look next at the executive skills students use when they write, it is important to mention that these five main areas of writing should be taught and practiced together. Do not wait for areas such as transcription skills or sentence complexity to fully develop before having students compose connected-text discourse, as in short paragraphs. While it is important to break down the needed skills in these five areas and target and teach each of them separately, they have been shown to all rise together simultaneously, or in close proximity, from the earliest grades (Harris et al., 2023; Klein et al., 2024; Saddler & Graham, 2005). Imagine a visual of pillars that represent all the areas growing upward together. Paragraphs grow longer, links between ideas become clearer, sentences become more detailed, and spelling improves as our lessons target and allow students to learn and practice these together.

Note to Early Childhood Educators

Even if only learning to transcribe (i.e., form letters, spell), students can still practice composing connected text (i.e., short paragraphs) orally via dictation. This dictation would mean that students "compose" orally or "in the air" in preparation for producing new text in writing as their transcription skills emerge. Unfortunately, this kind of early composing instruction is often underutilized in the early grades despite its importance (Kent et al., 2014; Pinto et al., 2015; Rodriquez et al., 2024; White, 2013).

Teaching handwriting, word spelling, sentence syntax, and text composing areas separately but close in time in a lesson is more effective for creating a functional writing system than working on a single writing skill for a full lesson or in isolation for an extended time. First, handwriting and spelling contribute to transcription skills (Fayol et al., 2012). Next, syntax and text construction contribute to translation of cognition and ideas into written language. All along, teaching children self-regulation strategies (executive functions) helps them coordinate these transcription and translation skills as they write to achieve different writing goals and across genres (Altemeier et al., 2007). For examples of lessons that teach these cascading levels of language close in time, see Berninger and Abbott (2020).

In essence, teaching the five areas of writing and practicing them together supports transfer (Berninger et al., 2017; Harris et al., 2023; Olive, 2014). Students learn right away how to strategically shift between the varied levels of language (Berninger et al., 2017) and to coordinate using their executive skills together as they do so. That is to say, students must draw on and integrate multiple levels of language whenever they write, from sounding out spellings to monitoring whether their sentences make sense and flow from one idea to the next.

Teaching writing via isolated skill exercises (think of worksheets or an exclusive focus on one area such as sentences for an extended time) removes the language and larger meanings that can bootstrap learning and mastering basic writing skills. Having students write paragraphs (or essays) about content that they are interested in, such as science topics, while teaching the skills and strategies needed to write about this content (Harris et al., 2023) makes learning to write easier and more motivating. Students become intrinsically driven by their desire to learn and to communicate.

In addition, content knowledge acquisition happens faster when related ideas are presented in connected paragraphs that students read—rather than in isolated lists of individual sentences (Chilton & Ehri, 2015). Likewise, students better learn content when they compose a paragraph about a topic rather than make a list of sentences about it. Think of a short story or article about birds in contrast to a list of facts about them. Students likely learn more about the topic when they create a cohesive paragraph about birds rather than making isolated lists of practice sentences. Learning and writing at the paragraph level eases working memory. The connectors within and between sentences (conjunctions, pronouns, synonyms) encourage learning. These offer repetition and create connections that deepen understanding of the topic far more so than churning out individual, isolated sentences on a topic would.

While reading, students will flex between the vocabulary words and words that refer back to them such as pronouns, referents (*that*, *those*), or synonyms. These offer repeated, varied exposures to the terms and the underlying concepts behind them. Learning words in cohesive paragraphs also aids inhibition since students don't need to filter out irrelevant information in an integrated paragraph as they might when reading disconnected sentences in a list (Chilton & Ehri, 2015). Likewise, coordinating the different levels of language (words, sentences that include connectors, paragraphs) and using them together to create writing that holds together is important (Berninger et al., 2017), and this approach likely supports faster learning of the material, as it does with reading.

When students learn and compose at the connected-text level, they see writing as something functional—something they are motivated to do for a purpose (Berninger et al., 2017). To make this clearer, I'll share a metaphor.

A Bike-Riding Metaphor for the Importance of Integrated Instruction

Think back and remember when you learned to ride a bicycle. Someone broke out and taught you every small action. Yet, they also showed you how to manage and coordinate them together from the start. Now, thinking about each small step would get in the way of riding smoothly. You automatized them all quickly and now naturally use them together.

Along these lines, some teachers may hesitate to break down all the subskills and the steps in the writing process, teach each one, and practice them together. They may be concerned that this could take away from the natural, fluent experience of writing. However, had you not been taught how to hold the handlebars, move your feet, and maintain your balance all together and in coordination, you would not have become the proficient biker you now are. We did need to teach each skill individually and provide integrated practice.

Or, on the other hand, teachers may want to break down the skills and spend time teaching each in isolation. Yet equally important to providing instruction for each skill is to teach how to orchestrate using all of them together. What if you had practiced peddling alone, but not along with balancing at the same time? This would have drawn out the learning process and the smaller skills might not have transferred easily. Breaking up writing skills to work on areas such as sentences in isolation without also showing how to use everything in coordination has not resulted in gains in writing quality (Graham & Perin, 2007).

Taking the metaphor a step further, you persevered because you wanted to get somewhere on your bike. Would you have persevered if you had to do an hour of skill practice of moving the handlebars in isolation? Likewise, writers write because they are motivated by a desire to discover and clarify what they think or to share an idea. They galvanize all the lower and higher language and executive skills needed because they are driven to communicate. Teach each skill but also apply them in short pieces at first, in an "and/both" way.

Writing Instruction That Supports Executive Skills Is Magic Pixie Dust

In the previous section, we broke down writing and explored why all levels of writing should be taught and practiced together. The next section breaks down executive skills. However, between these sections, I offer a personal note on my *why*.

Writing was something I always loved to teach. For the first 10 years of my career, I taught writing in structured ways. In a way, I was serving as the executive skills for my students. My students with executive skill challenges flourished with this structure. However, I did not understand that I could not only support executive skills but also teach them directly. My game-changer moment came when I road-tested teaching strategies that support executive skills (Graham et al., 2012). When I did, my students' writing improved (Laud & Patel, 2008). Over the next few years, I also discovered more systematic ways to support language skill development at the vocabulary and sentence level (Haynes et al., 2019).

Then, something unexpected happened. My students began to self-regulate. I felt taken aback at the speed at which their writing improved, when the adjustments to my instruction were so simple and minimal. At first, I did not have words to understand what I was seeing, but I knew it was special. I saw the "on" button click for my students, and they began engaging in far more effortful and self-directed ways. I remember hearing a tapping noise as a student wrote his essay and asking him why he was doing that. "I want to meet my correctly spelled words goal when I finish this essay," he told me. I was floored to see him suddenly able to coordinate so many levels of language as he drafted his piece.

When I began sharing these approaches with colleagues, in workshops and then through large-scale research studies I have led, I saw the same phenomenon repeat. Every spring, I'd hear from teary-eyed educators that their entire class used the scrap paper when taking the state assessments. Their students filled the page with encouraging reminders to themselves to do their best along with creating self-drawn detailed organizers. They too had never seen students self-regulate to this extent before. We discovered how to launch independent, skilled writers. Every single time it happens feels like a fresh miracle. In a moment of levity, the idea of magic pixie dust came to mind as a way to describe what we observed when using these new ways to teach writing. Teachers would follow up to share that their classes made the greatest growth on state assessment ever, and special educators would tell me that every child on their caseload received proficient scores, which had never happened before. But the greatest joy was always seeing students who previously felt defeated become empowered. Indeed, research has consistently found that not only does writing quality grow as a result of instructional strategies that support executive skills but also student confidence and enjoyment of writing grow as well (Harris et al., 2015; Limpo et al., 2013b). Let's move on to what these skills are.

Executive Skills Used When Writing: Breaking It Down

Now that I have defined executive skills and demonstrated what they look like in action in our school, let's look more closely at how they work when we write. Executive skills are interconnected cognitive processes that originate in the frontal lobe, prefrontal cortex, and related areas of the brain (Friedman & Robbins, 2022; Miller & Wallace, 2009; Otero & Barker, 2014). See Figure 1.2 and, for more on how these brain areas support literacy, see Cartwright (2023). When writing, students recruit their executive skills to exert conscious control as they initiate (*figure out what's being asked*), coordinate (*create and adjust plans*), direct (*compose*), monitor their writing processes, and draw on all the needed subskills (Harris et al., 2018). When they do not, we see the impact in the quality of writing they produce, but we may not understand the cause.

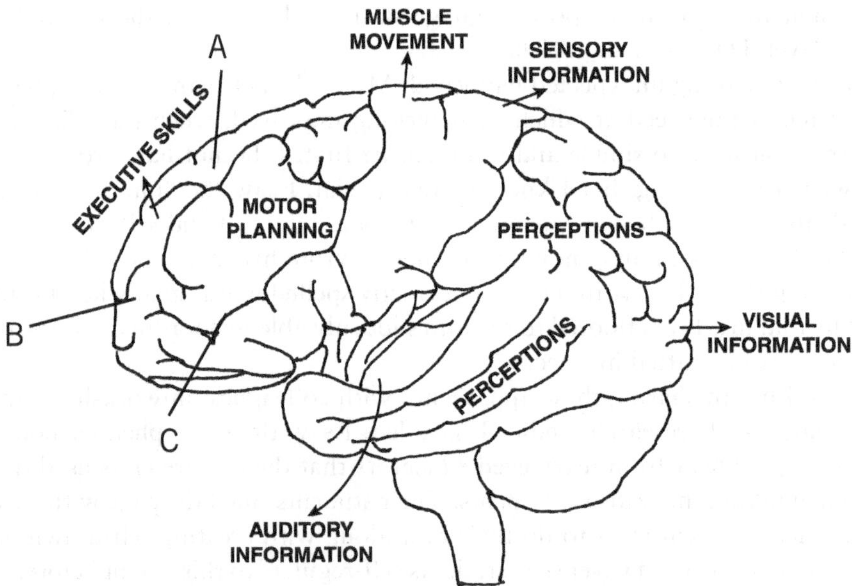

FIGURE 1.2. The human brain, with the approximate locations of major functions. *A*, dorsolateral prefrontal cortex; *B*, orbitofrontal cortex; *C*, ventrolateral, ventromedial, and medial prefrontal cortex. From Dawson and Guare (2010). Copyright © 2010 The Guilford Press. Adapted by permission.

To learn how we can best help our students, we need to step back and look at what is happening in the brain. Table 1.1 explains what these brain-based executive skills do as we write. Next, Figure 1.3 on page 13 depicts how the higher-order executive skills relate to and draw on the lower-order skills (Cartwright et al., 2023). Note that the lower skills, closer to the bottom, happen with less conscious awareness than those above. We don't usually think about how to direct our working memory, but we do make a conscious choice to engage our planning or organizing executive skills. Moving up in the flow chart, our instruction can, therefore, support the lowest executive skills and teach students how to consciously direct the higher ones.

Cold and Hot Executive Skills

Executive skills can also be broken into two larger categories: cold and hot. Cold refers to the more cognitive aspects of executive skills, while hot refers to more emotional, motivational, or self-regulatory processing (Diamond, 2013). Capacities such as working memory, cognitive flexibility, or inhibition would fall primarily under cold executive functions. On the other hand, social understanding or theory of mind (Zelazo & Carlson, 2012) and being able to self-regulate emotions have more hot, emotional, or motivationally laden components. The same cold skills become hot when they work to support self-regulation, such as using self-speech to encourage oneself when writing or to inhibit feelings of self-doubt. Both have been found to be surprisingly malleable, or easy to support (Zelazo & Carlson, 2012).

Unity and Diversity in Executive Skills

While executive skills work together in unified concert, there is diversity among these as well. They can be broken out into different capacities, but keep in mind that there is always overlap and coordination when students use them, often termed "unity and diversity" (Miyake et al., 2000). They could operate in isolation but usually do so together and in pursuit of achieving a goal (Doebel, 2020).

Integrate Reading and Writing

Before wrapping up, it would be remiss of me not to share a further word about the importance of leveraging the synergistic reading and writing connection (Kim & Zagata, 2024). Teaching these together strengthens both skill sets and better supports executive skills. For example, learning to form letters improves early decoding skills (Ray et al., 2021). Identifying elements in peer-written exemplars such as a compelling opening or ending helps students attend to and reproduce these (Graham et al., 2012, 2016). When reading, students can mimic the language, reasoning, and structures they see when taught to engage their working memory to help them analyze it and to make a plan for how they could use what they notice. Essentially, reading is "breathing in" and writing is "breathing out" (Allyn, n.d.).

TABLE 1.1. Executive Functions

Skill	Example	How it impacts writing
Working memory	We may learn about how an octopus can swim 50 mph. We hold this fact in working memory temporarily. We integrate it with other known facts such as the existence of predators in the sea. We juggle thinking about how being fast helps it escape harm. This allows us to integrate new information with what we know, like a mental scratch pad. (There is natural variation in how much capacity each child has on their scratch pad, and this executive skill is limited for all. However, the exciting part is that we can help students use it more efficiently.)	Working memory impacts every level of writing, from learning letter formation, spelling, and grammar to holding onto and sequencing a critical insight when constructing essays. Broadly, it helps us hold the overall text structure and big idea in mind as we write. This allows us to maintain coherence, which in simpler terms is the main thread that connects our ideas together.
Inhibition	Letter formation is aided when students subvocalize directions that they can follow and that help them stay on track and ignore distractions such as "I will start at the top of the line and go straight down." When reviewing which facts to include in a piece on octopuses, students might filter out an impulse to describe a turtle that was in a tank next to an octopus they saw at an aquarium.	Inhibition allows us to sustain attention to the task at hand and relevant information when competing thoughts come to mind.
Cognitive flexibility	When spelling, a student might consider two options and reflect on each. When composing sentences, a sentence may pop into a writer's mind, but before using it, the student might pause and consider other ways to structure the ideas. Essay writers might consider multiple pieces of evidence and choose the most effective, rather than sticking with the first that comes to mind. When writing multiple types of texts, inflexible writers might cope by writing about each separately rather than synthesizing information (Garner, 1987; Stromse et al., 2003; Wineburg, 1991).	Flexibility allows us to move between different ideas and consider alternatives ranging from when we spell to how we synthesize ideas across texts.
Goal-directed planning	When writing an essay, students must also hold the goal in mind, then find and generate ideas and choose which to use.	Writers must be goal driven, generate ideas, and then select which to use to meet their goals.
Organization	After picking ideas but before writing, students will put their ideas into groups and decide how to order them. When writing the letter *m*, students need to use correctly sequenced steps. When writing sentences, they organize words in grammatically conventional ways.	Organization involves putting components or ideas into groups and sequencing these in a logical fashion.

(continued)

TABLE 1.1. *(continued)*

Skill	Example	How it impacts writing
Self-monitoring	At the earliest phases, this might include circling the letter that they think they wrote most neatly. Later, this could mean reviewing their writing for spelling conventions or looking over an organizer to ensure it includes all their ideas. At the revision phase, this relies on having a deep understanding of the features of effective writing and the ability to compare one's own to these.	Students must step back and self-monitor themselves all through the writing process, particularly when revising.
Social understanding	When students give feedback on one another's writing, this allows them to empathize, consider another writer's perspective, communicate effectively, and navigate the social levels involved. Another example is when student writers need to think about who their audience is and whether they are expressing their ideas appropriately to reach it.	Social understanding impacts the ability to infer and understand perspectives, motives, emotional states, thoughts, and feelings of others and respond appropriately. Also termed *theory of mind*, it includes an understanding that others may think and feel differently from us (Premack & Woodruff, 1978). See Cartwright (2023) for a fuller explanation of this skill.

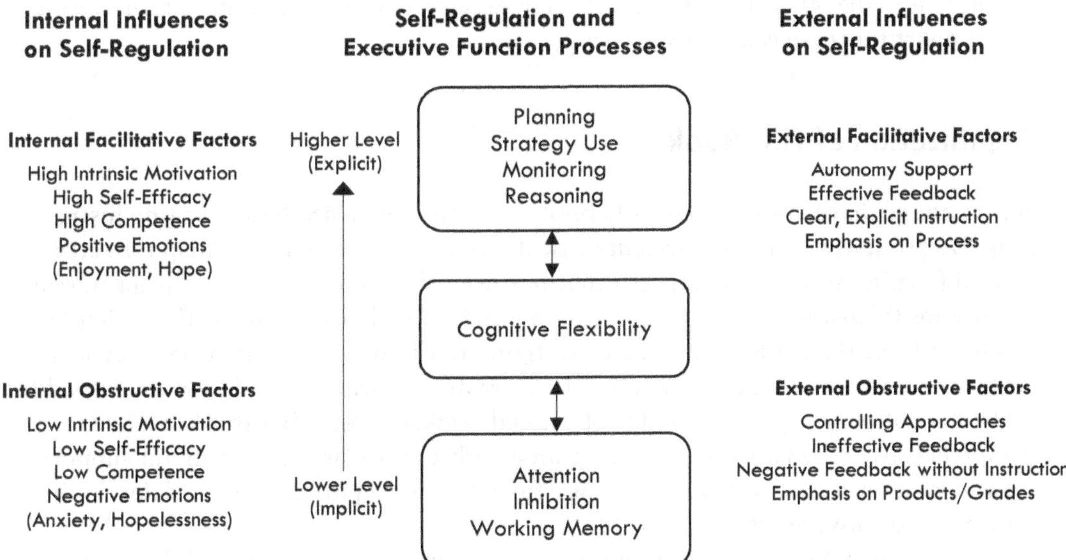

FIGURE 1.3. Processes involved in self-regulation. From Cartwright et al. (2023). Copyright © 2023 Taylor & Francis. Reprinted by permission.

Even more, research shows that writing about what we read builds knowledge and provides writers with a more thorough comprehension of a text (Graham et al., 2011), especially for those who struggle (Shanahan et al., 2024). In the past, I emphasized personal narrative as well as opinion "writing from head" (i.e., Should students have to wear school uniforms?). However, I found that these kinds of writing did not allow students to internalize the vocabulary, syntax, and reasoning present in academic language to the same extent that responding to complex sources does. While there is a place for this kind of writing, responding to sources offers greater promise toward closing gaps because of how it enables students to draw on, mimic, and internalize the academic language they encounter in the complex texts they respond to. To enhance the impact of our writing instruction and reach Hammond's (2014) vision of agentive, empowered, and critical thinkers, we need to teach writing with evidence-based practices. These practices include connecting reading with writing to build academic language and teaching in ways that support the invisible executive skills that can make learning these together more synergistic.

So, Why Did I Write This Book?

I wish I had known how important executive skills are to writing, and how to teach in ways that acknowledged this sooner. Many well-intended educators teach writing by primarily assigning and correcting, perhaps passing out organizers and offering lessons on spelling, sentence construction, or linking ideas. While teaching these language skills is necessary, it is not sufficient. Language development and executive skills overlap in some ways but are also independent (Gooch et al., 2016). Teaching only one will not build the other. Direct instruction in executive skills that occur within writing and support for these is also necessary.

Organization of This Book

We do not yet have a teacher-friendly book that offers evidence-based writing instruction, foregrounds attention to executive skills, and offers an easy road map for getting started (coming soon in Chapter 2!) that has been shown to have high impact in real classrooms (Hansford et al., 2024). Current practitioner books focus on the "what" to teach but leave the reader still needing to figure out how to integrate what they learn with their daily instruction. These books offer an important foundation and should all be part of our regularly visited professional bookshelves. What this book adds is a comprehensive, stepwise instructional framework that focuses primarily on supporting the most neglected and yet most powerful lever for supporting students' developing writing—executive skills.

As you read, I suggest you try out using writing, and the executive skill of organization, to further your own learning. You may want to keep a notepad nearby. Jot the name of each chapter and its subheadings down the side of one page. This will help you create and hold on to an organized mental model of this book's contents. Take notes on each chapter on your "outline-like" page. Rather than only summarizing, add your own thinking and realizations as you go. Doing so will aid your learning. You can begin by jotting down the following chapter topics and leaving space between each to fill in as your learning journey unfolds.

Chapter 1 has introduced executive skills, explained what writing is, and recommended integrating instruction in multiple levels of language while composing. It has also made the case for having students write about what they read.

Chapter 2 overviews the science of writing and research on models of writing instruction that emphasize the importance of executive skills. It then introduces simple yet comprehensive guidance for teaching writing with these skills in mind.

Chapters 3 to 8 are structured the same way. Each includes a definition of an executive skill, a visit to classrooms to see it in action, a sample lesson with the skill highlighted all through and then debriefed, and a wrap-up summary of key action steps you can take in your classroom tomorrow. One practical way you can use this book is to deliver each of the lessons in these chapters over about a week to understand the full approaches more deeply. Or you can try out each strategy or skill instructional focus, one at a time, adopting many if not all in a step-by-step way over time.

Chapter 3 dives into the first executive skill of planning and presents ways to teach students to plan before writing. It describes the essential components of planning—or the "what" to teach—and explains why instruction in how to plan before writing supports and harnesses executive skills. Each following chapter focuses on a specific executive skill that supports each phase in the writing process.

Chapter 4 moves forward to organizing, as students learn to use text structures to organize their ideas before writing, another higher-order capacity.

Chapters 5 and 6 discuss translating and transcribing one's thoughts into words when writing. Chapter 5 focuses on cognitive flexibility in the realm of language and delves into the language areas of word choice, sentence development, and cohesion (connecting ideas while writing), exploring how the executive skill of cognitive flexibility supports these areas. Teachers will learn about the unique demands that vocabulary and sentence composing make on executive skills, and how instruction can be delivered to develop and to scaffold these skills with concrete supports. Both vocabulary and sentence composing are capacities that can be front-loaded and directly taught, as well as scaffolded with tools such as vocabulary boxes and sentence frames.

Chapter 6 shifts from focusing on language development over to written transcription and the executive skill of working memory while looking at transcription. Specifically, this chapter addresses grip, spacing, letter formation, spelling, and sentence punctuation and overviews how the executive skill of working memory supports these processes.

Chapter 7 dives into how to teach revision, with a focus on the executive skills of self-monitoring and inhibition. Related to these, it also touches on the powerful force of goal setting, including how this fosters self-regulation in writers. Teachers learn how to instruct students to self-score their writing before revising it. The chapter shows ways to put students in the driver's seat by helping them to use self-monitoring to build their understanding of both the features of effective writing and the processes (i.e., planning, revision) they need to use to attain these features. This kind of self-evaluation is a challenging skill that draws on multiple hot and cold executive skills, which are explored.

Chapter 8 looks at theory of mind, audience awareness, social skills, and writers' communities as it moves from self-scoring and goal setting. This includes looking more deeply at peer collaboration and keeping one's audience in mind. It focuses on how peer feedback can spark and deepen awareness or perspective taking, and how this can be taught and developed. Leveraging this kind of peer feedback and discussion in ways that support executive skills benefits students as they reach to write about higher-order complex concepts and insights.

A Note to Primary-Grades Educators

You may want to skip ahead to Chapter 6, which covers early transcription skills, since you front-load these skills in your work with your students. The upper grades reinforce these skills and can follow this book sequence. For upper-grades teachers, if your students already transcribe efficiently, you might even skip this chapter. However, even if students do not have documented special needs, many still struggle with handwriting, spelling, and transcription, so the chapter includes tips for older students as well.

Following the eight chapters and a brief epilogue, you will find an Appendix of Resources and Reproducibles, designed to support your own executive skills to make it easier for you as you plan how to bring these ideas you learn to your own classroom. The Appendix is organized in five sections. The first group (Appendices A–C) provides a bird's-eye view of the recommended scope and sequence, the skills to teach at each grade level, and a progression guide of writing tools. The second group (Appendices D–H) includes materials that help you identify a preassessment and create writing assignments. The next three groups of appendices provide materials that support and strengthen the executive skills of planning and organizing (Appendices I–N), working memory and cognitive flexibility (Appendices O–R), and inhibition and self-monitoring (Appendices S–Y).

In all, I hope this book (1) illuminates for you what executive skills are and how they support writing; (2) provides you with tangible, concrete steps you can take in your classroom to better support these skills; (3) deepens your understanding of what the science of writing tells us works and *why* it works; and (4) inspires a vision for how students can become skilled and self-regulating writers. My fourth goal may be the most important.

In my 35 years of teaching, there is one clear career-defining before/after moment. Before using these approaches, I saw my role as imparting skills and strategies. Afterward, I revamped and developed a new goal—to teach in ways that enable my students to independently drive their own learning. When I did, their writing performance soared. I watched them literally "learn how to learn." The concrete and doable strategies in this book provide an evidence-based and easy roadmap to help you get your students there, too.

CHAPTER 2

The End Game

A Framework for Developing Self-Regulating Writers

Begin with the end in mind.
—STEPHEN COVEY

This chapter begins with the end in mind, as Covey (2004) recommends. Imagine students picking up pencils with a clear goal. Ideas come to mind; their writing demonstrates strong word choice; and rich sentences flow. They organize these into well-crafted paragraphs with a clear overarching structure. Their compelling message is a delight to read. They faced challenges while writing, but worked through them. Earlier in the year, they may have stared at a blank page or struggled throughout the semester. The students did not change, but the instruction did. This chapter describes how to introduce and launch a way of teaching writing that focuses on executive skills and helps students reach this vision.

First, we place this instruction within the context of the *science of writing* and the recent increase in research that stresses the important role of executive skills. Halfway through the chapter, our focus shifts to the practical application. We look at what instruction should include and how to carry this out in a typical week. We include a sample lesson plan, which is then analyzed for how each instructional element supports executive skills. This chapter concludes with simple next steps you can take to incorporate this learning into your own writing instruction.

The Science of Writing

The *science of reading* includes a vast interdisciplinary body of decades-old, scientifically based research evidence (see The Reading League, 2022) that points to the most effective instruction. Journalists have documented what is being termed a reading crisis (Hanford, 2022) in a call for schools to better use this science to inform reading instruction. Nearly all states have passed laws or implemented new policies requiring schools to use reading instruction backed by science (Schwartz, 2024).

Likewise, attention to the science of writing and its evidence base is growing, leading scientists to argue that neglecting writing instruction is "leaving money on the table" (Truckenmiller, 2024) and that the science of reading is incomplete without the science of writing (Kim et al., 2024). After all, reading and writing are similar in many ways, two sides of the same coin. Reading is decoding or pulling words off a page and making meaning of them. Writing is encoding, or putting down words designed to create meanings. They draw on many shared underlying language and executive skills (Kim & Graham, 2022). It is vital to address both the science of reading and the science of writing.

From Simple to Not-So-Simple Views of Writing

The sciences of reading and writing share many parallels. Central to the science of reading movement is the Simple View of Reading (Gough & Tumner, 1986). This view holds that reading is the outcome of two main factors: listening comprehension and word recognition. This model can be broken down to include greater attention to executive skills and self-regulation, as in the Active View of Reading (Duke & Cartwright, 2021).

In the same way, executive functioning has also been recognized as central to writing. The original Simple View of Writing similarly held that there were two main factors to writing. First, it included the flip side of listening comprehension, which *is ideation* or *text generation.* This relies on using oral expression (what we say) to translate our thoughts into words and create meaning. It also included *transcription,* or writing these ideas down (Berninger et al., 2002), also called *encoding*—the flip side of word recognition/decoding. However, Berninger modified this view shortly after its initial publication to become the "Not–So-Simple View of Writing." This view added a third factor—the central role of executive functioning, particularly working memory (Berninger & Winn, 2006; Bourke & Adams, 2003; Kent et al., 2014; Poch & Lembke, 2017). Continued research supports the contribution of executive skills to writing quality (Cordeiro et al., 2020; Kim & Graham, 2022), as do later models such as the Active View of Writing (Duke et al., 2025) shown in Figure 2.1.

Executive Skills Raise Writing Quality Directly and Indirectly

We can now connect how knowing these models helps us as educators. They explain that executive skills *directly* contribute to writing quality (think of organizing) and *indirectly* by supporting oral language and transcription (Kim & Graham, 2022; Ruffini et al., 2024). To illustrate the *direct* role that executive skills play, consider why making an organizer aids writers. The executive skill of organization supports students when they engage in the writing process. It helps them stay on track, group

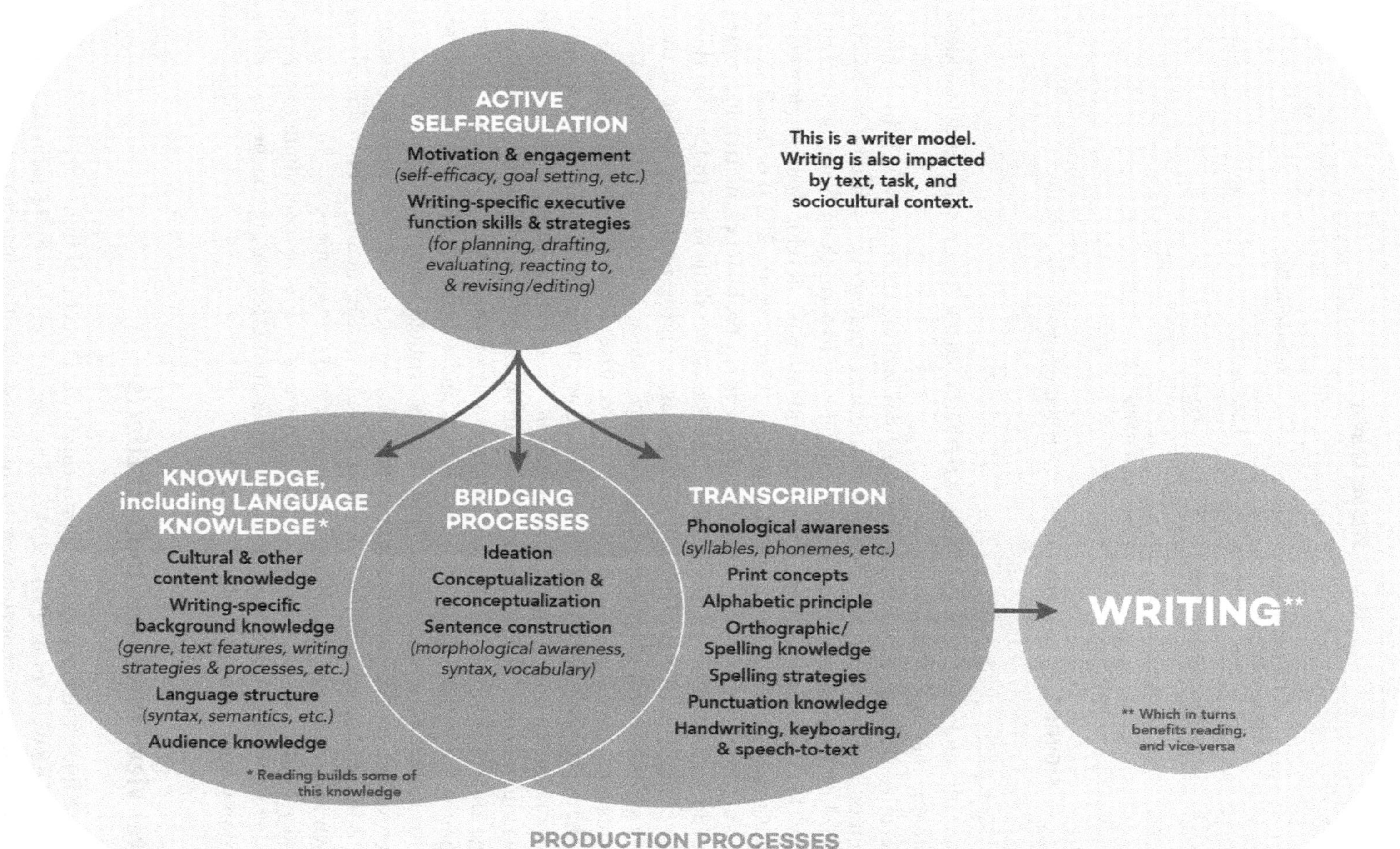

FIGURE 2.1. The Active View of Writing (Duke, Graham, & Cartwright, 2025). Reprinted by permission of the authors.

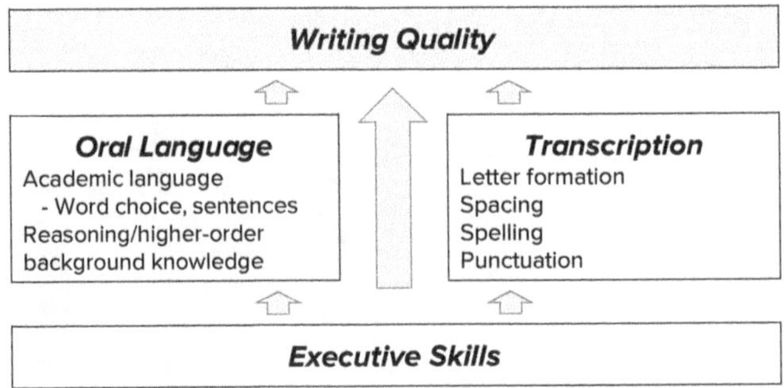

FIGURE 2.2. Executive skills' contributions to writing quality.

ideas logically, and make transitions clear to their readers. As a result, students' ideas then hold together and flow better.

Executive skills also *indirectly* support final writing quality as well by helping transcription and oral language. When transcribing, students can self-monitor by circling their best formed letters or verbalize aloud how to form them (Santangelo et al., 2016; Zwicker & Hadwin, 2009). Regarding oral language development, students can practice using conjunctions to expand sentences (Harris et al., 2023) or retell stories with a structured template (i.e., the character, setting, problem, plan/attempt, consequence, end, and emotion) (Kirby et al., 2021). Executive skills help students do these language-building activities. Through the language improvements they support, their executive skills help improve final writing quality. Figure 2.2 shows these three major ingredients (oral language, transcription, and executive skills).

In the figure, notice the thicker center arrow that goes directly from executive skills to writing quality. Teaching organization, an executive skill, leads *directly* to better writing quality. The smaller arrows go from executive skills *through* both oral language and transcription, *indirectly*. Students rely on their executive skills to attend and monitor when they circle their best letters and subvocalize how to form them. They also use them to hold, juggle, and flexibly arrange ideas when expanding sentences or to lean on story structure templates while doing retells. Teaching with executive skills in mind recognizes how they contribute to writing quality—both directly on their own and indirectly by aiding oral language and transcription.

Understanding how executive skills directly and indirectly contribute to writing quality better allows us to make sense of why the most effective approaches to writing instruction work (Graham et al., 2012, 2016).

A Newer View: Direct and Indirect Effects

Along these lines, the latest model is now called the Direct and Indirect Effects Model of Writing (DIEW; Kim & Park, 2019). This model offers a more refined, comprehensive, and research-supported way to think about writing instruction (see also the Active View of Writing for a similar framework with key ingredients) and positions executive skills as the foundation of writing instruction (Kim & Graham, 2022). It suggests that, to raise outcomes, we must address the following factors:

- **Social–emotional aspects** (*motivation, positive mindsets*)
- **Lexical literacy** (*transcription, spelling, handwriting*)
- **Discourse oral language** (*vocabulary, grammar, background knowledge*)
- **Executive functioning**

Stay tuned—coming soon in this chapter is a practical, teacher-created lesson plan that will show you how you can do this easily!

The DIEW model enables us to look at even wider contributions to writing quality, such as reading comprehension, inferencing, perspective taking, and monitoring, all of which draw on executive functions and have both direct and indirect effects on writing (Kim & Park, 2019; Kim et al., 2022). To make this expanded model easy to visualize, see the house metaphor in Figure 2.3.

The roof shows the reading and writing connection. These processes help each other, suggesting that instruction should connect these to raise writing outcomes. The horizontal beam just below shows that reading and writing fluency relate and also help each other. To the left, the pillar lists the print elements needed to produce letters, words, and sentences. These rest on phonology (sounds that make up words), orthography (written systems to represent sounds), and morphology (meaningful units within words). The right pillar shows oral discourse or the language we use to produce ideas. The base foundational block lists the needed self-regulatory skills of self-direction and

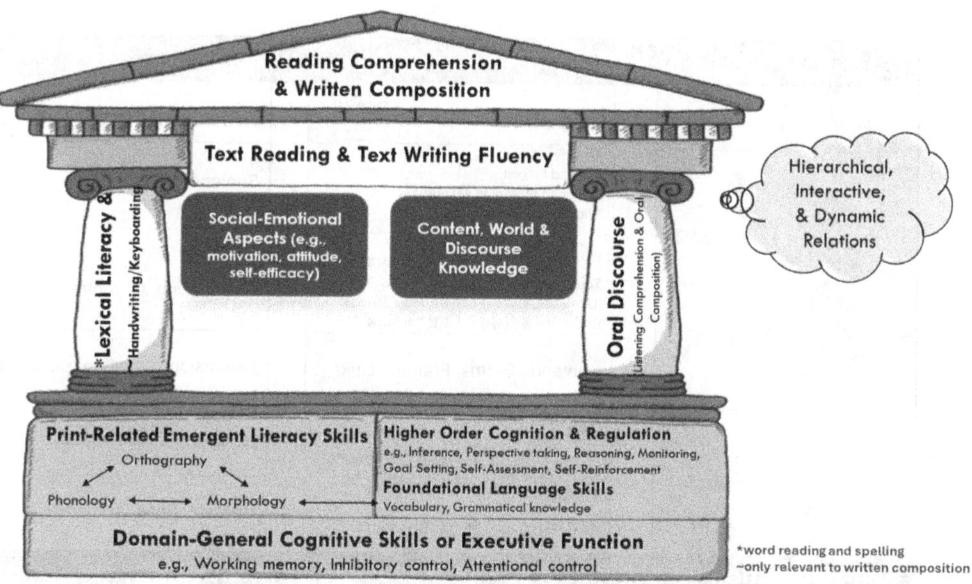

FIGURE 2.3. The Direct and Indirect Effects Model of Writing (Kim, 2020; Kim & Graham, 2022; Kim & Park, 2019). Reprinted by permission of the authors.

goal setting. Finally, at the broad horizontal base block, all elements stand on a shared foundation—executive functioning skills.

What to Teach: POWER and TIDE as Guides

Moving now to the classroom focus, Figure 2.4 translates the skills from the house metaphor to an instructional sequence that can guide how you think about lesson planning. The figure offers a way to consider the *what*—what strategies you will teach—in a way that brings forward and centers the importance of executive skills. I walk you through each section of this chart now.

Top Row: Self-Directed, Skilled Readers and Writers

This chart places the executive skill goal of building self-directed writers at the top and the needed self-regulation at the bottom as the foundation of writing instruction.

Foundational Skills

Moving down and left are foundational skills, such as letter formation or spelling, and all their subskills (phonemic awareness, orthography or morphology). The font is grayed out because these are taught in the early years of school, or only as needed in the upper grades.

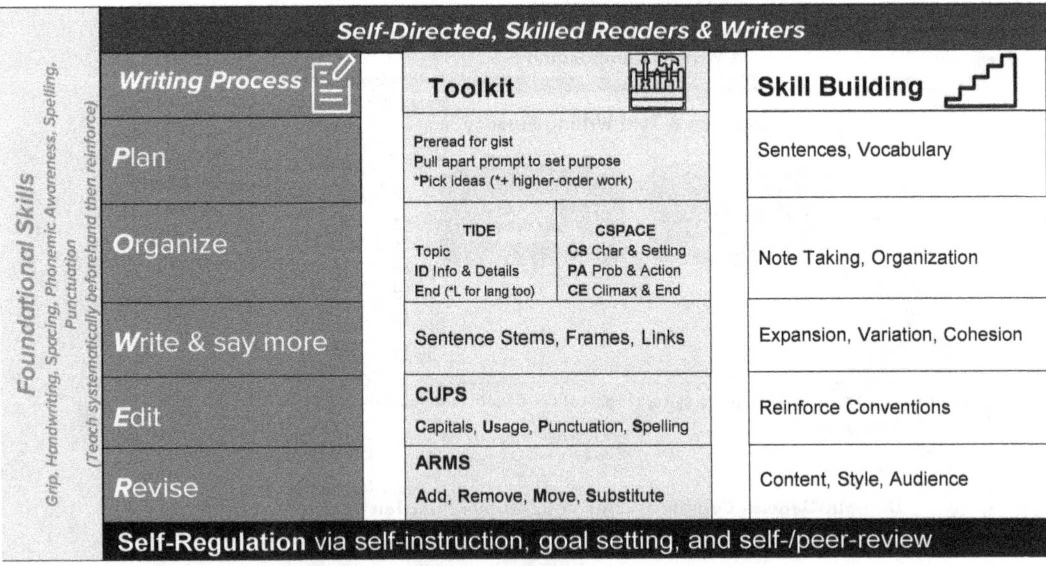

FIGURE 2.4. Framework for "what to teach."

The Writing Process Panel

The second panel, POWER (Englert et al., 1991), lists the kinds of strategic thinking processes (Murray, 2003) that all writers use (Plan, Organize, Write, Edit, Revise). Students can write this on their papers and use it to guide themselves when working through the writing process. Mnemonics aid students in remembering, calling up, and using sets of steps (Scruggs & Mastropieri, 2000). This puts them in charge as they write, rather than waiting for a teacher to tell them what step in the writing process to do next. POWER is one example of the kind of mnemonic that can support students in understanding and using the writing process.

Toolkit Panel: Support Each Phase in the Writing Process

The third panel provides product tools. In contrast to POWER, which is a tool that supports writing processes, these "product tools" now help students understand the product (writing) they will produce. These tools are only examples to illustrate ways executive skills can be taught and supported.

Plan: Preread to Find the Gist, or Main Idea

At the top of the toolkit, after P (Plan), you see three tools or strategies, the first of which is "preread for *gist*," or the main idea. Figure 2.5 shows examples of gist frames for grades 2 and 6.

> A *gist frame* is a tool we use to write a one-sentence summary. It can include key elements of a sentence such as who (subject noun) did what (verb), when, where (prepositions), or joiners (conjunctions) to indicate why or what happened. See Jennings and Haynes (2018) for more on these elements and how they can be taught as a way to "frame" sentences we write. The order of the parts of speech included can vary, and new grade-level grammar standards, such as past tense or subordinating conjunctions, can be built in each week. Introducing these elements regularly embeds grammar practice into your daily instruction routine.

Writing such a gist frame serves two different purposes. First, doing so provides practice composing at the sentence level. As students create short gist frame sentences daily, they practice including all the main parts of speech, starting with a noun and verb. They then grow to build in additional grammatical elements, as per their grade-level standards—such as prepositions in kindergarten, past tense practice in grade 2, or modals in grade 4 (see Appendix I).

Second, writing a gist, also considered a main idea statement, additionally supports reading comprehension (Boardman et al., 2015). This is particularly so when students write gists that also include causal or contrastive statements, then write short summaries and make inferences (Wijekumar et al., 2017). The better students understand what they read, the better they will write. Essentially, these gists help students

Main Frame					
Who (noun)	Did what (verb)	When/Where (preposition)	Why/What happened (conjunction/joiner)	Who	Did What
Octopuses	camouflage	in the ocean	so	they	can hide.

Example of Grade 2 Gist with Grammar Standards					
Who (*Collective* noun)	Did what (*Irregular past tense* verb + *adj*)	When/Where (preposition)	Why/What happened (conjunction/joiner)	Who	Did What (verb + *adverb*)
Children	*flew red* kites	outside	because	they	love to run *quickly*.

Example of Grade 6 Gist with Grammar Standards						
Why/What happened (*Subordinating* conjunction)	Who	*Appositive*	Did what	When/Where (preposition)	Who (*pronoun referent*)	Did What (verb + *adverb*)
After	Jonas,	*a leader who put principles before his own security,*	bolted	to the unknown,	*he*	risked it all, feeling motivated *deeply* by purpose.

FIGURE 2.5. Gist frame examples.

build a mental model of the main idea, hold onto it, and call it up when they begin writing. After teaching a tool such as writing gists, each week teachers can integrate further comprehension instruction, as described in Cartwright (2023).

Therefore, in the Plan phase, we begin with gist frame writing to provide daily instruction in sentence composition focused on teaching and practicing grade-level grammar standards, along with the second objective to also support comprehension of the topic when writing this summary statement.

Plan: Pull Apart the Prompt, or Task with Do/What

Next, after a first read, students might then establish a more defined purpose and do a second read in order to set a focus and a goal (Graham & Harris, 2007; Ruffini et al., 2024). To structure when responding to a prompt, have students pull apart the prompt so that they understand what they are being asked to do. Structured tools such as a Do/What strategy can help. To make a Do/What, students create a T-chart and ask themselves "What am I being told to *Do*?" (verb in prompt) and "*What* is the substance I'll write about?" See Figure 2.6 for examples. In these examples and throughout the book, I use the topic "Octopuses" to show how this process works for younger grades. To demonstrate how lessons might look for older grades, I base my examples on Malala Yousafzai, a Pakistani education activist who won the Nobel Peace Prize

Prompt: Describe how octopuses protect themselves. Cite examples from your sources.

Do (verb)	What
1. Desc (how)	1. Octo protect
2. Cite	2. sources

Prompt: Effective leaders persuade others and inspire action. Identify several ways Malala uses persuasion to convince others to agree with her, and evaluate each in terms of how likely it is to motivate others to act in ways that would support her cause. Be sure to use information from both the video and the text.

Do (verb)	What
1. Identify	1. Mal uses pers to conv
2. Eval (how)	2. Likely to motiv to act
3. Use	3. Info video and text

FIGURE 2.6. Example of a Do/What strategy.

at the age of 17. These two recurring topics are used to help you see the connected threads between the activities.

Plan: Pick Relevant Ideas

Next, while still in Plan, students can use strategies to help them pick ideas before writing. Picking ideas is often the longest phase where students do a deeper close read, take notes, annotate, mark up, and define key words. See Cartwright (2023) for more on scaffolding the self-regulatory executive skills that underlie reading comprehension. As they pick ideas, they can do so in unstructured lists, circle maps, Venn diagrams, or any format. See Figure 2.7 for an example of pick ideas.

Organize

Moving down a row, next to Organize (the O in POWER), you see mnemonics. You may already be familiar with popular mnemonics that aid organization such as CER (claim, evidence, and reasoning), OREO (Opinion, Reason, Example, Opinion restated), RACES (Restate, Answer, Cite evidence, Explain, and Summarize), or BME (Beginning, Middle, End). Two that are well validated are TIDE (Benedek-Wood et al., 2014; Collins et al., 2021; Harris et al., 2023) and CSPACE (Kirby et al., 2021;

MacArthur et al., 1991). TIDE works broadly for opinion/argument pieces, informative paragraphs, essays, quick writes, personal narratives, or even subgenres such as a friendly letter. See examples of organizers in Figure 2.8 and some blank organizers you can use in Appendices J–M. CSPACE is used to create stories, and its elements correlate well to overall story coherence and quality (Bourke & Adams, 2003). A blank organizer you can use is included in Appendix N. For the sake of simplicity, this book carries TIDE through each chapter whenever discussing organization since most of the examples in this book focus on informative and opinion/argument writing. This is the most common type of writing students will use in school, college, and their career. If you are thinking about narrative instruction while reading this book, you can replace CSPACE for TIDE whenever you see TIDE. For a chart of how TIDE and CSPACE can adapt vertically through grade levels, see Appendix C.

> *TIDE* = Topic introduction, Important evidence (or information), Detailed examination (or details), and End, or close variations on these terms (Mason et al., 2012). TIDE is used to structure expository writing such as informative or opinion/argument.
>
> CSPACE = Characters and Setting, then pose a Problem or set a Purpose (goal), followed by Action, Conclusion, and Emotion at the final wrap-up (MacArthur et al., 1991). CSPACE is used to structure how we tell stories.

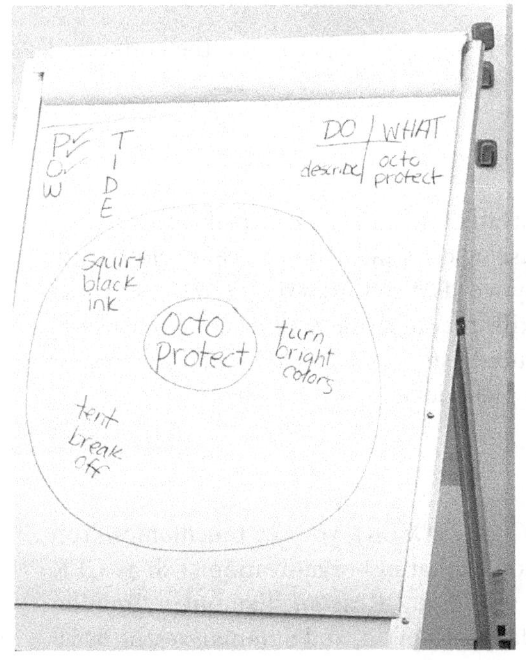

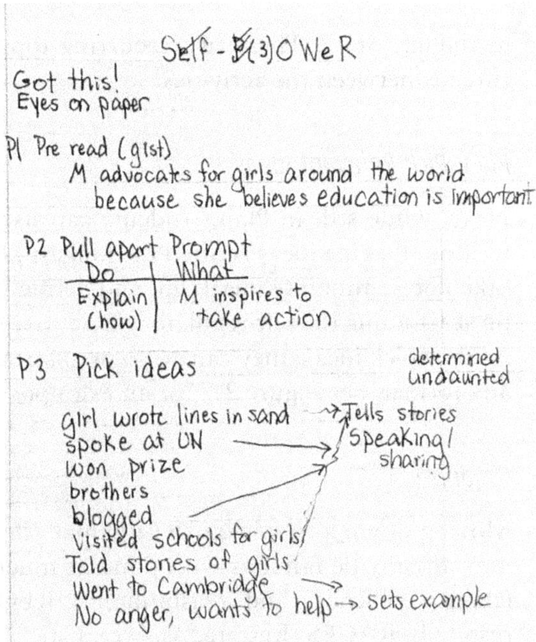

FIGURE 2.7. Examples of pick ideas.

FIGURE 2.8. Examples of TIDE organizers in grades 2 and 6.

Write

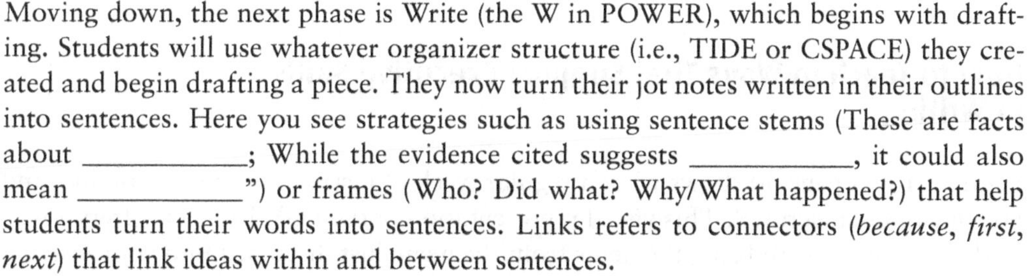

Moving down, the next phase is Write (the W in POWER), which begins with drafting. Students will use whatever organizer structure (i.e., TIDE or CSPACE) they created and begin drafting a piece. They now turn their jot notes written in their outlines into sentences. Here you see strategies such as using sentence stems (These are facts about ____________; While the evidence cited suggests ____________, it could also mean ____________") or frames (Who? Did what? Why/What happened?) that help students turn their words into sentences. Links refers to connectors (*because*, *first*, *next*) that link ideas within and between sentences.

Edit and Revise

Continuing down each phase in the POWER writing process are tools for Edit (E) and Revise (R). Tools for supporting these might range from reminders to use uppercase, periods, and check spelling (UPS) or ARMS (Add, Revise, Move, Substitute) and act as ways to guide oneself when revising. The mnemonics are all flexible and can be customized, but giving students tools to aid and support them in these processes helps them manage the underlying executive skills needed to carry themselves more effectively and independently through the process when writing.

Final Panel: Embed Skill Instruction and Reinforcement All Through the Process

The final panel in Figure 2.4, on the far right, lists examples of skills that can be taught and reinforced at each phase of the writing process. In a sense, the first and last panels are the skill bookends. Conventions such as letter formation, spelling, or grammatical accuracy would be front-loaded during foundational skills lessons (first panel), then reinforced during daily skill warm-up activities (last panel). The skills in this last panel, such as note taking or varied word choice, can be introduced and practiced at each corresponding phase of the writing process. By embedding direct instruction, deliberate practice, and reinforcement of these subskills into the actual writing that students plan, draft, and revise about the content topics they are responding to, they learn how to pay attention to multiple layers of language whenever they write.

Foundation Panel: Cultivate Self-Regulation All Through

Finally, the bottom bedrock in Figure 2.4 includes self-regulation skills that must be directly taught. For students who practice engaging in regular writing, using the writing process, the goal is to develop self-regulation. Students should internalize these routines and skills and receive regular self-, peer, and teacher feedback on their writing as they set new goals and work to achieve them.

In summary, Figure 2.4 shows the *what*—a menu of strategies, tools, and skills to teach that support writing in ways that include attention to executive skills. For a zoom-in that shows how these pieces all fit together as students work through each aspect of the writing process, see Figure 2.9.

Next, we turn to the *how*—how to teach these in a typical week.

How to Teach in Ways That Support Executive Skills in Writing

Figure 2.10 on page 30 shows what a regular week of instruction might look like and how it can be structured. This visual representation of the POWER cycle offers a way to think about how to bring the items from the menu just discussed into your instruction.

You may first notice the bolded arrows that suggest a cycle or repeated routine as the heart of this instruction. This ensures that students practice composing regularly, ideally every week or so (Graham et al., 2016). Introducing and practicing going through the writing process only a few times each year to produce lengthy essays will not likely lead to self-regulation, or give enough embedded skill application practice. Given how executive functioning performance improves with routines that are practiced repeatedly (Diamond, 2013), producing shorter pieces more often is important.

The three main features of this diagram include Self-instruction (top); Strategy Introduction (left); and the Teach, Model, Score cycle (center).

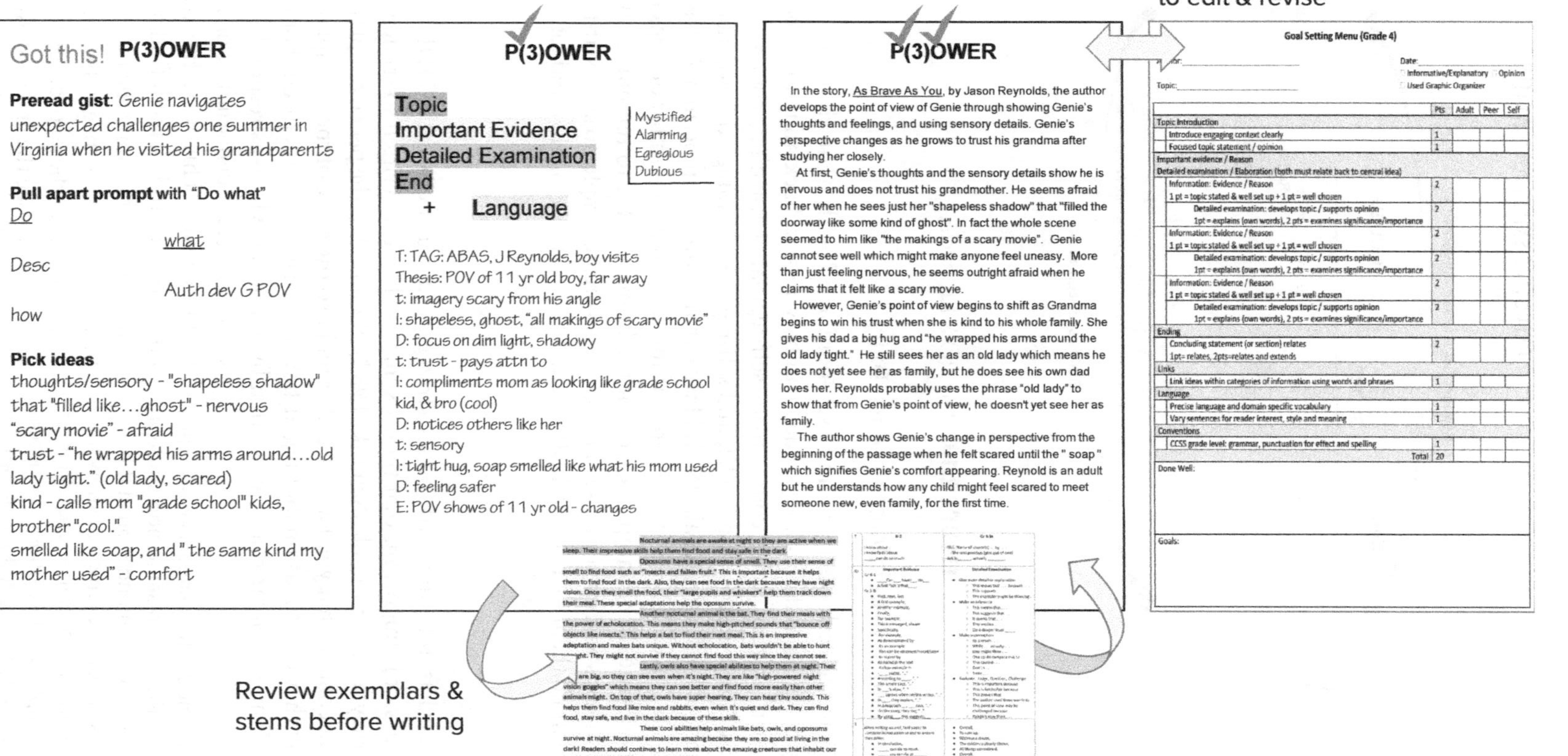

FIGURE 2.9. Writing process zoom-in.

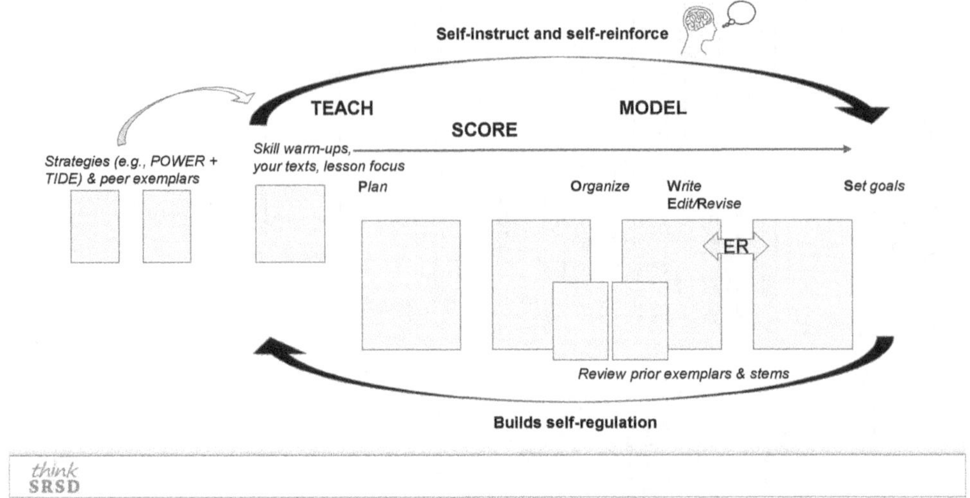

FIGURE 2.10. The POWER cycle.

Self-Instruct and Self-Reinforce Practice Daily

At the top, you see "self-instruct" and "self-reinforce," with brain thinking. This idea of explicitly teaching and coaching students in how to step back and guide themselves, or self-instruct, as they write comes from self-regulated learning, cognitive strategy instruction, strategic instruction model, and self-regulated strategy development models (Deshler et al., 1981; Englert et al., 1991; Harris et al., 2008; Zimmerman & Risemberg, 1997). Students can collaboratively create self-instruction plans—a list of steps they will follow as they write. For example, a student might make a list to remind themselves to follow certain steps as they compose. They can also create simple positive self-talk statements that remind them—"I've got this!"—which they can personalize and refer to daily.

Strategies

Over to the far left in Figure 2.10 you see strategies such as POWER + TIDE, as well as peer exemplars. It is important that these exemplars be peer-written so students believe the writing they see is attainable (Schunk, 1987). Be sure that the peer exemplar that you show is about content that you have already taught so the topic of the exemplar is familiar. This way they can focus on looking at how the writing is structured. For example, you can show an exemplar that was written by a student who was responding to your same science, social studies, or ELA curriculum texts. This way, the content is familiar and students will find it easier to look at and notice how the piece is set up. Instruction should begin by introducing strategies and these peer exemplars so your students see the end goal and how to get there right away. Seeing the end game

An *exemplar* is a model that shows an effective piece of writing written by a same-age student. In line with Covey's recommendation at the beginning of this chapter, exemplars show the end goal, or the finish line, in the sense that they give an example of what students can aim for when writing. They take out the mystery.

helps kick off goal setting, a powerful motivator. Students now understand what they are aiming for, and they want to get there.

To help students analyze and identify the exemplar's underlying text structure, you may highlight each section thinking about text structure (i.e., TIDE). Figure 2.11 shows examples of highlighting from preassessment essays in grades 2 and 6. Research supports having students study peer models (Graham & Perin, 2007), and you may have shown your students peer essays before. However, they may not have the working memory capacity to note and hold on to the specific features the writers used. When students are shown text-structure strategies such as TIDE, and instructed to think about this when writing on their own, this decreases their cognitive load.

Collect a Preassessment

The goal of this first launch lesson is to introduce the writing process along with organizer tools to use when writing. I also recommend showing a peer exemplar. However, before teaching this lesson, it is good practice to collect a preassessment. Doing so enables you to then show and analyze a strong exemplar response to that same preassessment that students just completed. When teachers collect the preassessment, they can identify strong exemplars from students in their class, write these themselves, or use artificial intelligence tools such as Claude or ChatGPT to create them. They can show it as an example of a piece written by a child who followed the writing process (POWER) and used TIDE to structure their piece. When teachers show these peer responses, not only can they highlight the aspects that make them effective, but they can also talk about how the writer planned and used the writing process. Later, students will review the preassessment they wrote, compare it to later pieces they produce, use it to set goals, and celebrate their progress as their writing improves. (For examples of preassessment tasks, see Appendix E.) You can also preassess your students' knowledge of key genre feature terms. Learning and knowing these terms also helps students set and pursue clear goals (see Appendix F).

Teach, Model, Score: What Does This Look Like Over a Week?

Finally, moving to the center of Figure 2.10, below the darker arrows, you see Teach, Model, Score. Below this figure are the elements of POWER that can guide you as you model writing with your students each week. You may also notice a small line just above the POWER boxes that says "skill warms-ups." If students are not yet fluent with foundational skills, be sure to add daily warm-ups, such as spelling practice or quick sentence production activities. For younger students, this would be in addition to whatever systematic program you use to teach these as needed. The following sections explain how Teach, Model, Score relates to POWER.

Teach

On the first day, perhaps Monday, we focus on "Teach." We might introduce and teach a new text or a new skill and/or strategy and even begin modeling how to

Grade 2 Samples

Task: Describe what octopuses can do to protect themselves. (Protect means to keep safe.) Support your answer with details from both texts.

Exemplar:

An octopus stays safe in different ways. They live near brightly colored coral reefs in the ocean, which keep them safe from harm because they can hide and escape through small spaces in these. Next, if an enemy grabs an octopus' tentacle, it breaks off. This 8-armed sea creature just grows a new one so it can swim away. Finally, an octopus is a strong swimmer and can move fast if it is in danger. Octopuses protect themselves in such different ways. In our community, we can stand up for our members to keep everyone safe too.

Grade 6 Exemplar

The article "Once Shot For Advocating For Girls' Education, Malala Is Going To Oxford" and the autobiography "I Am Malala" describe how Malala Yousafzai uses her voice to try to gain rights for girls even after she was shot by the Taliban. In both of these sources, Malala uses techniques to persuade others to use their own voices. By blogging, continuing to speak up even after being shot, and inspiring others with her words, Malala sets an effective model for how the average citizen could take actions to support their own causes.

In "Once Shot For Advocating For Girls' Education, Malala Is Going To Oxford", the author describes how Malala tried to change the world through her blog. When militants took control of Malala's hometown Swat in 2007, the Taliban "banned the education of girls". That same year, Malala began blogging about "life under Taliban domination". Since blog posts can be seen by anyone, Malala was able to use this to tell people all over the world about how many girls were being robbed of their educations. According to Malala in her autobiography "I Am Malala", "'Let us pick up our books and our pens,' I said. 'They are our most powerful weapons. One child, one teacher, one book and one pen can change the world.'" Malala certainly did this by blogging. She used her blog as a way for others to see what was going on in Pakistan. This can certainly be used to motivate others who would like to take action in support of their own causes. Using a blog is a great way to raise awareness about things that should be changed or a way to educate people. Blogs can reach people all over the world who can be persuaded to care about your cause and may help get millions of people involved.

In 2011, Malala returned to school and also "began publicly advocating for girls' education". On her way home from school one day in 2012, Malala was shot in her head, neck, and shoulders by a masked gunman. Malala survived this experience and continued to speak out against what was happening to girls in her community. In her autobiography, Malala writes "my only regret was that I hadn't had a chance to speak to them before they shot me. Now they'd never hear what I had to say." Malala did not want to be defined as "the girl who was shot by the Taliban." Instead, she wanted to be "the girl who fought for education." Malala teaches us that we should never give up when we face challenges. Standing up for something that we believe in can be difficult. We may not always feel as if we have the support we need or we may experience failure when we try. Since Malala never gave up when faced with her difficulties, her work can motivate average citizens to continue fighting for their own causes, even when things go their way. Her story can be used to remind people to never give up fighting for what they believe in.

Malala became very famous after she was shot by the Taliban for standing up for the rights of girls to go to school. She used this fame to inspire others through her autobiography and speeches. Malala gave a speech at the United Nations when she was sixteen. She said "If you want to see your future bright, you have to start working now and not wait for anyone else". In her autobiography, Malala states "I would do everything in my power to help educate girls just like her. This was the war I was going to fight". Malala inspired so many people with her words and even won the Nobel Peace Prize when she was eighteen. Average people can be motivated by Malala to use their own words to inspire others. Motivating people through words is a really good way to make your point and get more people involved in your cause. It also allows you to connect with people on a personal level, which might get them to care more about your cause.

In conclusion, Malala is an effective leader who can persuade others to do their best. Malala used her blog, continued to fight for a girl's right to an education after being shot, and inspired others with her autobiography and speeches. Malala is a great example of what a person should do when they are fighting for a cause

FIGURE 2.11. Examples of highlighted preassessment essays in grades 2 and 6.

use these. After you first onboard the writing process (POWER) and text structure (TIDE) in the initial lesson, then each following week, or instructional cycle, would return to Teach. For example, if last week's writing suggests that students did not master the writing skill or strategy of how to link ideas taught that week, then review again the teaching point. If they did, then introduce a new focus. This kind of formative, data-driven instructional planning is well supported (Graham et al., 2011). After teaching a new text (and new skill focus), you may begin modeling on the first day too.

Model

Over the next few days, we primarily "Model" each phase in the POWER writing process. We model less and less as students grow more independent in a gradual release model (Duke et al., 2011; Pearson & Gallagher, 1983). By modeling, a teacher leads composing in front of the class, writing ideas on the board as students contribute, and thinking aloud and subvocalizing the invisible thinking processes that guide them as they write. This can be called collaborative writing, co-writing, or interactive writing and is a key component in evidence-based writing approaches (Collins et al., 2021; Harris et al., 2023; McKeown et al., 2023; Olson et al., 2017; Wissinger et al., 2021). Students watch, take notes or copy, and adapt what they see the teacher writing, though this quickly fades as they break away and begin to write on their own.

Score

At the end of a cycle, we "Score" as a way to guide editing and revision and to help students set goals before they write again. Scoring is vital to the full Teach, Model, Score system and should be included in every cycle, even if only scoring for parts rather than a full piece. Scoring, along with modeling writing, are the key levers that encourage self-regulation. Scoring and modeling enable students to guide themselves and self-monitor what they write for quality as they go. Some coaches call the last day "Feedback Friday" to help teachers establish a regular routine that includes scoring. At this point, you can demonstrate scoring pieces in front of the class, taking student input as you go. Then, release students to self- and peer-evaluate their own and each other's writing so they can regularly self-evaluate and set goals.

All Through the Week: Practice Composing and Scoring with Short-Writes

Figure 2.10 demonstrates how writing can be taught over a given week. While students will practice writing at least weekly, those in the upper grades (grade 3 and above) do not need to produce full essays each cycle. To keep this regular practice manageable, students can work at the level of *short writes*, such as only a paragraph, and still see significant gains in overall writing quality (Benedek-Wood et al., 2014; Collins et al., 2021). In fact, frequent, shorter pieces allow more opportunities for formative feedback and practice (Graham et al., 2011). Older students can alternate spending a few weeks developing new skills at the paragraph level then apply these at the essay level every quarter or so.

As an additional tip, when even more pressed for time (and who isn't?!), during some weeks, students will only go through P3 with a text, or just "Take it to TIDE" and complete only P and O in POWER.

Build Self-Regulation by Repeating Routines Weekly, and in Manageable Ways

Overall, Teach, Model, Score enables us to bundle a set of strategies (such as POWER and TIDE) into one overarching (usually weekly) instructional routine. This allows for the amount of practice and regular feedback that helps students become independent in using these tools. It offers an integrative, overarching, and cohesive framework for instruction. The specific strategies included in the bundle can be deemphasized once students internalize them, and new ones can be added.

Teach the *Writer*, Not the Writing

Before moving to our sample lesson, we have a final word on self-regulation. When using such a system to teach, practice, and reinforce the kinds of strategies and skills students need to learn, the instructional goal shifts away from supporting them in producing a single piece of writing. It moves instead toward helping them to master the writing process, skills, and features they need to produce for effective writing on their own. The goal becomes teaching students how they can take themselves through the writing process and produce high-quality pieces, independently. Instruction would move away from teaching the *writing* to teaching the *writer*. This prompts a future-oriented outlook. Instead of helping students produce one well-written piece, we help them become able to produce writing pieces on their own. This is the difference between teaching skills only versus teaching in a way that also directly supports students in developing executive control and self-regulation right from the start.

See It in Action: Sample Lesson

You have just been introduced to a framework that supports students in learning the writing process and the most essential elements that underlie effective writing such as text structure. You then learned what comprehensive, cyclical practice in using these could look like over a given week.

The following sample lesson is designed to pull together these elements and make it easy for you to visualize what introducing this kind of framework to your students might look like. The subsequent chapters then break down and explore how to introduce and teach each aspect of the writing process. As they do, this kind of sample lesson plan will travel with us through the book. Think of these lessons as a scaffold for you to work your way through each chapter. My purpose in providing them is to bridge what you already know about teaching the writing process to the (possibly) less familiar executive function and self-regulation skills that are the focus of this book. You will see how much of what you already do supports these skills, and discover ways to further enhance your instruction around them.

More specifically, this lesson focuses on how to introduce the writing process, text structure, and the idea of exemplars to your students.

SAMPLE LESSON: Introduce the Writing Process and Teach How to Structure Texts

Note: Before teaching this lesson, it can be helpful to collect a preassessment of student writing. Have them read (or read to them) a short text and then invite them to write a response to it.

Goal: Introduce and preview the full writing process and expository text structure; then look at what an effective piece of writing looks like so students know what they are aiming for when they go to write.

Objectives:

1. Introduce the writing process.
2. Introduce the text structure of a paragraph or essay.
3. Analyze a peer-written exemplar.

Estimated Time: 30–45 minutes

Materials: Chart paper or smartboard, markers, highlighters for all students, copies of a peer-written exemplar, writing notebooks

Lesson Steps:

1. Tell your students that you will introduce the writing process, share a helpful way to understand how to set up or structure a piece of writing, and show an exemplar that was written by a child who used the tools you will share (5 minutes).
2. Write POWER on the board or chart paper vertically. Explain and write out what each letter stands for.
3. Do the same for TIDE (see the "What to Teach" chart from earlier). Students can write these in their notebooks if they are fluent at transcription (5 minutes).

   Reminder: Keep this anchor chart hanging all year. You can add to it as students flesh out how to do each element of POWER and TIDE better. It becomes an important reference that students will actively use throughout year.
4. Pass out an exemplar peer-written paragraph or essay. Have students read it, then discuss where they see the parts of TIDE in it. Use a different color to color-code each part of TIDE in it with a system such as green for topic, yellow for important evidence/information, orange for detailed examination (or details),

and pink for end. (If you collected a preassessment sample, this exemplar can be written in response to the same text they read for the preassessment.)

5. Move to peer and independent practice by having students color-code the latter parts of the exemplar in teams, then on their own.
6. When finished, have them draw a box in the upper corner and list the strong vocabulary words they found in that space.
7. On a sticky note, or in their notebooks, have them also make a list of what makes detailed examination (or details) differ from information. Elicit that it adds more and does not move to a new fact. It may include "my own thinking" (inferences or insights), particularly in grade 3 and up.
8. If time, have students draw TIDIDIDE down the side of a full page of notebook paper. Students write TIDIDIDE to remind them to include three body sections in their paragraph or essay. (Older students can use variations such as TIDID for shorter writes, or TtIDtIDtIDE to remind themselves to include subtopic sentences in each section). Then have them pull out the key "jot talk," not full sentences, from each section of the essay into this drawn organizer. If you have more or fewer body sections of sentences in the middle of the exemplar (not the introduction or ending), then TIDE changes accordingly.
9. Ensure students memorize POWER and TIDE. You can introduce songs, chants, and games to help them practice these until memorized.
10. Wrap-Up: Ask students to share what they learned. Have them repeat what POWER and TIDE stand for, and discuss how these tools can help them. Then remind them that these tools will help make writing easier.

Next Steps: In the future, students will now use these tools each week to guide them as they write. You will model how and support them in a gradual release using thinking aloud to show how expert writers use them, then fade the level of scaffolding. Each week, you will teach and model increasingly higher levels of writing as they use these tools together to build pieces collaboratively as a class, then more independently.

Mental "Shelving"

This sample lesson introduces the core processes writers follow, along with products (well-structured paragraphs) they create. By starting with introducing the big picture for both, you help students build mental structures, or *schemas*. They can see the whole and how all the pieces fit together. Doing so supports executive skills and gives students an organized mental framework, or shelving system (Nahna, 2024). Moving forward, students have shelf-spaces to neatly organize and place each bit of new learning to do steps in the writing process, and they know what to focus on next after first structuring their ideas into paragraphs. As they learn more nuanced and broken-down ways to plan, draft, revise, or liven up the language in their pieces, having the big picture of POWER in mind helps them hold on to each new strategy, skill, or scaffold, readily call them up, and apply them in an organized fashion. For example, as they master writing topic sentences, and learn more about how to set up evidence or facts, they organize these new skills under TIDE. This supports them in pursuing their goals by using the writing process to reach toward the kind of writing they see in the exemplars (Perone et al., 2021).

No More "Dash to Drafting"

Such tools also help students overcome distractions. For example, when they write POWER on their paper and cross off each element as they go, these clear steps and overarching plans help them to focus on important tasks and overcome distractions. These tools make sustaining attention, staying on track, knowing what to do, and monitoring themselves easier. Such tools empower them to take themselves through the writing process independently, in time. They make it easier for them to avoid rushing through writing. If your students are in the habit of dashing right to drafting and skipping over the needed prework beforehand, this kind of tool disrupts that impulsive behavior. These tools put speed bumps on the road that help students inhibit the impulse (another executive skill) to dash to drafting and offer a more manageable way to approach each of the steps.

Build Recall to Ease Working Memory Load

To help students memorize the phases in the writing process with mnemonics such as POWER, or how to structure their writing with tools such as TIDE, you can have students copy these by hand when you introduce them. They can also repeat them daily in chants or songs, as was recommended at the end of the lesson. The goal is for them to internalize these phases and use them independently, which helps students to reach gradual release and move to independence (Harris et al., 2008). Students can draw on them to guide them when these are in long-term memory. Once students have them internalized, they can juggle using the tools (and steps within them) more easily without taxing their working memory as much. They can also follow and use these in more cognitively flexible ways.

How Text Structure Awareness Supports Organization and Flexibility

Text structures such as TIDE bring order to language. Ideas do not naturally arise in organized structures. Students think in bursts that are ideas that arise preverbally then come into language in loosely connected phrases and sentences (Kim, 2022). Teaching students to make outlines of their ideas as they arise serves to scaffold their organization of these bursts, helping the executive skills used. All learners, especially the many who struggle with executive skills, can more easily structure what they would like to communicate when they have an outline. TIDE (or CSPACE) offers an easy way to remember and then use text structure from the start when composing. It's also easier to think outside the box when you know the box. Understanding text structure makes the box clear to students. They can then flex how to present their ideas more easily, yet still be understood because they work from a structured base. Later, TIDE also becomes important in helping students set and pursue goals.

Take It to the Classroom: Tips You Can Use Tomorrow

To bring the key ideas from this chapter to your classroom, you can take the following key steps tomorrow. Note that the Appendix at the end of this book is sequenced to provide a virtual starter kit designed to help you take this to your classroom. You may want to return periodically to Appendix A, which provides a "big-picture" scope and sequence, and Appendix B, which offers a comprehensive "bird's-eye view" of all the writing skills broken out that you would target over the year. For now, let's get back to the initial steps of getting started.

Collect a Writing Preassessment

Have your students read a slightly more complex but brief text and view a brief (1- to 2-minute) video. If you prefer, you can start with just a simpler text and video to begin and add more complex texts after your students learn the strategy. Yet, be sure to bring in and have students respond to challenging texts as soon as you can to ensure that you maximize opportunities for students to engage in writing and practice it using all the executive skills. If the task is not challenging enough, they may not need to recruit their executive skills. Assign a writing prompt and have them write in response for 30–45 minutes. Afterward, show an exemplar so they can compare their writing to it and set goals for themselves. There would be no preinstruction before this activity. The purpose is to see what students do when they write and whether they are able to structure and manage their writing without any direct instruction.

Introduce the Writing Process

Explain to your students that writers use a writing process and explain each part, as in the sample lesson. Post the list of steps and have them write this in their notebooks. Explain that all year as they write, they can jot down POWER and cross off each step whenever they write.

Introduce Text Structure

Tell your students that any text, such as a paragraph or essay, follows a basic structure. For informative or opinion/argument writing, this can include the elements of TIDE: Topic, Information, Details or detailed analysis, and End. After students have a handle on this kind of expository writing structure, show them the broadest form of narrative structure as CSPACE: Characters, Setting, Purpose, Actions, Conclusion, and Emotion, which was introduced and discussed earlier in this chapter. These structures can aid comprehension of texts (see Cartwright, 2023, for more on this) and guide students when they write their own pieces.

Analyze Exemplars for Text Structure, Initially

After explaining the writing process and discussing how texts can be structured, show peer-written exemplars that demonstrate the features of high-quality writing. Like a tour guide, walk your students through what makes the exemplar effective. Make this explicit through color-coding each section of TIDE or back-mapping it into an organizer so students clearly see each part and how the overall text is structured. Be sure to introduce the idea of a *language box*. Draw a box at the bottom or top corner of the exemplar. List the effective word choices there. Also, make a list of how the important evidence (information) differs from the detailed examination (details), such as that information is facts while details say more about these or add an inference about them. This helps students understand how information differs from elaboration. (Using a language box along with TIDE is often referred to as TIDE-L.)

As the year progresses, you can continue to analyze these exemplars for additional layers of elements such as linking ideas, making vocabulary choices, and crafting compelling introductions or inferences. Step by step, you can analyze them all for aspects of structure, language, and reasoning over time.

Begin with the End in Mind

Introducing the writing process and text structure and analyzing an exemplar response allows students to see the gestalt and understand what is being asked of them right out of the gate. Let students know where they are going right from Day 1 so they can set clear goals and have tools to get there. Returning to the opening quote, keep in mind Covey's admonition to "begin with the end in mind." Students initially analyze peer exemplars—that is, example end pieces of writing—for structures such as TIDE and CSPACE so that they can see how effective essays are organized and then use it during the planning stage. Once they reach the goal of improving organization of their writing, they keep going. They also look at levels beyond structure such as sentence variation and word choice to understand more deeply what makes the piece exemplary, again so they can mimic such features when producing their own writing. Seeing exemplars kicks off the force of volition because they give vision and inspire students to set clear targets and work toward them. (See Figure 2.11 for examples.)

That's a Wrap!

This chapter introduced the main models of writing instruction and how they underscore the importance of executive skills for effective writing. It then offered a framework for onboarding the kind of writing instruction that centers the importance of these skills. It also presented a sample lesson for how to launch writing instruction in a way that centers attention on supporting executive skills in order to develop self-regulated, thinking writers. The chapters that follow dive more deeply into how to teach each aspect of writing and highlight how the evidence-based practices for doing so draw on and support executive skills within writing. Each chapter follows the same format, which includes:

- Definition of the executive skill and why it matters
- Back Inside Our School: What It Looks Like When Students Are Doing It Well
- See It in Action: Sample Lesson
- Lesson Analysis (how the executive skill underlies each component)
- Take It to the Classroom: Tips You Can Use Tomorrow
- That's a Wrap!

CHAPTER 3

Planning

Teach and Model the Writing Process

Failing to plan is planning to fail.
—Benjamin Franklin

Planning well is an important factor in producing higher-quality pieces because it makes writing easier (Chai, 2006; Truckenmiller et al., 2022; Worden, 2009). Essentially, a stitch in time saves nine. When students plan carefully first, they write faster and more efficiently and need to revise far less (Worden, 2009). *Carefully* in this case means that students think first about the big picture of what they would like to say, as well as the details they will include. Some planning always happens, almost unconsciously. To write anything, we first have an idea in mind, a goal to express it, and then we figure out—or plan—how to write our idea. This natural process involves some level of planning, but usually small amounts. To write well, one should not plan minute by minute as one goes but, rather, create a more comprehensive and goal-directed plan upfront (Schunk et al., 1993). When students are not internally goal-driven and are unaware of the planning executive skill that their more expert peers use, we see the familiar list of disorganized ideas or just "staring at blank paper."

Planning is a future-oriented process of calling up and defining a goal, then mapping out steps to meet it. This includes understanding the task, setting a purpose, and brainstorming—all before starting to write.

While this kind of planning is a higher-order executive function, it relies on the lower-level core skills such as working memory (Vanderberg & Swanson, 2007), inhibition, and cognitive flexibility (Diamond, 2013). To plan well, students must hold ideas in mind long enough to jot them down (*working memory*). When multiple ideas come to mind, they need to filter out (*inhibit*) irrelevant ones. They need to shift course (*cognitive flexibility*) often to ensure they meet their goals. Based on the lower core executive skills, the higher-order skill of planning supports writing quality (Ruffini et al., 2024). These executive skills do not operate in isolation. Students recruit and use them together during writing. In this chapter, we focus on how they are recruited and used during planning.

One can have a plan in mind or write it down. Studies show that even by middle school, students cannot plan "online" (in their minds) as they transcribe their ideas, while adults *can* create and hold a plan more easily (Olive & Kellogg, 2002). This suggests that students should draft a plan. However, students do not naturally create a plan before writing (Limpo et al., 2014), likely because they do not know how. However, the good news is that this executive skill of planning can be taught and scaffolded. When taught how to plan well, students produce higher-quality writing (Collins et al., 2021; Harris et al., 2023; McKeown et al., 2023; Wissinger et al., 2021). This is particularly important when writing in the more complex genres, such as compare–contrast and teaching students with disabilities (Shen & Troia, 2017) or those who struggle in core underlying areas such as initiation and flexibility (Hooper et al., 2002). The executive skill of planning is important in written expression (Hooper et al., 2011), and it distinguishes effective writers from those who struggle, emphasizing its critical role (Johnson et al., 2003).

Making a plan may look simple, but it is not. Think about all that a student must call up and do in order to plan well, particularly when responding to a source that represents increasingly common forms of writing in schools (Graham & Perin, 2007). As soon as students open the source text, they must pull the words off the page and comprehend them. This includes decoding them, understanding the vocabulary and sentence structures, reasoning, making inferences, and noticing how the text is structured. Then they need to take notes while they read, which is a cognitively demanding skill in itself. To be efficient and to support deeper processing of the material they are learning, these notes should shrink and distill key ideas and be taken in shorthand, and not full sentences (see Figure 2.8 in Chapter 2).

To then create an organizer, students must draw on the cognitive skills that underlie the organization process. These include *salience determination*, or deciding what is relevant and important, which is intimately tied to inhibition (ignoring what's irrelevant) and requires significant mental effort. Likewise, they must also practice *summarizing*, grouping or categorizing, and sequencing the information while planning. They also need to learn shorthand or note-taking skills, or how to use abbreviations, symbols, or images so they can write their notes quickly and efficiently. Even more, they need *fluent transcription* (i.e., letter formation, spelling).

All through, it is important that they take notes by hand as they plan rather than type them. This promotes greater brain connectivity, which leads to deeper learning (Ihara et al., 2021; Mueller & Oppenheimer, 2014; Van der Weel et al., 2024). Doing so helps students hold the ideas in working memory longer and resist distractions. Writing notes by hand allows them to spend more time processing them. In buying this time, it may promote more cognitive flexibility as they have a chance to rethink or change their ideas.

Stepping back to teach and support the executive skill of planning, we can guide students in how to break the writing task down into manageable pieces and steps. This reduces the mental demands of writing so that subcomponents can be tackled one at a time. The multiple steps to planning, discussed in this chapter, culminate in creating written plans. As mentioned earlier, making a plan lightens the cognitive load for students. Using a plan decreases the amount of information students need to hold in mind as they draft because it places a concrete guide and reminders on paper. This helps them to get started and then hold onto ideas (while fine-tuning them) as they compose.

Students can then focus more easily on lower-order skills, such as forming their letters more neatly and spelling more accurately. They have more cognitive capacity to attend to these after they have their ideas down on paper. Doing so also enables students to better ideate (generate further ideas) and write with greater higher-order insight and depth because their mind (i.e., their limited working memory) is not tied up holding on to their basic ideas.

In the following section, we return to our school to watch students planning during a writing lesson. Following this visit, I analyze the lesson for how the instruction supports the executive skill of planning, then wrap up this chapter with tips for taking the key ideas to your classroom.

Back Inside Our School: What Planning Looks Like When Students Are Doing It Well

Let's head back inside the double red doors of our school. These students were lost before they learned the kinds of executive functioning support strategies described more fully in this chapter and had the skills in place to be able to compose more efficiently. At best, they might read an assigned text, then begin drafting. If they planned, they might overplan and produce a full draft on the organizer itself, which is not an effective planning method. Their drafts might include difficulties with conventions such as spelling or sentence structure. Their working memory may be consumed with merely holding on to their basic ideas. They likely could not attend to multiple levels of language at once. Emotionally, they may have started off full of hope that they would write something wonderful, but then quickly lost steam, felt overwhelmed, and gave up. They read the text, dove into drafting, then looked back at the text but struggled to identify which information was the most important, which information should be included, and how to organize their ideas.

In contrast, after learning the main strategies and tools described next, they had a plan and a way to get there. During today's visit, we watch how students gather ideas. This is part of the first phase, the P in Plan, from the writing process introduced in the last chapter, and the easily recallable POWER (Plan, Organize, Write, Edit, Revise) mnemonic.

These students have been studying animal and bird behaviors in science. Their Language Arts curriculum has a unit on this topic as well. The week began with the teacher showing slides that had the key words from the unit next to images. She also showed a 2-minute video that explained what *endangered* means and gave several examples. After the video, students might complete graphic organizers such as a Frayer map (Frayer et al., 1969) or create semantic feature maps (Jennings & Haynes, 2018) of the key vocabulary terms. They discussed how some raccoons were endangered. One student shared that these animals can live in icy temperatures and that she would not like to live someplace that is so cold herself. The teacher pointed to the title at the top of the fact list they were making where they were keeping the ideas they picked. It said "Endangered creatures." This student acknowledged that ice may not belong there but could be a small detail to include into writing. Students copied the words down, created a list, and made a web to show the examples, synonyms, and connected ideas. They then read several texts on this topic. Students had participated the day before in a shared, collaborative, classwide writing project concerning other endangered animals. As their teacher modeled going through each phase of the writing process while making notes on chart paper, students watched, contributed ideas, and copied them into their writing journals. They began making a fact list where they recorded information.

They continued writing about different endangered animals. They read some more information, viewed a short video, drew images of where the animals live, and listed what they eat, how they survive winter, and further specifics. Taking these steps sets the students up to have enough information to turn these notes into an organizer. As the teacher models the process, students copy everything into their notebooks. They use abbreviations and short phrases along with stick figures to be efficient. Finally, they will use their organizer to create a paragraph, which they will score together as a class as a way to find areas to revise in a next lesson. Doing so will help them to set a class goal, such as adding more details, which they will work to meet the next time they write.

After modeling and practicing how to plan, the teacher lets students work in small groups, on their own, or stay as they plan for their own pieces now. Inside one student's mind, you might hear:

> *OK, I don't like raccoons. I'm glad that was only a class example write, and I don't have to write my own report about them. They can bite you. Wait, I have to stay on track. I'm going to write about squirrels. I have my notebook open. I'll look at my Do/What to help me remember my focus as I plan. Right, my piece will be about squirrels. I'll look in my book at the part about squirrels. I see they are gray. That is a fact. I can write that down. Great, I have a fact already. I can do this. The book says they eat nuts. I can write that fact too. I'll also draw the large, bushy tail and write bushy. I know that when I plan, I'm only putting my ideas down in short notes. I will turn my notes into sentences later.*

Another student in upper elementary might struggle more to stay on task, but the mnemonics and self-talk help:

> *OK, I know I need to write an essay about a penguin rescue that I just read about. This is hard. When is lunch? Wait, let me think about my goals. My goal was to write down and follow all the steps. I'll use this scrap paper and write down the steps I should follow to make this easier. I'll start by putting positive self-talk. It's a little hokey, but it does seem to help me. I'll write that I've got this. Next, I'll write out POWER and check it off as I do each part. Alright, I'm moving along now. I feel better and less overwhelmed. I'll reread the text source*

and jot down the gist. Then I'll do a Do/What and make a chart that lists what the prompt is telling me to "Do," which is Describe. The "What" is the challenges the rescuers faced and how the penguins responded. I know it is helpful to keep repeating the "What" in my mind to keep me focused on what I will write about as I read, plan, and then write. Once I forgot and I went off topic. OK, the "What" is how the poor little penguins responded. Wait, how do I spell "responded"? I'll sound it out and write one chunk at a time. That will help me meet my correct spelling goal. It sounds like "did"—d-i-d—at the end. Wait, it already happened so it is past tense. This would be spelled -ed. My other goals are to analyze the information more insightfully and strengthen my ending. OK, I'll look back more carefully to find information on how they responded so I can come up with better ideas for how to analyze this. I'll jot that down on my scrap paper as I go.

See It in Action: Sample Lesson

You just visited classrooms where students were planning before writing. Remember the Teach, Model, Score cycle? The last chapter's sample lesson looked at how to "Teach" the writing process briefly, simply stating what each part of POWER stood for. This sample lesson will dive in more deeply and focus on how to "Model" the Plan (P) phase in POWER at the start of a weekly cycle. Learning how to plan—and, even more, internalizing this executive skill—requires explicit instruction, support tools, modeling, practice, feedback, and coaching. Without this, the students just described would not have reached the level of independence they have.

SAMPLE LESSON: Modeling the P in POWER

Goal: Model showing students how to use the writing process when they write. Focus on the P (Plan) in POWER. Show how to carry out each step in P.

Objectives:

1. Review the writing process and demonstrate how to do the first step of planning.
2. Preteach vocabulary and background knowledge needed for the lesson.
3. Model using self-talk to guide and encourage oneself while writing.
4. Model prereading to find a main idea gist statement.
5. Model pulling apart a prompt to identify what the task is asking you to do.
6. Model picking ideas to use when reading to write.

Estimated Time: 30–45 minutes

Materials: Chart paper, whiteboard or smartboard, markers, pencils, notebook paper, copies of a text that students will read

Lesson Steps:

1. Introduce and teach any vocabulary or background knowledge needed to understand the topic or texts being taught in this lesson. Encourage students to think about vocabulary use goals. Let them know they will have a chance to write about this topic and to meet their word choice targets when they do. They can use these words to help them do that. (*Note:* You would use your content and texts for this lesson—your science, social studies, or ELA materials.)
2. Write POWER on the board and review the meaning of each phase in the writing process. Students can write this down and cross off each step as they go (5 minutes).
3. Explain that today we will focus on learning and practicing the P phase in the writing process.
4. Tell students, "First, we will write down some positive self-talk, such as 'I've got this; I can stay focused' or 'I'll follow the steps in P.' This can help us stay focused, encouraged, and know what to do as we write." Create a class list of such phrases and post it. Students can copy these in their notebooks (5 minutes).
5. Explain that the P in POWER helps us plan to write. There are three steps:
   - Preread for a main idea or gist.
   - Pull apart the prompt with Do/What.
   - Pick ideas.
6. *Preread.* First, we will do an initial read and find the gist or main idea of the text. Have students look for the "who" and "did what" in the text they read, then turn that into a sentence. If they identify only one small section of the text, we call that a mini gist. We write a few more ideas, combine them, and then come up with the main gist. See Appendix I for how to expand and vary gist sentence practice over the year (10 minutes).
7. *Pull apart.* Next, lead students in analyzing the prompt with a Do/What T-chart. Under "Do," they write the prompt's verb. The prompt might say "Explain how" or "Decide which." Under "What," they write what it is the prompt is directing them to explain, such as how "octopuses protect themselves."
8. *Pick ideas.* Explain that this is often the longest phase in the writing process. The longer students spend reading, discussing, and thinking about a topic, the richer their final writing will be. Have students look at the What in their Do/What to help them focus as they now do a close read and look again at the text to find evidence that can help respond to the prompt.
9. Teachers can model in think-alouds how they would read each section, demonstrating where they would pause and mark the text or take notes to help them pick which ideas are best to use.
10. Students will also make notes, mark up, or begin copying strong vocabulary and phrases at this point. These will later go in their language boxes on their organizers when they reach the O, or Organize, phase in POWER.

Wrap-Up: Summarize that this lesson reviewed POWER and looked at how to follow the steps in P. To see an example of a think-aloud lesson in action in a real classroom, go to *https://thinksrsd.com/srsd-in-action/.*

Lesson Analysis: How Each Component Supports Planning for Effective, Self-Regulated Writing

Preteaching Vocabulary and Knowledge Support Planning

In this lesson, students write about what they read. Beforehand, their teacher pretaught key vocabulary and background knowledge with slide decks, images, videos, and/or discussion. This front-loading frees up cognitive resources and enhances comprehension (Chien, 2020; Peng et al., 2024). Students can then focus on applying the kinds of strategies that support the executive skill of planning more easily. See Cartwright (2023) for further insight on front-loading vocabulary and background knowledge. As you preteach, also help students discover ways to figure out new words or concepts they encounter in texts so that when you are not with them, they can do this on their own. To motivate them, link this to their goals. They may have set specific targets such as using more varied words. By identifying the meanings of new words and adding these to their planner, students actively engage their planning executive skills in a goal-directed way (Bruce & Bell, 2022).

Teacher Talk Example

Let's talk about the importance of planning. A plan includes a list of steps to follow and what to do at each step. Planning helps you meet your goals and make the activity easier. Today we are going to write about this passage on wolves, but before we can do that, we want to make sure we gather the important knowledge as we read about the topic and get ready to make a writing plan. Sometimes, texts include words or ideas that we don't know. We'll need to know meanings for those words—and the knowledge behind them—to write about the topic. We can write these on our plan to help us remember to use them.

Let's look at the passage about wolves. I see a few words that might be unfamiliar: habitat, endangered, *and* territorial. *Let's work out the meanings together now to make sure we understand them and can use them when we begin to write. Let's look for synonyms nearby or word parts we recognize. I see "place where they live" in the sentence just after habitat. And I know* cohabitate *because we used this word when we studied how rhinos and zebras live together. So, a habitat must be a place to live. We used words nearby and parts of the word itself to help us figure out what they mean.*

These are great strategies you can use when you read on your own in the future, too. They help you figure out what important words mean so you can note them on your writing plan. When you plan ahead for the words you will use, you get yourself ready to include them when you go to write later. This can help you meet your goal to use stronger vocabulary words in your pieces.

Self-Regulation Can Be Taught Explicitly

After this kind of preteaching, students begin using the writing process with increasing independence. This chapter focuses on the launch to this work, which begins with planning. During the planning stage, students should motivate themselves and set out specific steps to meet their goals, mentally. The POWER (Plan, Organize, Write, Edit, Revise) process will help them get started and self-regulate (Englert et al., 1991). We can do this even more explicitly as well. Remind students to use this positive inner self-talk before getting started with planning. Self-talk language ("I've got this; I will start with POWER") offers a way to jump-start and bolster students' calling up, recruiting, and using their executive skills.

Some teachers initially even add the word *self to* POWER: *Self-POWER*. Writing this kind of reminder helps students remember to activate their own inner self-speech independently to guide and motivate themselves as they work through POWER, starting with planning. Using self-talk, or self-instruction (Englert et al., 1991; Meichenbaum & Goodman, 1971), helps students initiate, set a plan, and direct their attention and is particularly important for students with developmental language disorders (Baron & Arbel, 2022).

Before students begin planning their ideas out, they can write these kinds of self-encouragement phrases ("I've got this") to support their initiation and to maintain their plan (Englert et al., 1991; Harris et al., 1985; Meichenbaum & Goodman, 1971). They will also use tools such as POWER and TIDE to help them get started, self-regulate, and stay on track. Teaching students through modeling and inviting them to practice this kind of positive self-speech along with following the steps in POWER both contribute to developing self-regulation. Instruction that teaches and supports such planning and self-regulation accelerates developing both cognitive and affective—or cold and hot, respectively—executive functioning capacities that support students in becoming independent, skilled, and self-directed.

As a personal example, I often had to redirect myself while still only in the planning phase when outlining this book. I often used this kind of self-talk, reminding myself aloud that "I can do this" and setting writing goals daily. Self-talk was introduced in the first sample lesson, will reappear in each chapter, and is meant to be integrated at each point all through the students' writing process. This kind of authorial inner-self speech can be regularly scaffolded and honed after it is initially taught, modeled, and practiced. Additionally, self-talk can be expanded to include any kind of verbal or nonverbal cues that help students regulate. These could include a picture on their desk that reminds them to refocus or nonverbal mindfulness practices that have also been shown to help students self-regulate and improve executive functioning (Flook et al., 2010) and advance writing skills in areas such as handwriting (Cordeiro et al., 2021) and increase the quality of opinion essay writing (Limpo et al., 2023).

Gist Writing Builds Coherence and Creates a Mental Model

After preteaching the needed vocabulary and background knowledge, as well as helping students get into a positive and self-directed mindset with self-talk, it is time to begin using the steps of the writing process. Students are ready to begin working through each phase, starting with the planning phase (P). It is important to break down each step and label it, as done in this lesson. The three steps for Plan (P) are fluid:

- P1: Preread for a gist.
- P2: Pull apart the prompt with Do/What.
- P3: Pick ideas.

It is important to break down the writing process, and teach and model each step, as students initially learn it. However, you can balance how much you break it down with how much your students (and you) can manage at a time. If you want to choose one or two steps to teach and model initially then add more steps, that can work. To ensure effective planning, it is important for students to see and understand the big picture: There is a writing process they should follow (i.e., POWER), and they should use a text structure to organize their ideas while writing (i.e., TIDE for informative or persuasive writing). They can learn the more fine-grained aspects of how to do this (how to write a topic sentence, ending, or analysis) a few steps at a time, rather than all at once.

Modeling and teaching how to write gists is an evidence-based practice (Vaughn et al., 2022; Wijekumar et al., 2017) that helps students see and hold on to the whole of the text. As defined earlier, a *gist* is a short, one-sentence main idea summary that identifies *who*—did *what*—*when/where*—and *why*, or *what happened* (Jennings & Haynes, 2018). See Figure 2.5 in Chapter 2 for examples. Creating a gist helps students identify, maintain, and update the main idea as they read rather than lose the central thread. It may also help with the kind of cognitive shifting needed to flexibly allocate attention during planning and the writing process (Butterfuss & Kendeou, 2018). While reading, students can integrate new content and adapt their main idea gist statements.

Wider Benefits of Using Gists

Teaching students to write a gist also offers the opportunity to slip in daily sentence construction, expansion, and variation practice too (see Appendix I) when they write this gist statement. When writing gists, students practice producing and varying grammatically accurate sentences, an evidence-based practice (Graham et al., 2012, 2016). Teachers can use this time to introduce and discuss what makes a sentence complete, fragmented, or run on and how to ensure sentence variation. Over time, each day, teachers can model introducing new grade-level grammatical elements or varied sentence structures as they expand and vary gist writing each week. For example, grade 2 teachers might have students write gists using collective nouns to incorporate practice of this standard, while grade 4 might use subordinating conjunctions. As you increase the complexity of your gist statements each week, you can help students identify and note text structures in their statements (Wijekumar et al., 2017). For example, the structure could be descriptive, cause–effect, problem–solution, or contrastive. Later, after students have a well-constructed plan, they will draw on these sentence writing skills as they turn the ideas on their planners into full sentences.

With the reading comprehension needed to make an effective plan, research supports that students who can create these brief summary statements (gists) receive the highest scores on what they write (Chai, 2007) and also improve globally on reading comprehension when using the more advanced main idea statements that focus on text structure (Wejikumar et al., 2017).

Support Inhibition and Attentional Control for Effective Planning

As a next step in preparing to support planning, the Do/What tool allows students to set a purpose, inhibit distractions, and maintain attentional control during reading and writing. In this chapter's Sample Lesson, you saw the student remind himself to stay focused on the What. In this case, the What was the penguins' responses. He kept repeating the What in his mind as he read, planned, and wrote. Doing so enables students to focus on what they will write about. This lets them inhibit irrelevant information, maintain attentional control, and shift focus as needed. Many students also write this "What" on a sticky note and refer to it frequently as they read to gather information or evidence, then also write the "What" on their organizer (which you'll learn about in the next chapter) and again at the top of their paper when they draft and revise. Such tools build out each element of POWER and continue to support students by giving them a clear set of steps or routines that are easy to memorize and can be followed whenever they write.

Planning Requires Filtering for Relevance

When picking ideas to write about (see Figure 2.7 in Chapter 2), teachers can demonstrate and practice as a class how to select and then filter the most relevant ideas. In this lesson, a child shared a detail about ice, but it did not go on their list of picked ideas because it was not directly related to an endangered creature. Teachers can also model and discuss how to prioritize these ideas in younger grades at the oral level above what students can produce in writing. It is important to teach and model at the academic language level—and slightly above it—that students use when they speak and read if their transcription (ability to write down) skills are below their speaking level, as is often the case in the youngest grades.

Teacher Talk Example: Explicitly Explaining Planning

Writers! Today we are planning for when we go to write later. This means we are jotting down ideas, facts, words, or images that will help us when we write our drafts. We plan with a goal in mind. For now, our goal is to figure out which ideas we should use. This is called prioritizing for relevance. We will think about which ideas are the most important and most relevant, or best related, to the topic we will write about. For example, here are some ideas from the text and the video. I will now cross out those that do not seem related to how they protect themselves:

> ~~blue blood~~, swims fast, changes color and shape, eight legs, ~~short life span~~, 50 miles per hour, sea, aquarium, coral reef, squirt ink, pens use ink, makes water black

We found a lot and we crossed off a few that we don't think relate to how they survive. We may find more when we later go back to organize them.

This phase constitutes the bulk of the thinking that students do before writing (i.e., their planning before writing). Teachers can begin by showing how to make a list of key ideas in a bulleted format and all the higher-order thinking that goes into choosing what to put on this list. Knowing which ideas to pick and making this summary list is an underestimated skill. While this may appear simple enough, it requires great cognitive effort—twice the effort as reading (Piolat et al., 2005). This aspect of planning may be so demanding because of how much it tugs on inhibition, filtering out irrelevant information (Altemeier et al., 2006). This step also involves paying attention to vocabulary and noting strong words and phrases that they could use when they move on later to then write about what they are now reading.

Routines Support Planning and Other Executive Skills

In the last chapter, tools such as POWER and TIDE were introduced. In this chapter, teachers model how to use these tools to plan for writing. Modeling how to use these kinds of scaffolds along with an exemplar is essential to preparing students for planning effectively and independently. Too often teachers may provide these scaffolds in a one-off lesson and even encourage students to use them, but then do not model them enough and do not give the time to teach students to practice and use them to mastery. Just like any other literacy instruction, such gradual release of responsibility is essential for effective writing instruction. First, the teacher models (*I do*). Then, the teacher works alongside and scaffolds students (*We do*), and finally, students (You do) are given the opportunity to apply strategies in independent writing (Duke et al., 2011; Pearson & Gallagher, 1983).

Remember: *TIDE* = Topic, Important evidence (information), Detailed examination (details), and End.

It is not the tools that make writing easier but teaching how to use them, then having students practice using them with feedback, repeatedly. Importantly, strategies are not the be-all, end-all of writing; rather, planning strategies, like those described in the current chapter, help writers gather knowledge in an organized way to reach their writing goals, particularly when used repeatedly, across many texts. This repeated practice is the critical element needed for supporting executive functioning (Diamond, 2013). To decrease the cognitive load that skilled writing places on students, you can introduce the key tools the day before modeling them in the ways described in the last chapter's sample lesson.

Discussion Supports Planning by Bolstering Attentional Control and Inner Self-Speech

It has been said that "Writing floats on a sea of talk" (Britton, 1970, p. 164). Prioritize discussion whenever modeling writing or writing together with your class. The more students talk, the higher their learning outcomes are (Sedova et al., 2019). Also, teach students to plan and rehearse what they will say by visualizing their ideas or jotting them on whiteboards. This allows them to plan better and make sense of what they are learning (Fiorella, 2023).

As the students in this lesson picked their ideas, they also discussed why they chose each. This discussion moves the modeling to independent application more quickly because students learn how their peers work through the writing process. In real time, they see the kinds of decisions their peers make and learn how to keep themselves motivated and on track. It opens up the black box of how more capable peers manage their executive skills when writing. This is a mystery otherwise. When I learned to write in school, I saw good writing in the sources I read, but I never learned how it was produced. I never understood the executive and self-regulatory skills that went into writing and never imagined I could learn how to better direct and control these skills. The purpose of discussion is not just to build content knowledge, underlying language, and reasoning but to make the invisible become visible. It allows students to realize that their own executive and self-regulation skills play an important role in their writing and that there are ways to manage these skills to make writing easier and more efficient.

One student shared that she did not realize some of the higher-achieving students in her class spent so much time picking ideas carefully, writing multiple drafts, and using tools she could use too. She had believed that they naturally wrote easily, quickly, and with minimal effort. She didn't know they were talking to themselves, guiding themselves, and using tools as they wrote. Having students discuss both the content and the metacognitive processes they use when writing enables us to coach the executive skills and shows students how to use these strategies flexibly.

During these discussions, students can use speaking stems such as "The text says . . ." or "This evidence suggests . . ." or "By using (e.g., a metaphor), the impact is that . . ." (see Appendix O). Students can also draw from vocabulary banks that they created while reading and use these words when discussing ideas with peers at this point. They can even learn to discuss their processes with stems such as, "To come up with creative ideas or to stay on track, I tried . . ." These kinds of structured discussions build not just oral academic language but also inner speech.

What students hear in class becomes the substance circling in their minds when they go to write in the future. Stay tuned! How this happens is explained more fully in Chapter 8. Being able to use self-speech to guide oneself while writing is a key way to harness executive functioning. The vocabulary, syntax, and reasoning skills that students practice and develop during these discussions may only be the tip of the iceberg. Seeing self-regulation modeled through think-alouds that show self-speech happening ("I can use POWER to help me stay on track") provides an additional benefit. Internalized self-speech that students develop predicts their executive skills, particularly around cognitive flexibility (Alarcón-Rubio et al., 2014), which is important to writing well. This inner self-speech becomes their own. More specifically, the vocabulary they hear, the syntax and ideas, the logical reasoning, and how to generate insight and guide their executive skills become internalized. They gain practice, all done orally at this point, when they contribute during modeling and during small-group "turn and talks" where they discuss their ideas with peers before sharing them with the full class. In this lesson, they did all this as they debated which ideas to pick.

Take It to the Classroom: Tips You Can Use Tomorrow

Write POWER at the Top and Cross It Off as You Go

Returning to the three-part framework of Teach-Model-Score, this chapter dove deeply into the first step of POWER, focusing on the first aspect, planning. Most students struggle with writing from the first step of initiation or knowing how to get started, sustaining attention, staying on track, and knowing where to go next. Writing POWER on one's note paper and crossing it off as they work through each phase gives students a concrete and tangible way to get started and stay on track.

Preteach Vocabulary and Background Knowledge

If you use a packaged ELA, science, or social studies program, you will find words to teach each week. You can also identify high-utility words, or Tier 2 words, to teach (Beck et al., 2013). These words are important to understanding the texts that students will read. Follow the lessons in your program and front-load and teach these before reading the text. Also, have students write them down so they can plan to use them when they go to write later. When students also use these words outside of the context of the text they are reading, and add them to what they write, they learn them more deeply and become more likely to retain them. Likewise, preteaching the key knowledge that students will need to understand the texts they will read and, later, to include or keep in mind when writing decreases the load on working memory; this enables students to more easily understand what they read and potentially to reap greater benefit as they apply the prereading planning strategies in P3 of POWER (Peng et al., 2024).

Model Self-Talk

Self-talk is essential to planning. Think about when you plan. This usually involves talking to ourselves in our minds and often even pepping ourselves up. To leverage this inner speech, students need plans and tools such as mnemonics and self-talk statements ready to help them direct themselves in using these. These could be posted on their desk or listed on a top page in their writing folders or notebooks. This should include positive, self-encouraging statements, strategies, and self-direction on how to use these tools. Teachers could model using self-talk such as, "I'll look at my language box on my organizer and my lists of sentence stems to generate several possible sentences and inferences. Then I'll decide on which ones I like best before I share my idea with the class. I'm excited. These tools are helping me!" Whenever you model in this way, invite your students to notice your self-talk as you go. Be sure to model encouraging yourself, getting stuck, coping with frustration, shifting approaches, and other ways to self-regulate.

Practice Self-Talk Every Day!

After I learned how to develop self-regulation, I used to confide in colleagues that I did not always have time to do this. I was caught up in using TIDE and other scaffolds to help me teach my content such as historical understandings or science concepts. After some time, it dawned on me that I should start every class period with a minute or so of self-talk, showing a video, sharing a quote, or having students share what they use with each other. This helped me integrate teaching self-talk permanently into my instruction.

Model Prereading for a Gist before a Closer Read

When responding to texts, students should engage in multiple reads. After a first read, they can construct a gist. Initially they can begin by writing a list of "Who" words—who or what was the text mainly about. They can then list "Did what" phrases. Choosing from these, they would create a simple gist statement that tells *who*—did *what*—later adding *when/where*—and *why/what happened,* as well as your grade-level grammar standards such as adjectives or irregular past tense when you create these. These statements can be gradually expanded into causal and contrastive statements (Wijekumar et al., 2017). See Jennings and Haynes (2018) for a fleshed-out progression and Appendix I for ways you can incorporate your grade-level grammar standards.

Model Pulling Apart the Prompt

As a next step while preparing or planning, students make a Do/What to set a purpose and stay focused. Students do this on a sticky note and refer to it frequently as they read to gather information or evidence, then as they make an organizer and again when they draft and revise. Such tools build out POWER and continue to support students by giving them a clear set of steps or routines that are easy to memorize and then follow whenever they write.

Model Picking Ideas

During and after watching a brief video, listening to a read-aloud, or reading a text on their own, students take notes. To decide which notes to take, they discuss the content and share how to choose the best information to capture. Discuss, collaboratively as a class, how they use the Do/What now (see Figure 2.6 in Chapter 2 for examples). This tool helps them focus on what the prompt is looking for. Quality student discussion should begin now and be embedded all throughout the writing instruction as students debate why certain information may be better and which words best capture the ideas. As students participate orally in the collaborative selecting of information to use in their outlines, teachers can explain that even though we are not yet writing, we will be looking for, paying attention to, and preparing to use more complex language at the word level and at the sentence level. Therefore, when noticing strong vocabulary or rich sentences that seem particularly well structured, annotate for these, copy them into word banks, and even copy notable sentences occasionally to be ready to use these words and mimic these varied structures.

Picking Ideas in Younger Grades

When the youngest students cannot form their letters, spell, or use periods and capitals appropriately, then they do not yet have the conventions to convey in writing the same ideas that they are able to say aloud orally at a far more advanced level. That is why drawing and dictation are helpful in the early grades to help them get their ideas down. While you are modeling how to pick ideas, students may start by writing (or drawing and dictating) in order to translate their oral ideas to paper, but this quickly shifts to more academic writing. Even in preschool, students can be encouraged to use academic rather than just oral language while learning to transcribe.

Students can be taught to read and write at a level that is higher than their current spoken language. Oral language is what they use informally with friends and family regularly. Think about early reading. Younger students begin to read simple decodable or phonetically controlled books, far below their oral language. Yet we would not limit them to a diet of only decodables. They hear rich picture books read aloud too. Likewise, they can write about these richer books or short videos that do include academic language and help build this for them. This is a reason why read-alouds are so important and can be used well at this phase of picking ideas. Students can share the rich ideas and vocabulary they heard, and this can be transcribed in front of them. These sources expose students to advanced vocabulary, sentence structures, and deeper concepts. As teachers transcribe, they hear the language again and see it appear. Teachers can jot line images of key concepts such as a chrysalis. Students can copy these if they are not ready to copy such full words yet.

As discussed earlier, if students are not yet ready to copy as the teacher scribes these notes, they can jot abbreviated notes or simple line-drawn images so that they have something to do to keep them engaged while the teacher is modeling writing in front of the class. They might jot these images on whiteboards or clipboards before they share them. This ensures their executive skills are engaging, they are focused and paying attention even if they are not copying or composing exactly what the teacher does.

Modeling in General

Be sure to model executive skill processes such as planning for as many lessons as students need until they can perform independently. It is important to model this process and not just tell students what to do. You will want to demonstrate each step, starting with planning a gist, pulling apart the prompt, and picking ideas. This first step of showing the normally invisible executive skills students use when writing is powerful. As you do, be sure to say aloud all the thinking a student would do for each step. In the younger grades, you can have fun and go into persona. You can act like a child as in this example.

Teacher Talk Example

Good afternoon, writers! Today I will show you how I would plan if I were your age. As I demonstrate this and share what I would be thinking, I want you to be great listeners. Right after, I'll ask you what you heard me say. Curtain up! OK, I'm going to write about octopuses. I love these. OK, how do I start? I'm stuck. What do I do? Wait, I'll use POWER. My teacher showed me how POWER can help me get started. Alright, first I do the steps in P. I will read this again and write a gist statement. Oh, I see the words Who, Did what, When/Where, Why/What happened on the poster in my classroom. I will think about the who—octopuses. Did what? Protect themselves. When/Where? In the ocean. Why? To stay safe. I've got this! I will write these down. Now, curtain down. You watched me act like a student and show you how I would get started.

However, one caution. Some teachers see the immense power in modeling, but then model for too long. Remember to use a gradual release. After you model the phases once or twice, then release in a supported way. You can begin modeling the first steps to get started, then have students continue in small groups. An engaging activity I have used is to have students stand in groups at chart paper and work together as they write. To ensure they all contribute, we give them each different color markers, and they write their name at the top in their color. This way, you can walk around the room and monitor or scaffold only as needed as they work.

A big "aha" moment for me was how much modeling students needed. I did not realize how much I could leverage by helping them to use their own inner speech when I modeled doing this orally. I even directly had my students talk aloud as if they were using POWER and TIDE in front of their peers. These tools and this kind of modeling speeds up the gradual release process. It's no coincidence that the development of executive skills is associated with self-regulatory language recommended in this chapter (Bodrova et al., 2011; Cragg & Nation, 2010)! In fact, the magic of moving in a gradual release progression from modeling to independent use of strategies comes from using a combination of the strongest tools, along with inner-self speech to help make this process happen more quickly and, critically, from repeatedly using the tools until they become internalized.

Embed Think-Alouds While Modeling

Think-alouds appear throughout this book as a reminder of how important they are for teaching executive skills and showing flexible ways to use them. These can help students to learn to manage all aspects of writing and reach independence more quickly (Traga Philippakos, 2021) and are a key part of most evidence-based approaches to writing instruction (Graham et al., 2012). These allow us to reveal the invisible, self-regulatory talk

A *think-aloud* is what it sounds like. You would literally take the train of thoughts going through your mind as you engage in writing and say this aloud as a way to teach each step in a process. Be sure to be explicit. Break down each action into its smallest substeps and state how to do each aloud.

happening in writers' heads as they get started, stay on track, focus, and cope with challenges while writing. Modeling a think-aloud becomes one of the main vehicles for instruction. Providing the *how* and *why* during these think-alouds helps with skill development and buy-in. You may have introduced tools designed to support the executive skill of planning in the past but noticed that students do not use them independently or effectively (Limpo & Alves, 2013a). A simple shift to incorporating think-alouds allows you to better break down ideas and ensure students know how to use their skills and understand why this process will help them. For example, you might project a circle map for collecting ideas. As you fill it in, you might say aloud:

> *OK, I know I need to gather facts about octopuses. I'll write that in the middle and circle it. Now I'll list facts around that inside the bigger circle. I want to rush to get to the writing so I can be done. Wait, I know that if I fill this in first, it helps me make an organizer and then write faster and more easily. I've got this.*

Use Rich, Complex Texts

Use complex, content-rich texts and videos as the material for students to write. Include text sets so they must practice synthesizing ideas across them. To learn how to plan, students need texts that will stretch them. If the text is too easy and they can recall the information readily, they may not need to use the executive skill of planning and will just go on autopilot. They will use the information they easily recall and not need to work at extracting key ideas if the ideas and text are too simple.

These can include vocabulary-rich short videos, primary artifacts, or other challenging sources. To make instruction more manageable initially, students can respond to a single source or several when writing. It is important that the text sources be complex, even if only using one at first. To build muscle, students need challenges. It is important to move to the most rigorous texts and topics that students can reach for. When encountering complex texts, students must engage the executive skill of planning to help them read, understand, and gather information that will help them plan their writing. Students need to be taught the scaffolds, skills, and behaviors that will equip them to approach these, as well as the stamina needed, rather than working in simpler books. See Cartwright (2023) for more on how to support students in accessing these stretch texts.

Read Source Texts with a Writer's Eye

One more note about the P (Plan) phase before moving on to O, Organize. Point out the higher-level vocabulary, syntax, sentence structures, and general craft as you read rich texts. Writing in response to rich texts is a triple win as it addresses students' writing, reading, and content knowledge. As students read and discuss these texts, they can highlight these language elements and jot them down in their notebooks while the teacher records them on the corner of the board. This helps them plan for which words, phrases, and sentence stems they will eventually include when they write. Here is an example of what such a teachable moment might look like.

Teacher Talk Example

Alright class, we will now continue our read-aloud about how animals survive in the desert. Notice how it opens by surprising you with, "I bet you thought deserts are hot. Well, think again!" I noticed that a few of you began your essays with a statement like this about bats. You mentioned that they seem scary, but they actually help us. This can be a great stem to use: "Did you think? . . . Well, actually . . ." Let's note that on our list of sentence stems in our writer's notebook. (Read on.) Did anyone notice that the boy did not say the traveler felt thirsty. He said his throat was so parched, it felt like a cotton ball was in there. That's a great word to use when writing about deserts. Should we include that in our word box too?

That's a Wrap!

The previous chapter laid the groundwork by introducing a system that you will use to model and students can internalize throughout the year. This chapter has zoomed in on how to teach and model the Plan (P) phase of POWER. The following chapters pick up after P and continue modeling the next steps in the POWER writing process from making an organizer to writing drafts, and then editing and revising.

CHAPTER 4

Organization

Text Structure

Wisely and slow; they stumble that run fast.

—SHAKESPEARE

Organization may be a popular step to skip when writing. Writers tend to generate ideas mentally, then often rush to write before organizing these carefully. However, organizing before writing leads to better pieces (Graham et al., 2012). As an executive skill, organization comes into play at all phases of the writing process, right from the start. When initially learning to form letters, students produce organized motor sequences in a specific order to ensure their letters will be neat and legible to their readers. When writing words, students must organize and sequence letters, syllables, and word parts such as prefixes, roots, and suffixes. Next, they must arrange words into a sentence, sentences into a paragraph, and then paragraphs into essays. The last chapter looked at planning—how to think up and find ideas to include in these essays. While organization plays a role all through, this chapter focuses primarily on organizing these ideas as a way to explore and understand this crucial executive skill.

Organization is the cognitive ability to arrange and structure actions or ideas in a systematic way.

When teachers think of organization, Roman numeral outlines or popular mnemonics such as RACE (Restate, Answer, Cite, Expand) or TIDE (Topic, Important evidence, Detailed examination, End) come to mind.

These kinds of organizers all serve the same purpose. See Appendices J–N for examples of organizers. When used well, these mnemonics give writers a place to structure their thinking and to lay out a road map that will help them meet their goals. On a deeper level, they serve as a way to teach and support the underlying executive skill of organization.

A well-created organizer offers an external visual that can support the higher-order reasoning needed to go beyond merely stating facts that have been gathered.

When moving the ideas they plan to use over to organizers, students revisit them. They further refine how they will filter, arrange, and sequence their ideas in an organized way. The goal in teaching this executive skill is to help students by making it easier for readers to understand and follow their thinking.

It is important to emphasize that the kind of thinking writers do while organizing differs from when they plan. Like planning, organization is a higher-order executive skill that taps the same core areas of inhibition, cognitive flexibility, and particularly working memory (Ruffini et al., 2024). Similar to planning, these areas work together to help accomplish the higher-order work of organization, the focus of this chapter. However, building an organizer requires more than just listing ideas. Planning involves idea generation or gathering information, while organization is the act of logically grouping and ordering these areas (Flower & Hayes, 1981).

Although the work of organization may begin during planning, it needs to be used as a separate step. Merely picking or listing ideas does not raise writing quality, while outlining that shows how they will be grouped and ordered does (Kellogg, 1990; Llaurado & Dockrell, 2019). When picking ideas, students filter for relevance and inhibit information that may seem interesting but is unrelated to the topic. On the other hand, organization requires more advanced filtering, reasoning, and categorizing. Perhaps in a natural effort to lighten this work, students often mistake organizers for essays and compose their full essay in a given graphic organizer without doing this challenging higher-order work, then feel they are done.

Just like with picking ideas, creating an organizer is important to teach and model. When students see examples and learn how to draw them, the organizer makes the executive skill of organization visible and concrete to students. This strengthens our students' ability to exert this executive skill when they prepare to write and helps them prioritize it while writing and revising.

After they draw an organizer, students should put a few notes, enough to hold their thoughts, but not too much on their organizers. Writers who overplan (write a full draft) and those who do not plan enough wind up with pieces that are lower quality than students who put a few words to hold each idea but not full sentences (Chai, 2007). Students who organize their thoughts before writing (Worden, 2009) at optimal levels (not too much or too little) perform better when composing all the way down to first grade (Arrimada et al., 2018; Harris et al., 2023). Organizers also take much of the sting out of writing because a well-created organizer serves as a comforting guide. They reduce the amount of overhaul revision that will be needed down the road (Worden, 2009).

Teachers may assume that students will naturally infer how to organize ideas because they see information organized nearly daily when they read texts. However, most younger students do not know how to plan and organize despite seeing well-organized writing daily when they read. Also, even if students create an organizer, they may not then use it to guide themselves as they write (Limpo et al., 2014), unless taught and coached in how to do this. The good news is that in my experience, when we model use of organizers in this way, students really enjoy the process of organizing their ideas after collecting them. They find it energizing to look for ways they can group and order them.

Organizers do even more than just help make writing clearer and more efficient. They help concretize, or make visible, mental schemas for grouping and sequencing ideas. By *schema*, I mean a framework for organizing knowledge (Kim & Burkhauser, 2022). Think of a tree with branches. The main idea is the trunk. The facts about it are the branches. Creating an organizer allows students to grasp the big picture (trunk) and to understand how their selected ideas relate and support it. Organizers act as a temporary scaffold in supporting students in understanding and internalizing new schemas (Kim et al., 2024), likely due to the way they build up and strengthen the underlying executive skill of organized thinking itself. Overall, organization is so much more than graphic organizers or outlines, but these do play an important role in developing this higher-order executive skill. Organization is about creating logical systems and then using them flexibly. Stay tuned; the subject of the next chapter is how to teach cognitive flexibility so that students can organize their ideas in versatile ways.

Consistent with the structure for previous chapters, this chapter provides another classroom visit and a sample lesson that demonstrates how to move from the planning phase of selecting ideas to organizing them with the goal of strengthening the executive skill of organization in our students. This is followed by a breakdown of how and why the lesson teaches and supports this executive skill. It also includes a section on organizing narrative writing. It then summarizes the key recommended instructional strategies before wrapping up.

Back Inside Our School: What Organizing Looks Like When Students Are Doing It Well

Peering into a lower-grade classroom again, we see students sitting on a rug, watching their teacher create an organizer on large chart paper. Students take out their clipboards from the day before and flip to a fresh page. The teacher is discussing the list of ideas they picked the day before, and students are weighing in on which to use. Today they learn that they will move from the P (plan/pick ideas) phase to O (organize their ideas). Depending on their grade level, they may see a horizontal TIDE (or CSPACE, if writing a narrative) organizer on their clipboard with large boxes on these letters where they can draw simple images or write words on lines just below each if they choose.

If they are in an upper grade, they will draw their own organizer. All students would contribute to the discussion of which ideas to use from those they picked while reading and discussing the text, then move them to the organizers. In this class, they just heard a read-aloud about Paul Bunyan. For the sake of time, the teacher did not read the full excerpt. Instead, she chose to read a few sections to save time for more writing. The students listened for examples of hyperbole or exaggerations. They shared instances they heard with peers, and each pair shared with the class. The teacher listed these examples. Students then looked for how to group them. Some were about Paul's size, appetite, strength, and actions. They put each example into one of these groups, then voted to use all but appetite since there was only one exaggeration about that. Each child jotted short words or line images in the middle sections of the organizers on their clipboards. At the top, they wrote the phrase from the "What" in their Do/What (see Figure 2.6 in Chapter 2). The "What" they will write about is examples of hyperbole in this tall tale. Next, they reviewed their facts and listened to parts of the story again, but this time listening for strong vocabulary words and exciting phrases to add to the language box at the bottom of their organizer. The lesson ended with students feeling excited to use their organizers to guide them while writing.

Heading upstairs to a middle school classroom, if we could listen in on how students think while composing, we might hear the following:

> *Okay. I have picked my ideas, but now I just have a long list. How can I arrange these into groups so I can write about them? I don't want my writing to sound like a list. I want to show how my ideas connect. The ideas need to be grouped. How they relate to each other and the main big idea needs to be clear. Well, I see I do have three categories—Malala helped others through blogging, speaking, and telling inspirational stories. Here is a fact about how her dad had to bring her sister to school. Hmm, that doesn't seem related so I'll cross it out. The other facts seem to fit into clear categories.*
>
> *Now I'll draw a TIDE* [see Figure 2.8 in Chapter 2]. *I'll move each category, or group of similar ideas, to its own ID section and fill those in, one at a time. Then, I'll put the "what" from my chart in the T and look for what my big idea is. I'll add that to my Topic to help me think of a thesis or overarching idea. Let's look at the overall text structure. Well, this is describing her actions, but they are all solutions to a problem, so I can use transition words that show this. Oh, I put a few full sentences. I'll cross out the smaller words such as* the *and* and *so I'm only using short "jot talk" on my organizer. I'll also look back at all the words I marked up while reading and those I noted during our discussions. I'll put those into what we call the language box and draw that on my TIDE organizer at the bottom so I'm sure to use those words when I go to write.*

Before learning how to pick ideas and organize them for writing, these same students would get stuck. They might stare at a blank page or screen and not know how to begin. If they marked up a text or participated in a discussion and were invited to write about this, they would often skip organizing and go right from picking ideas straight to drafting. During drafting, they could lose steam and confidence. They put down any ideas that come to mind. Some gave up, while others tried to revise but realized that they would need to revise substantial portions, and it might be easier to start all over again. In contrast, the students who put in the effort to organize have a clear plan and begin writing easily with far less structural revisions needed later (Rau & Sebrechts, 1996). After learning the organization tools and being supported as they use them, they know what to do, get started, and find the process more enjoyable overall. Once organized, they cross off the O in POWER. They feel a sense of accomplishment that they completed the organize phase in POWER.

See It in Action: Sample Lesson

Returning to Teach, Model, Score (see Figure 2.10 in Chapter 2), the following lesson continues the focus on "Model," moving ahead to modeling how to do the O in POWER and how to support the executive skill of organization that comes into play at this point. Recall that you would have already introduced POWER and explained it during an initial sample lesson, then focused on Plan (P) in the last one. Organizing is practiced midway through a POWER cycle.

For younger grades, you would still be modeling all the thinking orally and writing in front of your students as they contribute ideas, making drawings or taking simple notes on whiteboards or clipboards. By grade 2 or 3, when students can transcribe, they would be writing along with you now, initially copying what you model but eventually including their ideas, too. Chapter 6 delves into launching younger students into more fully transcribing their pieces. Yet, for this third lesson on organization, they would still be observing or making notes at a level that is comfortable for them. They can use a notebook, whiteboard, or clipboard to do this.

SAMPLE LESSON: Modeling the O in POWER

Goal: Model showing students how to use the writing process when they write. Focus on the O in POWER so students can learn how to logically group, order, and structure ideas before writing.

Objectives:

1. Review the writing process and demonstrate how to organize.
2. Model using self-talk to guide and encourage oneself while writing.
3. Demonstrate how to use or draw an organizer.
4. Model naming and grouping ideas (this can happen in P also, just before O).
5. Model sequencing ideas.
6. Add reminders to organizers to support transitions and sentence quality.

Estimated Time: 30–45 minutes

Materials: Chart paper or smartboard, markers, pencils, notebook paper (whiteboard or clipboard), copies of a text that students will read, organizers depending on grade level

Lesson Steps:

1. Introduce that this lesson will focus on organizing ideas before writing. For this lesson, it might mean reviewing transition words.
2. Write POWER on the board and review the meaning of each phase in the writing process. Students can write this down and cross off each step as they complete them (5 minutes).

3. Explain that today we will focus learning and practicing the phase O in the writing process.
4. Before we begin, as we do every day, we will first jot down positive self-talk, such as "I've got this, I can stay focused" or "I'll follow the steps in O." Review the class list of such phrases posted and ask for additional ideas to add. Students review those in their notebooks, add any, and share with a peer which they will use today (5 minutes). (They can also write this kind of self-talk on the organizer as they work through the steps below.)
5. Next, explain that the O in POWER helps us organize before we write.
6. Provide students with an organizer or more ideally show them how to draw one.
7. Look over the list of ideas collected during the stage of picking ideas. Review the What in Do/What to stay focused on what to select. Write the "What" phrase at the top of the organizer. The "What" helps students craft the T in TIDE, the topic introduction or topic sentence.
8. Looking at the facts collected during P, decide how to group these into similar categories. Explain that there is no one right way to organize ideas.
9. For facts about how octopuses protect themselves, you might use ways they hide (ink), get away (swim fast), and change (shapes, colors) (10 minutes).
10. Model writing these facts with jot talk in the body sections of the organizer. This process of learning to use short note taking (jot talk) often requires frequent modeling. It can also be helpful to create "jot talk" lists of commonly used abbreviations with your class. This can help the process of condensing ideas to short notes, as in Figure 4.1.
11. For each body section in TIDE, name each with one of these categories. Then, list the facts about each underneath. Add details or detailed analysis under each (see Figure 2.8 on p. 27).
12. If students are using quotes from texts, they should not copy the quote. Only

and	&, +
leads to	⇨
new idea	/
more	⇧
less	⇩
same/equal	=
because	bcs
important	imp

FIGURE 4.1. Jot talk examples.

copy as much as they need to help them to recall which quote they will use. Add the page number so they can find it again when they go to write.

13. Next, determine how to sequence or organize the ideas. Put them in order by which seem the most interesting or the most important.
14. Add scaffolds such as links (first, next, last) and synonyms to help with linking when you go to the next phase and begin writing a draft.
15. Add a language box in the upper corner or bottom. Students can refer back to the text, to vocabulary words they learned during the week or to word lists they made during class discussions. They can also include grammatical elements (adverbs), spelling words, or morphologically related words they may be studying that week.
16. If time permits, model how to take an exemplar and back-map it into an organizer to show students what an organizer looks like and how to build one. Model pulling the key ideas for the essay, turning them into short jot talk, and placing them in the correct part of TIDE (or CSPACE if back-mapping a story).

Wrap-Up: Summarize that this lesson reviewed POWER and looked at how to follow the steps in O.

Lesson Analysis: How Each Component Supports Organization

Organizing Intensifies the Cognitive Load for Writers

Organization may be one of the most difficult parts of writing. Students must screen again for relevance, categorize ideas, identify hierarchies, and sequence everything. When students pick ideas, particularly in response to a text they have read, they do not inhibit, filter, and arrange ideas to the same degree as when they move to organize. They now discard ideas that no longer seem relevant, decide which go together in groups, and figure out how to sequence them. In this lesson, students had gathered ideas for how Malala inspires in a long list. However, they needed to look at them again and find groups and relationships. Otherwise, their writing will be essentially a long list. I'm sure you have seen this kind of writing, just pages of facts. One student, in this lesson, figured out three main groups for categorizing facts and then showed common threads between them—blogging, speaking, and telling inspirational stories. Finding these kinds of groups will help him organize ideas so they hold together and read more easily.

Consider the cognitive strain behind this work—filtering, rearranging, and sequencing ideas. Perhaps due to the cognitive demands that are part of the executive skill of organization, students often skip this phase, or they might produce an essay inside the organizer (Llaurado & Dockrell, 2019) unless directly taught and coached in how to make an organizer. This heavy lift may help explain why research suggests that giving feedback on outlines before writing is so powerful. Reviewing organizational decisions is more efficiently done at the outlining phase than after the piece is drafted, especially when done with a buddy during peer feedback given on organizers, and doing so eventually leads to better writing (Cramer & Mason, 2014).

Crossing off POWER Steps Organizes How Students Move Through the Writing Process

You would have already introduced POWER in an initial lesson before this one. During each lesson, students follow and cross off the steps in POWER. In this sample lesson, you would more fully explain the O in POWER. You might start off by discussing the importance of this executive skill.

Teacher Talk Example: Explicitly Explaining Organization

Today we are going to look at how we can get ready before we write. We have already read the texts we will write about. We found the important ideas and words and wrote those down on scrap paper, in our notebooks, or on whiteboards. It is also important to move the ideas we picked over to an outline now so that we can organize them. This might seem like the same thing as planning, but it is different.

When we organize, we arrange our ideas into groups and put them in order. We might also decide now that we do not want to use all the ideas we listed at first. We might decide to put some ideas together into a bigger group and talk about some before others. This is what it means to organize.

Here is an example. Today we are getting ready and planning for when we go to write later. We already jotted down ideas, facts, words, or images that will help us when we write our drafts. We will make an outline now, with a goal in mind. For now, our goal is to figure out which ideas we should use. For example, after reading a text on octopuses we have made a long list of key phrases:

swims fast, changes color and shape, eight legs, 50 miles per hour, sea, aquarium, coral reef, squirt ink, pens use ink, makes water black

We need to put these ideas into groups and discard some of them. We can group them according to where octopuses live, how they swim, and how they adapt. We will get rid of ideas like the aquarium or pens since we will not use those. After we finalize what to include and make groups, we will move each group over to our outline now and copy them there.

On our organizer, we can even add links such as first, next, finally, *or* in contrast *to show the order or how our ideas fit together. Once we have the organizer ready, we are not done with it. As we use it, it is important to check it off. We will cross off each idea we use. If we change the order again when we write, we can note that on our organizer. Doing this makes writing so much easier!*

During the last lesson, students would have crossed off the P in POWER at the top of their page after they worked through the plan phase. As you saw in the lesson, students crossed out the letter O when they finished drafting their organizer. Doing so is particularly important for staying organized as one continues through the writing process phases after initially getting started. Having a way to stay on track helps students move along and work through each phase while writing.

Organization Supports Seeing the Whole

TIDE is a way to structure a text, or a *text structure*. Substructures of TIDE include Descriptive, Sequential, Problem–Solution, Cause–Effect, and Compare/Contrast. Students who identify such text structures, such as cause–effect or problem–solution, in what they read see significant gains in reading comprehension (Wijekumar et al., 2017). Cognitively, our brains do not easily grasp the whole and hold on to disparate facts, but this can be learned. Making a one-page outline facilitates organization, which is essentially what TIDE provides. When we list the categories in a way that shows how they relate to each other and fall under the whole, students understand and hold on to the big ideas more easily (Hebert et al., 2016; Strong, 2020). Creating an outline to follow a text structure such as TIDE helps students hold a bigger picture more easily and supports them in ensuring their writing is clearly structured for their reader as well.

Organization Facilitates Better Cognitive Flexibility

As students move their ideas over from the list of picked ones, they then organize them in varied ways. The beauty of writing, including how we organize our ideas, is that there is no one correct answer. There are many flexible ways to group, sequence, and organize the ideas generated in the P phase. As you saw, one student organized the facts about ways in which Malala inspires into blogging, speaking, and telling inspirational stories. He could have grouped them in many ways. Any logical system that he can defend can work. While the executive skill of organization allows writers to create a framework for structuring their ideas, it also allows for creativity and flexibility in how these ideas are presented.

In fact, after creating an organizer and moving ahead to drafting, writers often continue to add to their organizers, delete parts, and change them as they use them to guide themselves while writing. Organizers need to be a fluid tool that students come back to and revise. Having a written organizer likely frees up mental capacity that makes it easier for students to consider multiple ways to express ideas flexibly and shift between these. More on how to ensure organizers are used in ways that lead to voice-rich writing is coming soon, in the next chapter that explores cognitive flexibility. For now, organizers are a vital building block that contributes to good writing.

Language Boxes Create a Structured System to Hold and Retrieve Key Words

Organizers can include a section for listing vocabulary words to be used, offering a structured way to remember to use them. Vocabulary use, particularly vocabulary diversity, is one of the strongest predictors of overall writing quality (Bourke et al.,

2003; McNamara et al., 2010; Olinghouse & Wilson, 2013; Truckenmiller, 2024). Most curricula introduce and have educators teach sets of high-utility words each week. You can teach them too, but ultimately the bigger goal is to help students become more word conscious over time. We want students to begin to find and learn words on their own too, in an organized way. The students in this lesson might have caught and put words, such as *appetite* and *exaggerate*, in their boxes during an initial read or discussion rather than having them taught explicitly. Having a place to hold these new words organizes the process and better ensures students will use them during writing. Even more, language boxes serve as temporary scaffolds but also work toward helping students to grow to become more word conscious as well. Students who recall the key words from what they read are more likely to use them when they express their ideas and score higher on assessments that involve writing in response to texts (Gioia et al., 2023).

So far, we have discussed TIDE organizers and the importance of language boxes (the L in TIDE-L) as an organized system for holding vocabulary options. If we had to pick the biggest winners that hold the most importance to overall writing quality, they would include TIDE or text structure (organization) and vocabulary (Bourke et al., 2003; Truckenmiller, 2024). Both of these can be easily scaffolded by making an outline and including a language box on it. The goal is also to develop the underlying organizational awareness of text structure as well as to offer a structured way to bring better word choice to our writing.

Teach Narrative Organization, Too

Before we move to Take It to the Classroom, here is a note on narrative text structure and organization. The examples shown so far have featured informative and opinion or argument text writing because such texts are the most common form of writing students are asked to do. Narrative writing includes different genre features, but teachers can scaffold executive skills in the same ways across different text types. Teachers can introduce narrative text structure as an effective way to support reading comprehension (Bogaerds-Hazenberg et al., 2021) in combination with other instructional strategies. Once students understand narrative structure well, later in the year, they use their understanding of it to guide themselves when planning and writing stories (Harris et al., 2008; Vander Hart & Power, 2021).

However, it is recommended that students write in only one text type or genre repeatedly for at least a few assignments. Since information and opinion text types are so similar, students can learn and use both together but should wait a few months before also producing narratives since they differ significantly. This way they can achieve mastery before moving to produce narrative writing. See Appendix A for a recommended scope and sequence of a suggested order for introducing each text type and how much time to spend on each over a school year. Spoiler alert: When Common Core first came out, it listed three main text types (informative, opinion/argument, narrative). Over the years, we have not found that dividing the year up into three parts and spending equal time on each in isolation works best. Also, given how structurally similar informative and opinion writing are, TIDE works well for both. Therefore, teachers should toggle between opinion and informative writing throughout the year, as the tasks demand, and narrative writing does not need to be taught over a full third of a year (Laud & Zampitella, 2025).

Research has shown that students can improve their ability to write informative or opinion/argument writing pieces quicker than narratives (Harris et al., 2006). Therefore, it is recommended to begin writing instruction by teaching the informative or opinion/argument text structure at the start of the year. This helps students experience initial success more easily. Students will also use expository writing throughout the year when writing responses to literature they read, and in response to science and social studies texts. They can begin narrative writing later in the year, usually by winter, once they have developed as writers.

When writing stories, mnemonics such as CSPACE (Characters, Setting, Problem [or Purpose/goal], Action, Conclusion [or Conflict], Emotion) provide the same kind of executive skills support as students organize and prepare to write for a different purpose: to tell a story. Initially, CSPACE can help students understand stories they read. They can take apart any story, pull out the key ideas from each section, and map them into a CSPACE organizer (see Figure 4.2). When they understand and can name the elements of a story, they can use CSPACE as an organizational tool to prepare to then also tell a story.

Students can begin learning narrative text structure in the same way as informative and opinion/argument by mapping out stories for the elements of CSPACE and listing the features, including those that distinguish each subgenre such as science fiction or mythology. After doing so, they become ready to then tell stories in each of these subgenres as well.

Students would follow all the same steps in POWER when using CSPACE to write narrative stories. They would start by pulling apart the prompt, then picking ideas to include in their stories. They would then create organizers in the same way as described in TIDE except that their transition words would be more time oriented, or temporal, such as when we woke up or after the bell rang.

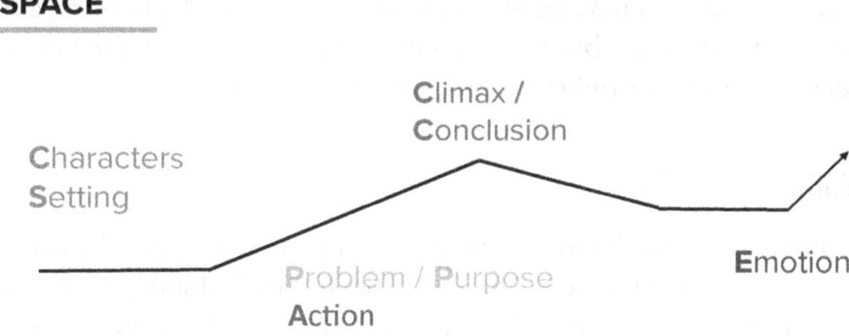

FIGURE 4.2. CSPACE map.

Take It to the Classroom: Tips You Can Use Tomorrow

Have Students Draw Linear Organizers

You may have passed out organizers before but not seen students use them independently. Move to teaching students to draw their organizer as soon as you can because doing so helps them internalize the structure behind the organizers quicker than when we hand them copies of premade ones. This may be because drawing them is less passive and more generative (Fiorella, 2023). Remember that the goal is to develop the underlying executive skill of organization when creating outlines so that when students go to write, this executive skill is activated and thus becomes strengthened. Students will grow to think about how they structure, order, and present their ideas even if not looking at their outline.

Even in the earliest primary grades, we see most students are able to draw TIDE-L down the side of lined paper and use this as the structure for their organizer. You can model this structure by making one on a Doc Cam as your students follow along:

> *First we start at the top, over where the highest blue horizontal line crosses with the red vertical line on the left, and we put the T. Then we move down four lines to put the first ID section. We make a place for each ID section, and there are often three, so our actual TIDE might look like: TIDIDIDE-L (or TtIDtIDtIDE, as a reminder to plan one's subclaims for each section too).*

This also allows for flexibility in case students want to write more or fewer than three body sections. In the upper grades, students can customize how they draw this to include extra I's, D's, or both within each section. They also include smaller t's to remind them to state the subtopics for each section. Using small t's (or "baby t's" as teachers in early grades call them) leads in well to becoming the topic sentence for each body section as their pieces become longer over the year.

It is important that organizers be linear, set up in straight lines that go sequentially down the page, rather than circular webs. Our schools have found that students see the flow of ideas more readily and this eases the transition from planning to writing. See Figure 2.8 in Chapter 2 for examples of linear organizers, as well as Appendices J–N. Web or circular organizers may be effective for supporting the reading comprehension phase of the writing process, but when preparing to write, students benefit from moving their ideas to a more straightforward, linear structure.

Teach Jot Talk

At several points, you have heard the term *jot talk*. As students take notes while reading sources, viewing short videos, or listening to read-alouds, they should capture these in the briefest way possible. To keep the focus on the organizational structure, students should use just a few letters to represent an idea, rather than full words or sentences—the smallest amount needed to hold the thought. Seeing a brief outline helps them think about how the piece is organized.

Jot talk also helps them conserve their energy for writing. They can learn to use class-created, shared abbreviations and also use small images such as arrows to show direction or causal relationships or initials rather than full names. For some students, using jot talk is more challenging. Those students may need to write in full sentences on their organizers but can shrink their ideas afterward or use a highlighter to mark which words they would have used if they had written them in jot talk. Be patient. Be ready for this to take longer than you expect. With enough modeling, think-alouds, and having peers discuss how they do this, students do improve at using jot talk.

The Lowdown on Language Boxes

Earlier I shared the importance of the language box and how it offers an organized structure to help students learn and use new words independently. Moving to practical tips now, students can literally draw a large L for language in the upper corner or bottom of their organizer. They can put the words they would like to use in this box or underneath the L. You can invite them to write definitions next to the words or to break the words into syllables and practice spelling them as additional phoneme segmentation, phonemic awareness, and spelling practice.

To teach and support this stage, teachers (and peers) can model think-alouds to teach when and how to pause, recognize, and think about these kinds of words, paying attention to them and using strategies to decipher what they mean. During the Pick Ideas step or when moving words to the language box, you can support students in figuring out what the words they pick mean in an organized small routine. Four strategies have been found effective. Students can work through trying each of these as they work to determine the meanings of the words they collect and add to their language boxes: (1) use context clues, (2) break it down to morphemes, (3) identify part of speech, and (4) look it up (Elleman, 2017).

A special note on morphology or word roots. The second strategy above includes paying attention to morphemes. A morpheme is the smallest unit of meaning in a word, including its base, prefix, and suffix. For example, the word *intractable* has three morphemes. The prefix *in* means "not." The base *tract* means "to pull." *Able*, the suffix, means "capable of." By learning to identify such morphemes, students can learn new words (and spell them!). While we can lead activities that build targeted vocabulary and support students in actively using stronger word choices when writing, we cannot teach all the words they should know. Students need an organized system to set them up to become self-propelling or word conscious in their ongoing learning (for more, see Cartwright, 2023). As mentioned earlier, letter formation, spelling, and morphology all depend on sequencing, which is part of the executive skill of organization.

Wider Benefits of a Language Box

Keeping a list of vocabulary words jotted down during read-alouds and independent reading sets students up to encounter such words several times. They will use words from these lists during discussions, on their organizers, and while writing. Later, they will also copy these over to the scoring system scales and count how many they used toward vocabulary bonus points. (Scoring scales are more fully explained in Chapter 7.) When students add words to their language boxes, practice identifying them, try to figure out what new words mean, and use them repeatedly, they become more word conscious, naturally curious, and even driven to learn new words and to use them skillfully.

Beyond Only Outlining: Organizing Your "Junk Drawer"

Beyond adding language boxes, students can also include self-talk, reminders to use conjunctions, stems, and other scaffolds that will support them when they go to write. They can learn specific places to put these on their organizers, then cross them off when they use them. Over time, these become internalized. The organizer can serve as a revolving door where students can bring in higher-order supports and jot them down. Organizers become a broader workspace that continues to help students save time and ultimately produce better pieces. Students begin to refine and group their ideas during the Pick Idea phase. However, this can continue when they move to organizing. Creating an organized plan helps students to further develop and refine their ideas before they move to write, which raises the quality of the final writing.

Post Organizers Next to Writing on Bulletin Boards

After students use organizers to write, be sure to post these next to any writing samples you put up on your bulletin boards. This further demystifies the writing process. When students see only final drafts from peers, all the planning and organizational executive skill work behind them becomes invisible.

Teach the Why Behind Organizers

Starting instruction by teaching text structure (TIDE or CSPACE) helps students see the big picture and understand what is being asked of them. It gives a launch point as they think up and begin to organize their ideas. Studies on writing instruction that have shown overall writing gains begin with teaching text structure in the ways outlined in this chapter (Graham et al., 2012, 2016). While sentence-level instruction could happen in parallel or in isolation for a few lessons, it is important to let loose the tidal wave of motivation that happens when students write connected texts (paragraphs or essays) about a topic they are interested in.

This is why organization is introduced so early in studies that show strong gains in overall quality and is the rationale for the full Teach, Model, Score weekly cycle. Students should not be practicing skills in isolation but should be producing writing weekly, and initially in short pieces. The next chapter delves into how to move from an organizer to a draft.

"Check it Off!"—Self-Evaluation

The next chapter moves into how to use organizers. When students use the notes and language boxes on these, they should check off each idea on their outline. This helps them keep themselves on track as they go and stay organized. Doing so also helps solidify the connection between the organizer and future drafting. Often students create an organizer but then discard it and do not reference it when they write. Also, when they use one, they should not feel locked into it but use it flexibly. They may add new information to it or rearrange parts. Fortunately, just like the other executive skills, this skill of cognitive flexibility can be modeled and taught. You can demonstrate flexible thinking while deciding which ideas to use or how to reshuffle them when modeling moving from the organizer to writing a draft. The following chapter now dives more deeply into this next executive skill: cognitive flexibility.

That's a Wrap!

Research clearly demonstrates that starting with the largest organizational level of text structure (TIDE) leads to writing gains. Seeing how a text is structured helps students understand what is being asked of them and gives them a launch point. The majority of studies on writing instruction that have resulted in overall writing gains begin with teaching text structure in the ways outlined in this chapter (Graham et al., 2012, 2016). The next chapter delves into how cognitive flexibility supports moving from an organizer to a draft. Be wary of assumption-driven instruction. We often assume that once students make an organizer, they will know how to use it. This is not the case and needs to be taught directly. Fortunately, moving from an organizer to a draft is actually a lot of fun for students when they have tools and understand how to do this.

CHAPTER 5

Cognitive Flexibility

The Key to Varied Vocabulary and Strong Sentences

A bird does not sing because he has an answer.
He sings because he has a song.
—Joan Walsh Anglund

Now the pulse quickens and the music begins! Your students are ready to begin writing their first drafts, or singing their songs. We move from the mechanics of picking ideas and organizing them to creating the music of beautiful language that flows and carries meaning to readers. The focus of this chapter is turning ideas from notes into rich vocabulary choices within well-constructed sentences and well-connected paragraphs.

Cognitive flexibility contributes to and supports this work alongside other executive skills (Altemeier et al., 2008; Drijbooms et al., 2017; Hooper et al., 2002, 2006; Niedo et al., 2014). This chapter looks at how this executive skill comes into play at drafting as a way to explore and understand how cognitive flexibility can be taught and supported. This kind of flexibility is important to creating this kind of writing that sounds like music. Sometimes also referred to as switching or shifting, cognitive flexibility is a later executive skill to develop (Best & Miller, 2010; Diamond, 2013) and is particularly difficult for students who struggle to write (Hooper et al., 2002). Cognitive flexibility requires and builds on the earlier core executive skills of attention, working memory, and inhibition (Dajani & Uddin, 2015). To be cognitively flexible, we need to attend to and hold ideas in mind, juggle them, and inhibit or stop interfering thoughts. This kind of flexibility happens in many phases of the writing process. We now turn our attention to how this skill supports translating ideas into the three main levels of writing: word choice, sentences, and linking ideas together in paragraphs.

Cognitive flexibility is the ability to shift mental strategies, adapt quickly to new rules, and change activities or direction fluidly.

Cognitive flexibility is the opposite of perseveration, where students may struggle to shift course or get stuck easily. Such students continue to use the same strategy or take a familiar path in new situations where it is no longer helpful. I'm sure you have seen such students. They may struggle with transitioning from one activity to the next or with any changes in routines. We see these students wanting to continue reading a book when it's time to go to art class. What we don't see are the invisible cognitive mechanisms in their brains that make shifting gears harder for them than for others.

In writing, students with low cognitive flexibility might use limited vocabulary, compose about the same idea every day, or use repetitive sentence structures in an inflexible, robotic way that reads not as music but as formulaic writing. Alternatively, such students might list facts in sentence after sentence without making the connections among them clear. Teaching in ways that support cognitive flexibility addresses these problems.

Let's look at how this can be accomplished. Stepping back behind any piece of writing, oral language is the foundation of word choice, syntax, and cohesion. Students draw from their oral language banks when composing. While multiple executive skills support this level of oral and written language (Drijbooms et al., 2017; Rocha et al., 2022), cognitive flexibility also plays an important role in writing quality (Berninger et al., 2017; Borne et al., 2024; Cordeiro et al., 2022; Hooper et al., 2002; Kalliontzi et al., 2022; Niedo et al., 2014; Spiegel et al., 2021; Valcan et al., 2024). Moreover, cognitive flexibility supports the rapid shifting that happens as we arrange words or notes into sentences (Altemeier et al., 2006). This underlying flexibility enables writers to mentally test out and revise varied ideas when forming sentences. It helps students to shift between subprocesses such as planning, reviewing, pulling up linguistic rules, or drawing on background knowledge (Quinlan et al., 2012). More specifically, flexibility contributes to word writing fluency and sentence combining, which require students to reorder and consider multiple ways to arrange words in sentences (Altemeier et al., 2008).

> *Syntax*, part of grammar, refers to the conventions or rules that govern how words are arranged in sentences. *Cohesion* refers to connecting ideas locally from sentence to sentence by repeating key terms and using synonyms or little referents such as *it* or *that*. Cohesive writing also links globally to the larger text structure with transition words such as *first*, *next*, and *finally*.

Think about what happens when you express a thought. First, you have a preverbal idea that turns into words and fragments. You quickly string them together, inwardly listening for the grammar and word choices, then you make rapid revisions mentally before speaking. Likewise, when we compose on paper, preverbal ideas and vocabulary choices come to mind. They move into phrases and clauses that we stitch together but often rearrange to ensure they make sense. Finally, we reread our writing as a whole to ensure it coheres or hangs together from sentence to sentence and from each paragraph to the whole. We need to remain flexible and make changes if writing is not coherent. This process requires the ability to shift quickly as we construct, arrange, and revise our ideas for clarity.

To ease and support this kind of flexible thinking, students should capture their ideas in their organizers first, as described in Chapter 4. Recall how doing so helps them hold on to their thoughts, freeing room in working memory to filter, juggle, and reconsider what they are thinking in flexible ways more easily without losing their ideas. Likewise, they should list potential word choice options (language boxes) and conjunctions as well as have lists of sentence-level scaffolds on hand so they can more easily think flexibly. Otherwise, we may see the kind of familiar writing in which students use limited vocabulary across sentences that draw on one repeated structure (The __________ does __________ because __________) throughout a paragraph and do not link ideas from one sentence to the next. Decreasing the cognitive load with scaffolds and systematically building flexibility support creative, fluid, and flexible writing.

We now head back to our school to look at how students can move fluidly from the O (organize) to W (writing a draft) phase in POWER, with our attention directed to how cognitive flexibility emerges in these processes and how it can be supported. After watching the lesson and seeing a sample plan, we break it down to analyze how cognitive flexibility comes into play at each moment. This analysis is followed by teaching tips for supporting this important executive skill.

Back Inside Our School: What It Looks Like When Students Are Doing It Well

Returning to the same school, we enter the red double doors again and step into the early elementary classrooms on the ground floor. It's been a few weeks since our last visit. The teacher has helped students create organizers. She modeled thinking aloud how she would take an idea, turn it into a sentence, add the sentence to the paragraph, and then cross it off on the organizer. Students copied along on their own paper and offered suggestions that she took. She literally thought aloud:

> *Now I need to move from my organizer to write a draft. Argh—what time is it? When is lunch? No, I've got this! I can do this. Let me start by reading the jot notes. It says "octo ink hide." I'll look at my language box too. That says "squirt." I remember my teacher jokingly turned this into a silly phrase like "Octo squirt ink hide" and we talked about how that doesn't sound like a good sentence at all. We have to stretch it out and add more now. Hmm, I'll think about a gist frame: who . . . did what . . . when/where . . . why/what happened. That helped: The octopus squirts black ink to stay safe. This sounds better and makes sense. Oh, and I can look at last week's exemplar about frogs to get ideas too. Let me see. It says that frogs can hop fast, and that helps them escape predators. I can add this kind of detail about octopuses too. Swimming fast is the same. It helps them get away too.*

This week, she invited her students to begin drafting independently. She modeled this think-aloud to help them get started. They have drafted a few pieces together as a class over the past month. Today she wants to see how they will do on their own. Just before they go off to continue writing their pieces, she leads a quick warm-up as well. Students are practicing irregular past tense verbs this week as their grammar standard. They look over their lists of picked ideas about octopuses and generate a few gist sentences that include these. They make one together as a class, then work in pairs to generate several more. They each self- and peer-check to ensure they used the verbs correctly, then move on to take out their organizers and begin drafting.

We see students sitting at their desks with their organizers in hand. One student is looking at a few words on her organizer about how an octopus's arms can break off. She then glances at her language box and sees the word *detach*. She writes, "An octopus can detach a leg." She remembers how W stands for "write and say more." She pauses and thinks of her gist sentence frame and how that can help her expand sentences as she writes, then adds *when*—"when a predator grabs it." She is glad she added another word from her language box and even expanded her idea when she used a *when* clause to grow her sentence in ways she practices daily during gist warm-ups.

She then looks at a list of sentence stems in her pocket folder. She thinks more about how to elaborate on the I in TIDE—the information she just wrote by adding a D or detail. She knows her next sentence should explain more about how the fact supports the overall topic of staying safe in the dangerous ocean. She decides to add, "This is important because if a predator bites them, they can break off that part and get away." She then remembers that sentence stems can sometimes be crossed off. They are a tool that help get our thinking going, but we don't always need to keep them after we get the idea. She pauses to reread and decides she can cross off "this is important" now and leave just "If a predator bites them, they can break off that part and get away" as her sentence. Without the stem (this is important), the idea still makes sense and is clearer. "Oh, I can also include the word *swam* in my sentence! That way I'll get a bonus point for applying one of our grammar standards for this week—irregular past tense action words."

"Phew! Another ID is done. This is going well!" she thinks. Then, humming to the tune of Taylor Swift's "Shake It Off," she whispers, "Check it off, check it off, I'm just gonna check, check, check it off"—in the same way they do at times when they cross off each step in POWER. She checks off the ideas from her organizer and the words she used from her language box as she turns them into sentences and writes her draft. She also pauses for a moment to imagine the octopus losing a leg but getting away safely. She thinks about her next idea about how they can swim fast to get away from enemies as well. She wonders if these special skills are the reason they can survive in the dangerous ocean. Larger connections and insights are happening. Turning her ideas into sentences helps her visualize them and make connections she hadn't made before. She begins to see how octopuses stay safe thanks to so many skills and defense mechanisms. She looks for ways that she can show how these ideas link and work together. Writing is serving as a tool for deepening and solidifying learning.

Heading back upstairs, we see older students moving from their organizers to essays as well. At this stage, they have already shared their ideas with a peer, received feedback, and changed their organizers. They added fresh insights that came up as they discussed their plans before writing. If you could listen in on what students are thinking, you might overhear:

OK, now I need to look over my organizer and begin drafting. I feel stuck. I want this to be really good! OK, wait, I remember we talked about this during our last classwide collaborative write. We discussed how we can hold off on writing a hook right away. I can be flexible and do this later. We can get our ideas flowing and put them down on paper, then go back and add a way to rope in the reader.

Alright, I've got this. I'll start by reading the notes I had next to T for topic introduction on my organizer. I know I need to start an essay with TAG—title, author, and gist. I'll open with this. Now, I'll give a one-sentence thesis. Let me look back at the "What" from my Do/What to see the topic of my thesis, and I'll look at my IDs on my organizer. OK, I see the big ideas. I'll use a conjunction to show how they relate as I write my thesis.

Next, as I write my first body section, I'll step back and look at how it connects to the thesis. I want to make that clear to my reader and show how each sentence links to the last one. I'll use my transition words to help with that. Let me quickly turn to the page in my Writer's Notebook where I keep a growing list of transition words. OK, I'll use the fancy linking phrase "in contrast" to show how the author used dirt, which is typically dry, and rain as symbols for the different experiences the main character had in A Farewell to Arms. *Let me think again about my analysis. I remember that the I–important evidence comes "from the book" and the D–detailed analysis comes "from my head"—from me. The analysis is my favorite part, but hard too. Hey, this is going smoothly. I think I did the really hard work when I made the organizer. Now I'm looking for fun ways to turn these into sentences that will be clear, hang together, and be enjoyable to read.*

I'll keep going. I noticed a few repeated patterns in the use of dirt, rain, and mud, and I found great quotes about each. Now, these are opposites in some ways, but how else do these connect? Well, dirt and rain cause mud. The dirt was a symbol for the terrible events the main character witnessed, and the rain symbolized his depression. I listed a few conjunctions such as after *and* although *on my organizer. "After" might help. The rain and dirt, figuratively speaking, combined to cause his muddiness, or lack of mental clarity. "After" this happened, it caused him to make poor choices.*

Wait, I also remember that when I go from one sentence to the next, I should always have a connector. I'm repeating the words rain *and* dirt *a lot. That can work to connect, too, but here it sounds repetitive. I'll try "these two" instead of saying "rain" and "dirt" again—yes, that little phrase sounds better.*

Hmm, every day we use positive self-talk in school. This character did not do that. I could show a cause—that bad events and depression cause us to think less clearly and make poor decisions. In further contrast, if we speak positively to ourselves, we can stop this chain reaction and make better choices. I had another thesis but I don't need to stick with it. We talked about being flexible and changing it if new ideas seem much better. I'm really excited about my thesis now! It helped to have all my notes, my word boxes, and lists of conjunctions that could help move my thinking along to a bigger idea that I'm excited to share. Also, my grammar goal is to experiment with using participle phrases. We made a few

> *gists with these as we warmed up today. I'll introduce my quote with "Feeling down that day, he thought . . . "*

Another student nearby might be thinking:

> *OK, while I read the novel, I marked up a few words that seemed important to understanding the content. I put these into a list in a "language box" I made in the corner of the texts* [or on a separate notes page students might keep]. *Then I also added some of the words that were part of our vocabulary lessons during class to this language box. Let me look at these again. I tried to figure out what they mean and noted possible definitions by thinking about context clues—the word parts I understood. For example,* excavate *seems to be a verb in the sentence, and it starts with* ex*—and I know that means "out" so this must mean something about moving things out, or I could look up the word. OK, I can do this. I've got a good list of words. Now as I start to turn my ideas into sentences, I'll check off my word list and be sure to use the words on it, or synonyms that come to mind as I write.*
>
> *As I move from one sentence to the next, I have to think about linking my ideas. I'm writing about how the character changes. To link from my sentence that used a quote, I'll repeat one key word from the quote as a way to link to my analysis of it in the next sentence.*

Previously, these students would likely have not made organizers. They would have moved right from reading a prompt to drafting. If they did make one, they might have written their entire essay in the organizer, then become too depleted to revise it and rewrite it. However, now these students use organizers, scaffolds, and strategies that help them know what to do to stay on track. They have also built language boxes and found sentence stems they can reference while writing. (See Figure 5.1 for examples.) As they draft, they recall the words of their classmates from when they wrote together as a class, and the metacognitive conversations they have had about how they each work through the writing process and draft all come to mind. Hearing remnants from these discussions in their own mind now when they write alone, they are careful to sew each sentence together by using linking words and synonyms or repeating a key idea so that each sentence leads into the next like puzzle pieces. This is starting to happen naturally for many, and they don't need to think about it as consciously now.

See It in Action: Sample Lesson

Specifically, this lesson showed how to "model" and support students in taking the short-note ideas on their O (organizer) along with various scaffolds such as sentence stems and turning these into a W (write) that includes sentences and paragraphs in flexible ways. It also depends on students having learned and beginning to internalize varied sentence structures through daily gist main idea practice. Thinking of Teach, Model, Score, this is the end of the "Model" phase. When students complete writing a

Younger grade stems (discovered by students in peer exemplars they read):

	Section	Sentence Starters
1	Topic Introduction	In the story /article... Title Author Context Thesis:
Body 2	Important Evid.	The first example that shows Another example... Finally...
	Detailed Exam.	This explains... This example shows... This proves... It seems
3	Ending	In conclusion - restate idea All in all... As you can see... To sum up... It is true...

Older grade stems:

By ___________, the author emphasizes ___________.

In using the word choice of ___________, the effect is that ___________.

In the passage, the author foregrounds ___________ as a way of ___________.

The use of ___________ helps the reader to ___________.

The author presents ___________ as ___________ in order to ___________.

It remains unstated whether ___________.

This sends the message that ___________, except that ___________.

The main contrast is between ___________ and ___________.

___________ veers off from the expected by not only ___________, but even more so by ___________.

FIGURE 5.1. Student-discovered sentence stem banks.

draft, they will be ready to move to "Score." This lesson described how to support the three important language levels of writing:

1. Choosing words
2. Expanding notes into sentences
3. Helping students cohere, or link together, the ideas within and between their sentences

It also emphasized promoting metacognitive awareness of choices we make while writing and how to be cognitively flexible in these decisions.

It also included—a lot! As you read, you might have wondered how long it takes to get students to this level and manage coordinating so many scaffolds. Writing is complex. To write well, there is so much that students must coordinate, and flexibly. As in previous chapters, we now present a lesson plan then debrief it by illustrating where the executive skill for the chapter, in this case cognitive flexibility, comes into play and how it can be taught and supported. We also include teaching tips and practical ideas to support students in managing everything. If you are curious now, you can look ahead to see how the Writer's Toolkit Notebook (Appendix P) can help students navigate using these resources in real time while composing, as you saw the students do in this lesson.

SAMPLE LESSON: Modeling Moving from O (Organize) to W (Write) in POWER

Note: If students are not yet transcribing, see Chapter 6 and have students participate orally in this lesson.

Goal: Model showing students how to move from an Organizer to turning ideas into sentences.

Objectives:

1. Engage in skill-building warm-ups, such as speeded gist sentence production that includes deliberate practice in the grammar skills your students need to learn.
2. Support word choice to strengthen the vocabulary they use, primarily through using language boxes.
3. Turn organizers into grammatically accurate and rich sentences.
4. Ensure that sentences cohere, flow from one to the next, and hang together in ways that make them easy to read and ensure that the overarching ideas they convey are clear.
5. Use scaffolds, such as stems and gist frame structures, to help students generate complete and complex sentences.
6. Help students gradually expand and vary their sentences by regularly introducing and practicing new grammatical elements in ways that vary their structures until each is internalized and automatized.

Estimated Time: 30–45 minutes

Materials: Chart paper or smartboard, markers, pencils, notebooks, pocket folders, copies of a text that students read, and filled-out organizers (drawn or provided)

Lesson Steps:

1. Warm-up: Have students brainstorm "gist lists"—words from the relevant ideas they picked. Use these to create a gist frame sentence as a class. Incorporate your grade-level grammar standards, such as irregular past tense words. Then have students work in pairs to generate several gist sentences in a gamelike way. Count how many they produce and set a goal to write more and use even richer vocabulary the next day.

2. Take out and refer to the organizers students created the day before as students work to turn their organizers into sentences.
   a. *Note:* As you go through the next steps, have students check off the content and tips used while coming up with sentences and writing them down. If students are not yet ready to write ideas down, see the following chapter.)
3. Tell students that the main lesson will now focus on turning short notes on organizers into full sentences and revising ideas.
4. Write POWER on the board and review the meaning of each letter.
5. Share that we are moving from O to W today (5 minutes).
6. Remind students that whenever we write, especially when moving from the O to W in POWER, we use positive self-talk, such as "I can stay on track" or "I can write powerful sentences." Have students review earlier statements the class has created and decide which they will use today (5 minutes).
7. Explain that after making an organizer, it is important to understand how to use it. Be sure to check off each section as we turn that part into a connected-text paragraph.
8. Begin by looking at the jot notes in the Topic section of the organizer. In upper grades, write an introductory TAG (title, author, gist) statement to introduce the topic. For shorter writes or in younger grades, create an opening topic sentence.
9. To write the opening topic sentence, draw from the notes on the organizer and refer to the gist frame. The "who, did what, when/where, why/what happened" statement often works well as a topic statement. Check the "What" in the Do/What to ensure the topic sentence responds to the prompt.
10. Next, work down through each section of the TIDE-L organizer, moving each section from jot talk to fuller sentences. Model this and have students work in pairs to help them get started.
11. In younger grades, students can expand the jot talk, putting words from the fuller sentences they create on their fingers to guide them as they turn ideas into sentences. Older students can practice this on whiteboards. They are not yet transcribing and creating a draft, only turning notes into sentences at this point. They can also look back at the gist sentences that they make at the opening of class each day for ideas.
    a. Over the year, you can show different elements to include and ways to expand and structure a gist. For example, if your goal is to teach irregular past tense or participle phrases, you can include these in the gist frames for that week.
12. Have students share their ideas for sentences and write this on the board together. Invite others to help revise it. Once you agree on a sentence, scribe it in front of students on a Doc Cam or whiteboard. As with pick ideas, students can choose to copy what you put or change this on their own papers.
13. Once students agree on sentences for the topic introduction, be sure to model checking this off on the organizer so they track where they are. When they use language box words, cross those off too. (Later, return and check off to ensure they used all ideas and all words from the language box.)
14. As you continue collaborative modeling in this way, have students draw from the language box and use sentence stems to support them at each step. Be sure

to encourage fading reliance on stems and personalizing them as quickly as you can. (See Appendix O for lists of stems to support each area of TIDE.)

15. Also, pause and take out older exemplars from prior weeks. Review these for additional stems and to note how the writer cohered, or linked together ideas all through.
16. Links should be included that show both global (paragraph to whole piece) and local (one sentence to the next) connections.
    - For global cohesion, students can use *first*, *next*, and *finally* to link globally, but be sure to vary these up and move to using synonyms quickly to keep the writing voice rich (see Table 5.1 for sample links).
    - For local links between sentences, use synonyms to hold together the flow and transition words such as *as a result* or *on the other hand* to show the logical relationships between one sentence to the next.
17. As you go, model in a think-aloud, coming up with a bare-bones sentence. Model referring to the language box to strengthen it or expanding it with stems. Then have students practice doing this as well.
18. In lower grades, students might think about using rich synonyms to hold their reader's attention rather than repeating the key word over and over. In older grades, they might think about how to end with the point they most want to stress when writing complex sentences. To encourage flexibility, model testing out a few options and how you would flexibly decide on the best.

    As an example, if they want to show Malala's influence, they would change "Malala reached so many because of her creative efforts." This sentence stresses that she is creative. On the other hand, "Malala's creative efforts allowed her to reach so many" puts emphasis on the last idea—her influence.
19. As students move to use their organizers, be sure they cross off each section or word as they use it to ensure they actively use the organizers to guide them when they write.

Wrap-Up: Summarize that this lesson offered practice in how to move from O to W and help students turn their jot notes, ideas, and words from their language boxes into sentences, while drawing on scaffolds such as stems, conjunctions, and other supports.

Lesson Analysis: How Each Component Supports Cognitive Flexibility for Effective, Self-Regulated Writing

Drafting Itself Facilitates Flexible Thinking and Insights

As students turn notes into drafts, cognitive flexibility comes to the foreground. Students move from planning and organizing to making connections and more advanced decisions. Drafting consolidates their learning, activates new perspectives, and enables insights (Galbraith et al., 2006).

However, students need to be cognitively flexible for this to happen. They must shift between ideas and possible interpretations and integrate them. For example, the student in the primary-grades classroom in this lesson had merely listed facts about how octopuses protect themselves. However, after she turned these into full sentences and put them together in a paragraph, the idea that *the sea is dangerous but octopuses are so skilled at survival* dawned on her. Prior beliefs may even be rejected and replaced, all requiring inner shifts in thinking. A student may have noticed a few interesting points while picking and organizing ideas. However, when preparing to draft through discussing ideas with peers and turning notes into sentences on whiteboards or early drafts of sections, they see relationships, discover a larger coherent focus, or reevaluate them in a new light.

This kind of flexible thinking enables students to "say more" or elaborate. Elaboration is key to high-quality writing (Crossley & McNamara, 2016). Quality elaboration does more than knowledge telling (listing facts) but moves to knowledge transformation. This is believed to happen mostly after the organizing phase and during drafting as ideas come together in new, unexpected, and exciting ways (Scardamalia & Bereiter, 1987).

Even more than just elaborating, students assemble puzzle pieces, seeing how one idea can connect to the next in multiple ways, and together they build up to construct and convey an overarching idea or theme. As Joan Didion has said, "I don't know what I think until I write." During this drafting stage, especially as we link ideas together, cognitive flexibility takes on a greater role (Altermeier et al., 2006) and helps make these leaps forward possible.

Flexible Word Choice

Let's break this down. To reach these higher insights, students start with vocabulary words. Generating labels for objects or ideas draws on cognitive flexibility (Filipe et al., 2023). To support flexible vocabulary choices, teachers would have modeled creating language boxes and showed how to use them. This child might have included *predator*, *camouflage*, and *squirt* in her box. Her teacher would model how to choose words from these boxes and weave them into sentences orally and use the words in flexible ways. You can also model thinking and testing a few options, then come up with several possible varied sentence choices for arranging these words. Recall that flexibility can be one of the last executive skills to develop. Supports such as language boxes, sentence frames, or stems can help to ensure that students include varied vocabulary and structures despite this being a more challenging or only emerging skill for many.

Cognitive Flexibility Supports Sentence Composing

Similarly to vocabulary, sentence writing draws on cognitive flexibility (Berninger et al., 2017). Children are born with a general tendency to seek social communication (Tomasello, 2003), and some view their natural acquisition of grammar as underlying the need to communicate and propose that they have an innate grammar learning mechanism for this (Miller et al., 2023). This facilitates their learning of syntactic rules that govern grammar, if given enough exposure. Most children learn to speak with grammatical accuracy without direct instruction in rules as long as they have sufficient language acquisition opportunities and do not have a language disorder (Pinker, 2007).

However, spoken grammar does not translate to written grammar. In other words, the kinds of language we use when we communicate orally are not the same kinds of language that is presented in texts or in writing, and the amount of experience in written language varies from one student to another (Snow, 1983). This is where cognitive flexibility comes in. Sentence writing can be so challenging because during writing, students are expected to use more complex vocabulary and syntax than during speaking. They need to shift to use more formal academic language. This includes more precise word choice, longer sentences, and more coordinating or even subordinating clauses, as well as other syntactically advanced grammatical forms than what they normally use when they speak (Sarmiento et al., 2024).

They also need to shift between lower-order letter formation and spelling skills and the higher-order work of holding the sentence's surface form in mind while choosing the next word in the sequence (St. Clair-Thompson & Gathercole, 2006). While holding the sentence in mind, they evaluate it to ensure syntax rules are followed. This evaluation step depends on executive skills to help retrieve these patterns from long-term memory and to coordinate using them flexibly (Larigauderie et al., 2020).

Pause and reflect on how much is happening here with language as well as with the executive skill of cognitive flexibility. This explains why having notes on organizers, language boxes, and sentence stems and doing gist sentence writing daily is so important to enable the flexibility needed to produce high-quality writing. For students who shift naturally and easily, this instruction and these scaffolds may not be as necessary. Yet, for most students, especially for those who struggle with this executive skill, these kinds of supports are essential in leveling the playing field.

Emphasize Applying Skills Over Isolated Drill to Promote Flexible Use

In these examples and in the prior chapters, you saw students and teachers working through the full act of composing rather than pausing to do worksheets or isolated practice activities. Instead, teachers may lead quick warm-up "gist practice" or sentence-composing activities at the start of class but spend most of the time during class embedding deliberate, repeated practice within the actual writing students produce every week. This way students learn and practice how to flexibly integrate each sentence within the whole and how to show the connections between ideas as they do.

Decades of research show that such isolated sentence-level or grammar instruction and practice does not raise overall writing quality (Graham & Perin, 2007), even when it connects to the content being learned (Myhill et al., 2018). Focusing on a target skill such as sentence production, in isolation on worksheets without quickly linking this skill to use in connected text (paragraphs), is not recommended (Berninger & Wolf, 2015). There is a place for explicit instruction and deliberate practice warm-ups in sentence writing, as in the quick-paced gist exercises. However, overfocusing on sentences exclusively for weeks at a time may slow or impede flexible use and transfer of these skills to the regular writing. For example, if students overpractice conjunctions or appositives in drills, they may overuse them in their actual writing and not draw on them in cognitively flexible ways.

Build Syntactic Awareness

Rather than only aiming to get students good at producing sentences, reach even higher to develop *syntactic awareness*. Think of how differently these same words land: (1) She left feeling surprised; (2) Feeling surprised, she left. Notice how the last word drives home the sentence's impact, stressing either that she was surprised or left. Like with word consciousness, covered in Chapter 4, students with greater syntactic knowledge show better reading comprehension (Brimo et al., 2017) and are more likely to produce better writing. You may already be aware of *statistical learning*, which is what helps build this awareness. Statistical learning is a process where students unconsciously notice and learn patterns such as letter combination and sound–symbol correspondences. Although this aids them in learning to spell and read, systematic, explicit instruction in sound–symbol–meaning relationships and spelling patterns is critical as well (Moats, 2020). Students who are cognitively flexible pick up and internalize these patterns faster (Feng et al., 2020).

> *Syntactic awareness* is the understanding that how we order and arrange words in a sentence impacts meaning.

Likewise, this implicit statistical learning contributes to students' syntax development as well (Kidd, 2012). This process of naturally detecting and integrating regular patterns of spoken language (Romberg & Saffran, 2010) can be supported with the kind of systematic modeling and practice (Montgomery et al., 2024) that daily gist writing practice offers. This instruction is particularly important for students with less English language exposure (i.e., multilingual English learners or emergent bilingual students) or those with disabilities.

Students can also be coached to notice, jot down, and appreciate effective sentence stems in ways similar to building word consciousness with language boxes. For example, you might marvel aloud while reading the peer exemplar, "Notice how this writer explained a quote by saying, 'This might mean A, but on a deeper level, it could also mean B.' " This is the type of sentence stem students can take note of and use in their own writing. Students can jot these down on a page in their Writer's Notebooks. The more of these that students collect, the more flexibly they can use them.

Cognitive flexibility and syntax are further related since students must shift between different sentence structures and integrate these when they read (Borne et al., 2024). When writing, the better they metacognitively understand this kind of shifting that readers must do, the better they can design their transitions between sentences for their readers. This leads to the next level of drafting: cohesion.

Variation and Cohesion Rely on Flexibility

After choosing words and putting them into varied sentences, students need to master yet another important level of writing. This is a level that is often overlooked and least well known, but it is critically important as well. Sentences do more than convey an idea with (1) words and (2) in rule-based, or conventional, order so they can be easily understood.

A third level is that sentences link ideas both locally and globally. They link together from one sentence to the next, helping to build local cohesion within and across sentences. Yet, they also link back globally to the larger idea, helping to build global text cohesion. This kind of connection is supported by executive skills that include switching (Bourke et al., 2003). Cohesion is sometimes found to be the most important factor in quality writing (Crossely et al., 2010, 2016). Yet it may be the least well understood.

Writing cohesively requires students to quickly test out varied ways to link ideas, hold these in mind, and flexibly pick which work best as they connect ideas within a sentence and from one sentence to the next. It also requires students to hold the big picture in mind while connecting each section to the whole. In these lessons, one student thought about sentence-to-sentence cohesion when he realized he was repeating too many words. He knew this would lose his readers' attention. He flexed and decided to use a referential phrase instead, calling rain and dirt "these two" as a way to actively link the ideas across sentences. Even simple variation, called anaphoric devices, such as inserting a pronoun or synonym can also help hold the reader's attention and cohere ideas within and between sentences.

> *Anaphoric devices* include using synonyms, similar phrases, or pronouns to refer back to a prior idea as a way to hold the reader's attention and create cohesion.

See Table 5.1 for a chart of such connectors, adapted from García-Sánchez and Fidalgo-Redondo (2006).

Early writers often miss the importance of connecting sentences. They write in a list where they tell one fact after another, repeating one key word over and over and lacking cohesion or links between ideas. Grouping ideas on organizers can help, but students still want to avoid "list-y" sounding writing. Using connectors that make relationships between ideas clear helps.

Teacher Talk Example

Today we will do the exciting work of taking the ideas from our organizer and moving them into a draft that we will finally write! As we do this, we will try out different ways to say what we mean and decide which we like best. This means we will think flexibly and not lock into the first way to say them that comes to mind.

We have done the work of finding our ideas and vocabulary words we can use. We have also been practicing gist frame sentence writing every day as a warm-up before writing time. Even more, we have collected sentence stems that we noticed in peer exemplars we liked. We noted those down in our notebooks. Now we will look at those and our organizer. We will begin turning our words into sentences. Let's think about octopuses. Our outline says, "swim 50 miles per hour." That's a good note, but not a full sentence. Let's turn that into a sentence. Watch me carefully. I'll put the sentence on my fingers, then share it with you. "An octopus can swim 50 miles per hour." Did you notice how I did that? Soon you will have a chance to turn

TABLE 5.1. Transition Word Banks

Ways to Link Ideas and Create Cohesion in Writing: A Maturity Continuum

Type of link/cohesive tie	Age range	Example	Description
Temporal links	K–Gr 1	*first, next, last, finally, later*	Move beyond these quickly, as they can stunt quality.
Connectors that emphasize relationships	Gr 3+	*for, and, nor, but, or, yet, so*	FANBOYS (coordinating conjunctions)
		after, before, until, when *where, wherever* *for example, for instance* *although, because, since, yet, unless, as a result, despite, in order to* *however, instead of, rather, despite*	Show more complex relationships than do coordinating conjunctions. Use cue words to reveal text structures, such as cause/effect or compare/contrast. They not only create cohesion but also show relationships.
Semantic repetition (synonyms, pronouns, etc.)	All	*Birds can soar. They soar or fly to the sky.*	Synonyms or exact words repeated
Anaphoric	All	*Sue is a cook. She makes food.*	Refer back to idea from prior sentence (pronoun referent).
Global	Gr 3+	*Now I will describe . . .* *In the prior section . . .* *Another way in which . . .*	Use linking phrases or sentences leading to or linking back to next or prior content globally.

Additive/intensifying	Contrast/change in direction	Causal/logical relationship
Time: *first, next, last*	*whereas*	*therefore, consequently*
moreover	*despite*	*accordingly, since*
furthermore	*in contrast, yet*	*as a result, so*
additionally	*however, while*	*consequently, then*
equally	*nevertheless, although*	*hence thus, therefore*
similarly	*nonetheless, but on the contrary*	*it follows, then*
significantly	*by contrast, on the other hand*	*let us now turn our attention to*
crucially	*conversely, regardless, despite*	*having just argued that*
notably	*even though, whereas*	*although some readers may object*

Note. Adapted with permission from García-Sánchez and Fidalgo-Redondo (2006). Copyright © 2006 SAGE Publications.

words on your organizer into a sentence in the next section. But first, let's keep going and add a detail. My organizer says "get away." Hmmm. My language box says escape and predator. I'll use those words in my next sentence. An octopus escapes from predators because it goes fast. Wait. I don't need to repeat the word octopus. *My reader already knows I'm talking about that. I'll say, "This helps it escape from predators." Now I linked the two sentences by using "it" to stand for octopuses. Also, since this is my first idea, I'll add the word* first *before my other sentence.*

An octopus can swim 50 miles per hour. This helps it escape from predators.

I am showing you how I might think while I draft. I would then cross off the ideas. It is important to think about how ideas will fit together and use my tools when I turn ideas into sentences. You have watched me do this. Remember how we always try out a few different ways to say what we mean before landing on what we will use? Doing this means we have to be flexible thinkers, shifting between word choices and ways to arrange your ideas in sentences. Now you will work with a partner to discuss how you could turn the next ideas into sentences, then decide which options you like best and want to use in your draft. [Students would also write this if they are able to transcribe. If they would like to write it differently, encourage this to help with gradual release and moving them to writing on their own.]

Cognitive Modeling

The teacher taught this kind of flexibility when she modeled turning words from a planner into sentences in this lesson. She did not just tell her students to do this. She thought "out loud" each step of the way so that her students could then mimic the invisible mental processes she used. When modeling thinking in this way, remember to show how to use self-talk to remind oneself to remain flexible when turning ideas into text. For example, a teacher might model selecting a word from the language box, testing it out, then discarding it and trying another. Students might do the same as they work through trying out different stems or expanding and varying sentence options before choosing which one to use. In this way, we teach cognitive flexibility by modeling it.

As an aside, I often noticed students writing in rigid ways, but I did not understand why or how I could help them. I was genuinely surprised at how quickly cognitive flexibility can be improved when I taught this directly and modeled it.

Note to Early Childhood Teachers

First you will model writing in front of your students. You will model at a much higher level than they can initially produce but still within the range for them to eventually produce by the end of the year. To figure out how high to model, listen to how your strongest students speak and nudge them to aim a little higher. Then, you will move to gradual release after students have watched you for a few weeks. You can invite them to draw, dictate, or try out using letters now when they go off to write on their own. Let them take the lead. They saw you model planning, writing, and using scaffolds such as sentence stems and word boxes. They will also see you model how to evaluate writing quality. As they watch you model and score writing, they are learning the processes and features they need to know to compose connected text.

Remember that you will also frontload and teach targeted skills (i.e., spelling, grammar, expansion) through warm-up gist frame sentence-level writing exercises at the start of each class. Students can practice writing these daily, then practice sentence variation and progressively master all their grammar standards (see Appendix I). Your students' early, initial efforts to write on their own will show you where they are in all levels of writing and what to teach next. You might model five or eight sentences. Yet they may only produce two or three. If they write in fragments or lack a topic introduction, details, or an ending, you can use think-alouds to teach these and continue sentence skill practice daily. You can provide them with lists of stems that they can rely on temporarily as they discover their own voices. Resist the temptation to tell them how much to write. Keep modeling and observing what they produce after watching you, then using this to inform your modeling and targeted extra skill instruction each week.

Use Exemplars to Develop Cognitive Flexibility

As a further way to support cognitive flexibility when drafting, review exemplars regularly. When preparing to write a draft, students should also have on hand a few exemplars written about topics studied in prior weeks. These can be kept in their writing notebooks. I was genuinely surprised when my students would ask me for copies of exemplars that we had written or analyzed in prior weeks until I realized the importance of these tools. Revisiting several older exemplars while drafting enables students to build a flexible vision of how varied effective writing can be. Writers can fixate and lock into narrow understandings of what is expected at times. In Chapter 7, you learn about scoring and how rubrics (ways to give feedback on writing) can help students understand what they should do. However, rubrics and strategies such as TIDE (the structural tool we've used for expository text writing) are necessary but not sufficient. They only go so far. Seeing and analyzing many exemplars go much further in helping our students think flexibly about writing. These ensure that students see multiple ways that they can structure their writing or meet different criteria. Without these, they may write in a way that is rigid and robotic and not understand how flexible effective writing can be. Teachers sometimes worry that providing mnemonic structures such as TIDE or scoring systems can result in a rigid writing style. However, the cause is more likely that students have not seen enough exemplars to understand all the different ways that effective writing can look.

A Note on Exemplars

Exemplars become the primary tool through which students learn over time and throughout their lives. The exemplar sparks motivation and helps students reach toward higher levels of writing. Your strongest writers need increasingly complex exemplars to challenge them. Teach students to actively seek these out so they become *exemplar conscious*, a term we coined to help students realize that every year, even during the year, the criteria they will strive to meet advances, and exemplars provide concrete examples of these advances. To ensure students become self-regulating over time and into the future after they leave your classroom, they need to become aware that seeking out and using exemplars is necessary each new year and for each new type of writing. As writers often say, "My bookshelf is my greatest teacher." Exemplars become the most important scaffold for good writers.

Take It to the Classroom: Tips You Can Use Tomorrow

Build and Continuously Reference Writer's Toolkit Notebooks Over the Year

At the start of the year, students can begin creating a toolkit in their notebooks (see the example in Appendix P). When you introduce POWER and TIDE, then each new tool or resource list weekly, students can organize them here. I had my students add each new item to the last available page and number it. For example, POWER and TIDE might go on the very last page in their binder or notebook and be numbered as "1" at the bottom of the page. A next resource might be strategies for helping us think up detailed elaborations. This would go on the second to last page and be numbered as "2." The third to last page could be numbered "3" and include a list of stems for opening a piece or setting up quotes. Students can handwrite such stems and add to the page every time they notice and find new ones. Having a growing bank of stems enables them to use these more flexibly, but it is important for them to be able to access these in a structured and easy way. Each time you model using an older resource, you can add it to the back and give it a page number so the class can know how to find them efficiently.

Model Using TIDE-L

The two most important factors for students to keep in mind when moving from an organizer to writing a draft are cohesion and varied word choice. To ensure the writing coheres, support students in drawing on a conventional text structure such as TIDE. For varied word choice, teach students to identify, hold on to, and use diverse vocabulary in language boxes. Using cohesive structure and varied word choice enables students to write more flexibly. Once students have a box, they can think outside the box. When they understand TIDE, they can vary how they structure their writing more creatively, yet ensure it holds together. You may want to use TIDE-L to remind your students of the importance of both TIDE and the language box. The kind of cohesive structure that TIDE promotes and word choice variation are the two front-runner predictors of overall writing quality (Truckenmiller, 2024). This is why we launch instruction on Day 1 by teaching text structure (TIDE) and language boxes, then reinforce this all year.

Teach Varied and Appropriate Vocabulary Use

As students begin drafting, they can highlight their vocabulary words in blue (or any color). This draws their attention to how many blue words they have and cues them to make more flexible choices, if needed. They can later set vocabulary goals such as using more blue words and varying how they use these words. If students overuse certain words or use terms awkwardly in ways that reflect not understanding them, students can set goals to use them more appropriately. For students with language retrieval difficulties or those learning English, you can add a step before creating gist frame sentences where you have students first list several possible "Who" terms, several "Did what," and other categories. See Figure 2.5 in Chapter 2 for an example. Students can then draw from these gist list word banks when they create gists and when they reach moving from their organizers to their drafts. Doing so supports students in using synonyms rather than robotically repeating one key word, better holds their readers' attention, and gives the writing cohesion (Jennings & Haynes, 2018).

Talk It Out First

Before students move to think about drafting and begin doing so, they should talk through and revise what they have on their organizers (Cramer & Mason, 2014). We covered the importance of discussion in earlier chapters, but we need to revisit it from a new angle. Once students build an organizer, they can work in teams or small groups to share and take feedback on them before they write. Doing so increases the likelihood they will use the feedback (Cramer & Mason, 2014) to refine their ideas. Once students have drafted, they may be less inclined to change course. It is likely easier to tap cognitive flexibility at this earlier phase before they become more wedded to their ideas when the draft is complete.

Teach and Practice Sentences in the Context of Connected Text

At this point, students are looking at their organizers and preparing to turn their notes into sentences. While modeling how to do this, you can pause and have students put the words they will use in their sentence on their fingers or on a whiteboard. They can whisper their sentence, then say it to a peer. At this point, they are not transcribing yet. You can jot down the sentences they say as they share their ideas and create a paragraph. You can discuss varied options for how they could construct each sentence, debate the impact of each possibility, and help them become more flexible in this process. Also, model integrating how to draw from the language box; use conjunctions, stems, and other scaffolds; and have students practice these. These can be as simple as "These are facts about" that you might use in kindergarten up to "By using (name a literary device), the author achieves the effect of . . ." (Levine, 2019), which the middle school student used in the opening chapter anecdote.

Provide Memorable Scaffolds

FANBOYS: *for, and, nor, but, or, yet*

AAAWWUBBIS: *after, although, as, while, when, until, because, before, if, since*

As shown in this lesson, students can list familiar conjunctions such as FANBOYS or AAAWWUBBIS (Anderson, 2005) in their organizers to prompt them to remember to expand and vary sentences until doing so is internalized. The child in this lesson chose to use the word *after* from this mnemonic. In my experience, AAAWWUBBIS is particularly helpful given that students take to it. They like to say and chant it in entertaining ways. When creating organizers, they can call it right up from memory and jot it down without needing to find it in their Writer's Notebook.

Academic sentence-level writing includes more connectors that link and embed multiple ideas within one sentence. Sentence-level composing also requires thinking about and revising for issues such as redundancy and ensuring there are enough connectors without overdoing it. Research on the use of connectors in writing is mixed, with some showing that using too many can bring down writing quality (MacArthur et al., 2019). A drawback of practicing using conjunctions outside the context of connected text writing is that students miss out on learning how to vary sentences in flexible ways to meet their purposes.

Teach Sentence Variety within Connected-Text Paragraphs

To introduce and encourage the concept of flexible sentence variety, begin "in the wild" so when they connect this work to real writing they will do so immediately. To do this, have students look at an exemplar. Direct them to note sentence variety. Look for a mixture of simple, compound, and complex sentences in the piece, rather than all one type. It is important for them to learn right away that better writing is not about longer sentences, and no sentence type is more important than another. Sentences must all work together to carry meaning, and this involves using varied types. As a way to evaluate the exemplar, students can highlight conjunctions in purple or put triangles around them. This helps them see the difference between simple, compound, or complex sentences instantly.

They can even write sentence types, such as S, S+, Cd, and Cx, in the margin to help them see how writers naturally vary these:

- **Simple (S):** One independent clause with a subject (noun) and predicate (action) at minimum
  —*The cat purrs.*
- **Simple Plus (S+)** (from WELL Lab): Includes infinitives
  —*She walks the dog to get exercise.*
- **Compound (Cd):** Two or more independent clauses that can stand alone and are connected by a coordinating conjunction such as *for, and, nor, but, or, yet, so* (FANBOYS)
  —*She walks every day, but today she stayed inside.*
- **Complex (Cx):** One independent clause that can stand alone and one dependent

clause that cannot, connected by a subordinating conjunction such as *after, although, as, while, when, until, before, because, if, since* (AAAWWUBBIS; Anderson, 2005)
—*She wanted to visit the park because her dog likes to walk there.*
- **Compound-Complex (Cd/Cx):** Combines elements of both
—*Although it was raining when the day began, she took her dog to the park and they played outside.*

Students can also go through an exemplar essay and circle the first word in each sentence. This helps them see that sentences begin differently and are structured in varied ways. They can even chant N2SSTSW (No Two Sentences Start the Same Way) to make this fun (Fisher, personal communication, July 2020). To front-load this instruction, vary how your gists are set up during your daily writing practice. Have students move to starting a gist with a where/when statement (Jennings & Haynes, 2018) or a subordinating conjunction or phrase such as *instead of* or *as a result of.* See Appendix I for a sequence that shows how to vary gist statements by grade level, according to the grammar standards that are taught. Students who struggle to write such statements can make gist lists where they make a list of possible "Who" terms or "Did what" terms, then draw from these lists when they go to create their gists, as shown in Figure 2.5 in Chapter 2.

Sentence- or grammar-level instruction in isolation increases the quality of isolated sentences but has little impact on overall writing (Graham & Perin, 2007; Myhill et al., 2018). The only studies that have shown that sentence instruction raises quality used both sentence-combining with text structure instruction as well (Olson et al., 2017; Saddler & Graham, 2005). Daily gist writing practice offers a sound alternative for students to practice identifying main ideas and summarizing, as well as to learn and practice their grammar standards.

Emphasize Sentence Correctness over Complexity

It is also important for students to compose sentences flexibly as they move from grade to grade. In younger grades, the number of clauses per sentence predicts overall quality, but this changes in important ways as students get older (Carvalhais et al., 2021). Sentence correctness (punctuation) may become a more worthwhile objective than complexity when students move to upper elementary and beyond. Offer regular practice in how to create a complete, well-punctuated sentence rather than overemphasizing the importance of extending length or variation. Sentence correctness, rather than complexity, is a stronger predictor of quality in elementary and middle school grades (Truckenmiller, 2024). Time is always limited. Cohesion and word choice are the strongest predictors. Prioritize strengthening these first.

Teach and Practice Sentence Cohesion Daily

As mentioned previously, there are two main types of cohesion: global and local. Global cohesion is when writers show how a whole piece holds together with words such as *first*, *next*, and *finally*. Local cohesion is how writers show how two ideas flow and relate together with words such as *even more*. Writers might also use a synonym or referent as a way to hold the reader's attention. For example:

> **Cats are fun. These feline creatures [synonym to cats] like to chase small objects while they [referent to cats] pretend these are mice.**

Notice how using a synonym ("feline creatures") as a between-sentence cohesive tie (Jennings & Haynes, 2018) holds your attention better than repeating cat twice. Likewise, the writer used *they* to refer back to cats rather than repeating this word. Literally every sentence we write must connect in such ways to those that come before and after. Table 5.1 on page 88 provides a chart that could be shared with students that present these. For more on how cohesion supports reading comprehension as well, see the chart in Cartwright (2023, p. 196).

Revisit Peer Exemplars

To support teaching cohesion and flexible ways to cohere or ensure writing holds together, analyze exemplars again in this light. You will first analyze these for text structure, such as TIDE for expository text or CSPACE for narrative text. These are the building blocks that support cohesion by organizing ideas clearly in ways readers expect, based on the most common organizational patterns they find in texts. Next, show students how exemplars also cohere ideas with linking words such as *first, next,* and *finally*. Then move quickly to showing another way to link ideas by strategically using synonyms or referents in more flexible ways.

Regularly Raise Rigor with Higher-Level Exemplars

For a graphic that shows the phases of growth in content and reasoning per grade level, see Appendix Q. Keep in mind that within a class each year, you may be teaching students who perform within a range of five or more grade levels. See Appendix R for stems that help move students forward through these phases.

This is just one example of how to strategically raise expectations around rigor. Each year, and even throughout one year, students quickly move forward and need new, higher goals even by midyear. The best way to keep the target moving ahead is by using the exemplars they see (and produce) each week. As you co-write with your students as in the sample lesson in this chapter, they will help produce and then see exemplar writing. These exemplars will be written in response to what they are reading and learning about each week. Be sure to keep raising the level of writing they see. This ensures that you continuously nudge their learning forward. Students see higher and higher exemplars all year long and will need to do this anew each year.

When planning their pieces, students need to gather the information or evidence they will include and to brainstorm what they will say about the topic. How they will do this, regarding what kinds of information to collect or how to analyze, will change each year. The genre features taught in prior years will not carry up year to year. Analogous to math, as students move up each grade, we need to teach new ways to use each of the scaffolds and strategies to meet the new higher levels of rigor. Raising the rigor in the exemplars shown and produced each week supports this process. This approach supports cognitive flexibility. By seeing many exemplars and increasingly higher levels, students know they cannot sit still. They must be continuously varying and improving. Varying is a hallmark of cognitive flexibility in writing.

Let Your Students Weekly Writing Data Drive Instruction

Teachers in the schools that achieve strong ELA proficiency gains, such as in the think-SRSD schools cited in Hansford and colleagues (2024), collect writing tasks each week at a minimum. If asked what they will teach the next week, they use their curriculum and state standards as a springboard that they reference. However, they look over their students' writing each week to decide what to teach next.

In a recent data meeting focused on which parts of speech to teach, teachers shared that they wanted to do lessons on prepositions. That was in their standards to teach. However, as we looked over their student writing for that week, it was clear their students were using these already and using them well. This data-driven observation allowed the teachers to move to the next grammatical area they were to teach and check to see where their students were. For a list of grammar skills to include in daily gist writing practice, per grade level, see Appendix I.

Also, when breaking down and teaching each element, be wary of those students who are already proficient. Keep watching your learners' writing each week. In line with the Goldilocks principle, offer just enough executive skill support but do not overdo it for those who may not need it. Once students become more cognitively flexible, continuing to overly break down and scaffold their writing could actually slow them down and even cause confusion. Err on the side of fading too quickly. After you model writing a piece once or twice, have students work in groups to respond to a similarly structured prompt and perhaps a slightly less complex text. Watch how flexibly they work. In order for them to build their self-regulation skills, they must have ample chances to practice using them. If needed, pull them back and model again. However, they may surprise you and be ready for release sooner than you predicted.

Along these lines, be wary of modeling for too long or giving too many scaffolds. Yet, do keep in mind the importance of breaking down the writing process and the features of strong writing carefully. We often find adults become irritated when they see how broken down all the steps of the writing process are in models that teach this way. However, novices and experts differ. When learning how to do something initially, we recruit and use more executive skills than when we become experts. Students may need to subvocalize, "I will be sure to vary my sentences." Yet, after they become naturally flexible at this, activating this same executive skill and speaking to oneself this way could prevent them from moving to higher, more intuitive ways of thinking. Be sure to discard such instruction and scaffolds to help learners remain fluid and continue to improve performance (Diamond, 2013; Miller et al., 2003).

That's a Wrap!

This chapter looked at the executive skill of cognitive flexibility and how this unfolds while moving from an organizer to writing a draft. An "I wish I'd known before I began teaching writing from the start" is not just how long we should model (all year long!) but also how high we can model. I kept seeing that my students' language and reasoning could go higher and higher when I modeled orally and transcribed the ideas we generated together as a class, and when I was there to support them as we came up with these if they needed help along the way.

When well supported, the O to W transition in POWER becomes the high-energy moment in writing. As students begin drafting, their ideas crystallize and come into better focus. Language is often trapped behind the executive skills when our instruction is not considerate of these. Teaching in ways that scaffold the executive skills helps liberate students' language. The sky is the limit!

CHAPTER 6

Working Memory

Transcribing Ideas While Holding Them in Mind

Isn't it amazing what can spring from the tip of a pencil?

—Quino

Pencils can have infinite magic inside, but for that magic to be shared with the world, students must pass through the gateway of transcription, or putting their ideas on paper. So far, we have focused on how executive skills underlie generating ideas, organizing them, and turning these into impactful and cohesive sentences that flow and hang together. Now we move on to transcription, picking up our pencils and moving them to write down those sentences.

Transcription includes skills such as forming letters, spelling, punctuating sentences, or keyboarding. As adults, we transcribe our thoughts nearly effortlessly. We have fully automatized these lower-order skills and do not need to think about them. Our minds are free to focus fully on sharing our ideas, as our magic flows through our pencils onto the page.

This is not the case for our young writers. Putting ideas on paper before these transcription skills are developed requires far more cognitive resources than we may realize, particularly *working memory* (Berninger et al., 2010; Kim & Park, 2018; Kim & Schatschneider, 2017; Limpo et al., 2017; Niedo et al., 2014; Vanderberg & Swanson, 2007). The areas of the brain that activate as students engage in transcribing their ideas overlap with those that support most executive skills, including frontal lobes. This suggests that students draw on executive skills when doing so (Planton et al., 2013, 2017; Rapp & Lipka, 2011). Even more, working memory is an important skill that comes into play and can be better supported while learning how to form letters and spell words. While multiple executive skills support learning and automatizing transcription, this chapter focuses primarily at the role of working memory.

> *Working memory* is the executive skill that allows one to temporarily hold thoughts in mind while monitoring, juggling, and updating them.

Working Memory Capacity Is Limited

Working memory capacity directly impacts writing quality, especially for young students who have not automatized transcription skills such as spelling or handwriting (Kim, 2022; Salas & Silvante, 2019; Valcan et al., 2024). If students are not yet fluent in such areas, they need to recruit and rely on using more working memory. Since this executive skill is limited, such students have fewer resources left to support the higher-order thinking needed for strong writing. This matters because we may not be aware that some young students struggle to write not because of low effort or not caring but because these invisible cognitive skills are being stretched beyond what they can easily manage.

Moreover, executive skills are more limited for certain students. Even for typically developing learners, it is important to recognize how taxing it can be to hold ideas in mind while also mentally juggling other tasks. When our students' limited working memory processes are tied up thinking about transcribing letters or spelling, they are not free to support higher-order language and reasoning. Relative to other academic areas, writing taxes working memory even more so than listening and reading do (Trindle & Longstaff, 2015). The good news is that we can teach lower-order transcription skills to automaticity in ways that better support working memory. When we do so, advanced thinking can happen more easily for students.

To be clear, higher-order thinking, such as idea generation, is also demanding of working memory. However, for students who struggle with transcription, those lower processes take up available working memory capacity and prevent higher-order processes from happening. Thus, we focus primarily on teaching and scaffolding transcription in this chapter. Doing so makes more working memory available for the higher-order processes described in other chapters. Teaching transcription in ways that recognize and support the role of executive skills in learning them frees up students to engage in the kind of higher-level mental juggling that leads to better composing (Olive, 2014; Olive & Kellogg, 2008; Salas et al., 2020).

Flipping this idea may explain why automatized transcription skills such as spelling proficiency predict higher-quality writing outcomes (Truckenmiller et al., 2024). Students were freed from sounding out words to focus on deeper thinking. It is important that students learn and practice such letter formation and spelling transcription skills until they are not only proficient but automatic as well. This includes keyboarding. When students hunt and peck, slow typing rates similarly impede their ability to think about the content they are writing (Connolley, 2007).

Explicit Transcription Instruction Is Important

Given how crucial it is to free up our limited working memory, comprehensive instruction in transcription skills should be delivered in explicit and systematic ways. This includes using a carefully sequenced skill curriculum with direct instruction (Pfeiffer et al., 2015). In fact, brain imaging studies have shown that students who struggle with transcription activate areas of the brain in less efficient ways than those who do so more proficiently (Costa et al., 2022). They may be forming letters haphazardly and guessing at spellings without drawing on sound–symbol correspondences. You may see greater effort but also exhaustion, frustration, and struggles when students do not receive effective instruction in the foundational skills of effective spelling and transcription. They may actually be trying and working harder than peers but not reaping the benefits.

Direct instruction that helps students recruit and use their executive skills efficiently equips them to work smarter rather than harder. They learn to form letters in an organized way, starting all straight-line letters from the top or hooking all curved letters around in the same way. They develop routines for segmenting and sounding out how to spell words. Such organized systems are particularly important for students who have less working memory capacity and who are more at risk for writing difficulties in elementary school (Costa et al., 2018) right from the time they first put pencil to paper.

Engage Higher-Order Language and Reasoning to Support Attentional Control

Recall the Simple View, the Not-So-Simple View, the Direct and Indirect Effects of Writing (DIEW) model, and the Active View of Writing (AVW) model from Chapter 2. Each divides the higher-order (language, reasoning) from the lower-order (physical act of transcribing writing) processes. Often, particularly in younger grades or with students who struggle, writing is mistakenly associated with these early transcription skills (letter formation, spelling, and sentence production). It can seem logical to target and teach these entirely in isolation first. Yet, reaching back to Chapter 1, remember that we must work to develop transcription and composing in parallel. Many early-grade teachers overemphasize code (lower-order) skills at the cost of neglecting attention to higher-order skills (vocabulary, reasoning), and this leads to lower gains in all areas (Farrow et al., 2024). Focusing on higher-order language and reasoning skills makes learning more fun for students, which helps them to inhibit mind wandering and maintain attentional control longer, promoting more efficient learning.

Here is an example of how to do both at the same time. I recently taught a group of young writers about Paul Bunyan. During their school day, they received regular, explicit instruction in foundational skills. I slipped in reinforcement of this instruction around how to form and spell letters as we wrote down rich vocabulary and facts they enjoyed about his life. I modeled how to form letters and sound out words while writing the facts they recalled, such as the fact that his sneezes could cause earthquakes. They persevered, or maintained attentional control, during the lesson because they were curious about Bunyan's amazing feats. Yet, I wove in transcription skill modeling and practice to bolster the handwriting and spelling skills they had already learned through their systematic foundational skills curriculum. I also wanted to show how to use these skills in real contexts at the same time. Keep in mind that if students have not had this foundational skill instruction, they would need more in-depth, direct instruction and support in these areas.

It is worth repeating how research shows that teaching transcription at the same time as providing instruction in broader language and reasoning levels of writing leads to increases in *all* areas, from the earliest grades. This includes transcription, vocabulary, reasoning, and final composition gains (Harris et al., 2023; Limpo et al., 2020; Puranik et al., 2019; Rocha et al., 2024). Recall also that executive skills are the third major factor, or ingredient, needed to write well. Writing rests on transcription, language, and executive skills. From the start, students engage these three areas when learning lower- and higher-order elements needed to write, as they did while putting down facts about Paul Bunyan. Then, when writing independently, they further use their executive skills to help coordinate using all skills together.

Reminder: Do Not Postpone the Higher Order—Teach in Parallel

If you are an early-grades teacher, you may be thinking that your students can't write whole sentences yet. Remember, transcription skills develop gradually. We cannot wait for or focus exclusively on these skills before students learn to compose. Students can use a combination of drawing, dictating, and writing as scaffolds initially as they grow more secure and fluent in letter formation, spelling, or sentence production. There isn't time to delay teaching the higher-order language and reasoning processes needed to compose connected text while we work on transcription. When we make time to work on both the higher- and lower-order processes daily, students who have learned to transcribe jump in right away with rich ideas, vocabulary, and sentence flair. They can also manage and coordinate the executive skills required for writing and the language demands needed in integrative ways.

Continue to Scaffold, While Also Directly Teaching, Transcription

While students work to learn, practice, and automatize transcription skills, additional scaffolds described in previous chapters remain relevant. For example, Chapter 4 explained how TIDE outlines aid and scaffolds the higher-order executive skill of organization. Continuing to use these and adding further scaffolds such as a language box (TIDE-L) helps reduce the working memory demands of transcription. (Adding the L to TIDE emphasizes the importance of strong language/vocabulary use along with text structure when writing.)

These outlines serve as a prosthetic, or artificial limb, in a way. They almost make the kitchen counter longer as students hold ideas mentally and juggle them before writing. When students jot their ideas on such outlines, their thoughts are not lost, trapped, or dominating their working memory. Students now have an outside place not only to hold ideas but also to plan and store the larger structures, connections, and vocabulary choices they will use. Having some ideas in an organizer enables students to coordinate between thinking about areas such as spelling and generating higher-level insights without their core ideas being lost. Further work-arounds that can scaffold transcription include using sentence stems or voice-to-text dictation and new assistive technologies. All these scaffolds can be used side-by-side as you also spend time daily directly teaching and practicing transcription lessons.

Wider Benefits of Transcription Instruction

Back to transcription instruction, as mentioned at the opening of this chapter, the transcription skills we teach draw from and rely on executive skills, particularly working memory. You may be wondering if all the cognitive effort needed for students to learn them is worthwhile, particularly with all the technology work-around scaffolds students can now easily use. It is! Transcription, forming letters, spelling, or punctuating sentences may seem separate from what we consider to be a high-quality essay or story. Yet these skills, particularly letter formation speed and spelling, predict writing quality, especially in the early grades and for those who struggle to write (Alves & Limpo, 2015). When we put in time to teach these skills, we help students produce better pieces both directly by improving these areas and indirectly, given how being fluent in them frees up working memory to support higher-order writing skills.

As an added benefit, transcription instruction builds early reading skills too. As students' lower-order transcription skills improve, overall composition quality and early reading skills increase (Fancher et al., 2018; Graham & Santangelo, 2014; Hand et al., 2024; James, 2017; James & Engelhardt, 2012; Kiefer et al., 2015; Longcamp et al., 2005). This may be because handwriting and letter perception recruit the same area of the brain (James, 2017; Moats, 2005–2006).

Note to Upper-Grades Teachers

If you teach upper grades (skill levels beyond grade 3) and students who already transcribe fluently, you may want to only skim this chapter. However, do be sure your students are fluent in all areas of transcription. Being proficient in areas such as handwriting and keyboarding predicts future levels of organization in writing through grade 4 (Wagner et al., 2011) and overall text generation through middle school (Salas et al., 2020).

In line with the previous chapters, we visit our school and see a sample lesson. Then I analyze the working memory supports in this lesson and provide suggestions for ways to support working memory while teaching writing in your classroom.

Back Inside Our School: What It Looks Like When Students Are Doing It Well

Let's check back in now with the students working in the early-grade classrooms and some in a special instruction setting. Students created notes during P (Plan) and O (Organize) phases over the past few days. Yesterday they reviewed their organizers with peers and began discussing how they would turn their short notes into fuller sentences and link their ideas together.

Today they are moving ahead to physically write drafts in W (Write) in POWER. In this grade 1 classroom, we see students turning their notes into sentences. Before we return to the writing lesson that we began the day before, we will step back in time a few minutes. We reach back to the earlier section of the literacy block where teachers focused on delivering foundational skill lessons. After watching some of that first lesson, we return to see how students are moving from O to W in the realm of transcription and now writing down their ideas.

Today, during foundational skill instruction, students are midway through a systematic handwriting and spelling curriculum. The handwriting lesson focuses on reviewing forming the letters *c* and *o*. Students practice verbalizing how to begin and form each. The teacher reminds them that the letter *o* is a circle. Students make a circle in the air with their fingers, starting at the left, moving right, and closing it up fully. She invites students to echo her words as they form these on lined paper and tell themselves: "To write the sound for (short) *o,* start over just to the right of the middle line, curve around in a circle, sit on the lower line, and come up to close by touching the middle one." These letters had already been introduced, but the teacher noticed students struggling with forming them. This prompted her to do a quick warm-up review of these. Next students practice spelling two-syllable words that have these letters in them such as *cotton*, *rocket*, and *pocket.* After the full lesson and practice in these types of skills, students return to writing about what they are reading.

Today students are looking at their organizers and quietly reviewing how to turn them into sentences. They had begun doing this the day before. They are whispering as they draft possible sentences and put their words or phrases on their fingers (or whiteboards) before they will then transcribe them on paper after formulating them. They hold each word or phrase in mind while testing out possible sentences, as described in the last chapter. They then share these sentences with a peer. The classroom is humming as students talk to neighbors, sharing their sentences and ideas. They review their language boxes and look at their lists of sentence stems as well, deciding which words and stems to use. All of this preparation eases the next step of transcribing these on paper.

Now they pick up their pencils and begin to transcribe their ideas, paying attention to grip, letter formation, spacing, spelling, and punctuation skills. They have already thought carefully and practiced discussing with peers how they will turn their ideas into well-chosen words. They thought about using varied and cohesive sentences that link their ideas together with transition words such as *first* and *next* or even better through using synonyms for the main words. These help hold the reader's attention better than repeating the one main topic word, and they help the writing hold together and flow from sentence to sentence. One child is writing about how animals hibernate. She sounds out the word *animals*—a-n, i, m-a-l-s—breaking the word into individual syllables and phonemes. She thinks to herself, "I'll imagine a rubber band. I'll stretch the word out and say it slowly so I hear each sound." On her organizer, she had only written *anim* because that was enough to hold the thought. She now thinks again about how to form each letter, how to spell the word, and she remembers to put a finger space between each word. She also knows to begin her sentence with a capital letter. In her language box, she also has *creatures* written. She will use it in the second sentence to refer back to this idea without repeating the same word over and over.

> *OK. I've written the word* animals. *Now I need to write* hibernate. *That word is written in the story we read. I'll look at the story to see how to spell it—"h-i-b." I'll write those three letters first. Next, "e-r." I'll remember to make my letters sit on the line and the* e *will be a careful circle, like when I write* a *and* c. *Now, the last part is "nate." That is spelled "n-a-t-e." I write an* e *at the end, even though we don't hear it when we say that part, but I know that's because it helps the* a *make the long sound in this CVCe spelling pattern. Alright! I've got two words. I remembered to capitalize "Animals," and I'll add a period after* hibernate. *I'll also put my finger between the words to make sure I have spaced them out far enough, but not too far. For my next sentence, I will use* They *to begin. I hear "th" but then "ay." Wait, that is a word on my special word list. It starts out with* th, *but the "a" sound is spelled "ey." OK, I've got that. We talked about how we don't want to use the main word* animals *over and over. We can use a word like* they *instead. This makes my writing more fun for my reader when I use varied words.*

Heading upstairs to an upper-grade small-group class, the teacher is leading a quick spelling warm-up activity before writing block formally begins. These sometimes last between 10 and 15 minutes depending on the skill needs of the class each year. Some students sit off to the side and continue their writing since they do not have these skill needs. The teacher is dictating a list of words with common morphemes. Today the morpheme is *tract.* Students write *tractor*, *intractable*, *retract*, and even *abstract*, which means "to pull away from the concrete *or* tangible meaning." The teacher then dictates four words that students misspelled last week, such as *finally*, and discusses why it has two *l*'s. She then has students generate extensive gist lists related to the content they are learning and writing about. These are lists of nouns (*Who* or *What*) and verbs (*Did what*) that they can practice using in sentences (see Appendix I). They also make a list of subordinating conjunctions (see Table 5.1 in Chapter 5) and practice composing sentences that open with a subordinating conjunction, then have two *Who*'s and two *Did what*'s, as any sentence with a conjunction would usually have. Students read their rich sentences to peers and mark a few that they would like to use when they go to compose today.

As they then transition to return to the pieces they had begun organizing the day before, you might hear students thinking:

> *I've created my organizer and thought through how I will write my opening and thesis. I need to start by writing the TAG—title, author, and gist. The book title was* A Long Walk to Water, *and the author was Linda Sue Park. I'll begin by indenting and writing "In the book." OK, pause. My goal is to have neater handwriting. I'll remember to have my letters start at the top of the line and go all the way to the lower line, make my circular letters round, and touch the middle and lower lines. Hey, they look good.*
>
> *Where am I? Right, now I'll write the name of the book, the author, and what the book is about. I'll use the Who (noun), Did what (verb) gist sentence*

frame to ensure I don't write a fragment. I'll also tap out the longer words to ensure I'm spelling them accurately and check the book or look up any words I'm not sure about. For now, I can circle the words that I'm not sure if I spelled accurately. This reminds me to come back later. For now, I get my ideas down first. I'll also look at my language box and sentence stems as I go. I can also think about word parts that I know to help me. I wanted to say that Salva becomes less tractable as the story goes on. I remembered the word retract *means to pull back and ends with a* t. *"Intractable" has the same root so I think it has a* t *at the end of the root "tract" too.*

The younger student already learned how to grip a pencil, match sounds to letters, and form letters before this lesson. However, her teacher did not wait until these were in place to begin modeling instruction in the writing process and text structure. All along from the start of the year, the teacher was modeling orally how to go through the writing process and produce sentences while writing in front of the class. This way, as students become more proficient at transcription, they understand how to use the writing process. As you model writing, you also develop your students' oral academic language and higher-order thinking so they are able to produce stronger writing right away when transcription kicks in. Students can begin to put letters and words on paper once they have learned grip, letter formation, and sound/symbol correspondences. They can also spell phonetically and reference word lists to help them write common irregular words correctly. Most states have standards that include having students write multisentence opinion, informative and narrative paragraphs, and stories right from kindergarten. Yet, in the earliest grades, before having the needed transcription skills, students should use a combination of drawing and dictation when learning to form letters. To do this, even before they can transcribe, they would need to see the writing process modeled in the ways described in the earlier chapters.

See It in Action: Sample Lessons

Still in the "Model" phase of Teach, Model, Score and midway through a weekly cycle, we turn now to see what a transcription lesson might look like during the Write (W) phase of POWER. This chapter includes two sample lessons.

The first lesson shows how a fuller lesson in handwriting, spelling, or sentence composing and transcription might look. This lesson would be taught as part of regular instruction in K–2 or for students with extra needs in older grades.

The second lesson is for older students who have learned basic transcription but continue to have areas of need around letter formation, spelling, or punctuation that require additional instruction and practice. It offers an example of what transcription "warm-up" instruction could look like in the upper grades. This lesson would not introduce transcription skills for the first time but would offer additional practice and reinforcement for students who no longer need this instruction front-loaded but do still require additional warm-up practice.

SAMPLE LESSON 1: Transcription Full Lesson—Before Modeling How to Move from O (Organize) to W (Write) in POWER

Goal: Teach targeted transcription lessons as part of a fuller, explicit, systematic and sequenced program.

Objectives:

1. Review how to form circular letters (*c*, *o*, *a*).
2. Practice spelling two-syllable words that have these letters in them.

Estimated Time: 15–20 minutes

Materials: Chart paper or smartboard, pencils, appropriate line-size paper, notebooks, or curricular spelling books

Lesson Steps:

1. Introduce that this lesson will focus on letter formation and spelling.
2. State that today we will practice forming circular letters such as *o*, *a*, and *c*.
3. Verbalize aloud as you form these letters and students watch.
4. To write the sound for (short) *o*, start over just to the right of the middle line, curve around in a circle, sit on the lower line, and come up to close by touching the middle one.
5. Then invite students to echo your verbalizations as they write them in their handwriting practice books or on specially lined paper.
6. Have students return and circle the letters that they believe they formed best and encourage them to tell a peer why they circled these letters.
7. Next, tell students we will move to spelling practice.
8. Say, "Now, we will practice spelling two-syllable words that have these letters in them."
9. Say, "I will dictate the word. We will clap out how many syllables it has and then sound out the letters in each." Use *cotton*, *rocket*, and *pocket* as practice words.
10. After students attempt to write these, model writing them on the board, stating the sound and using the letter verbalizations again as you write each letter.
11. Wrap up by having students practice spelling a few more similar words, working in pairs then on their own. Show the correct spellings. Have them score their own attempts and count how many words they spelled correctly out of 10. Then set a goal to increase the score in the next lesson. Have students also circle their two best-formed letters in their spelling list as well.
12. Let them know they will use these skills during the sentence and paragraph writing they will do next.

Wrap-Up: Summarize that this lesson allowed us to practice letter formation and spelling.

SAMPLE LESSON 2: Transcription Short Lesson—Warm-Up (Beforehand) and Modeling Moving from O (Organize) to W (Write) in POWER

Goal: Move from O in Organize to W in Write by transcribing ideas on paper.

Objectives:

1. Lead a full transcription lesson or warm-up activities, depending on age and students' needs.
2. Review the writing process and discuss how to move from sentences that students discussed.
3. Model using self-talk to guide and encourage oneself while writing.
4. Demonstrate how to take ideas we have discussed and put them in writing on paper or screen.
5. Use gist frames, stems, and reminders on organizers to support transitions and sentence quality.

Estimated Time: 30–45 minutes

Materials: Chart paper or smartboard, markers, pencils, notebook paper (whiteboards or clipboards), copies of a text that students will read

Lesson Steps:

1. As a warm-up, tell students we will do some quick spelling and sentence writing practice.
2. Dictate words that provide practice with common spellings or morphemes that students have not mastered from previous weeks. Draw these from a systematic curriculum. Follow the sequence of the curriculum, but only deliver the lessons that students have not mastered, as evidenced in their writing. You should follow the sequence if they are older students who would have already received this fuller Tier 1 curriculum, and this is follow-up reinforcement. For example, demonstrate how straight lines should touch the bottom line.
3. Dictate words such as *tractor*, *intractable*, *retract*, and *abstract* and explain what each means and how they share a common morpheme. Give the spelling right after and have students self-correct. Next, dictate words such as *finally* that they misspelled in writing they produced the week before and explain rules for why these are spelled as they are.
4. Transition now to the writing about reading portion of the lesson.
5. Have students then make "gist lists" of words from the topic they are reading and learning about. List *Who* (nouns), *Did what* (verb phrases), and subordinating conjunctions.
6. Have students use these words in sentences, read their sentences to peers, and self-check to ensure that each has two *Who* words, two *Did what* words, and an opening subordinating conjunction. Invite students to circle sentences they will use when we move to composing on paper or screen now.

7. Write POWER on the board and review the meaning of each phase in the writing process. If students have this already written in their notebooks, they can prepare to check off W as they move now to write (5 minutes).
8. Students take out the texts they read, their notes, and organizers.
9. Remind students that yesterday they discussed their organizers with a peer.
10. Explain that today we will now do the work of transcribing our ideas as we complete the W—write a draft phase in POWER.
11. As a regular routine, have students jot down positive self-talk, such as "I've got this," "I can stay focused," or "I'll use tools such as an organizer and stems as I transcribe my ideas today" (5 minutes).
12. Explain that the W in POWER is when we begin to write our ideas down.
13. Remind students to use their tools as they write. Model doing this and use think-alouds to reveal how writers might think as they move from ideas they have discussed to writing these now in full sentences.
14. Lead mini lessons as needed for how to set up quotes, add citation references or page numbers, and elaborate on their points as they write.
15. Be sure to reference and use the words from the language box in the upper corner or bottom.

Wrap-Up: Summarize that this lesson looked at how to transcribe ideas during the W in POWER and how to follow the steps in O.

Note: Oftentimes, the sample lesson in the last chapter on moving from O to W and this one take place hand-in-hand rather than separately.

Lesson Analysis: How Each Component Supports the Working Memory Needed for Effective, Self-Regulated Writing

Letter Formation—Rooted in Executive Skills

Although it involves physical work, handwriting is sometimes mistakenly viewed as related to hand strength. Writing is not entirely about physical capacity in one's arm or hand but is rooted in executive skill functioning and working memory skills taking place back up in the brain. As explained, executive skills play a significant role in all areas of transcription, particularly with letter formation (Klein et al., 2010; Niedo et al., 2014; Salas & Silvente, 2020), with working memory playing a central role (Valcan et al., 2024). Stronger executive skills, including working memory, are associated with letter formation quality (Chandler et al., 2021), particularly sustained attention (Feder & Maimener, 2007).

This is true for students even up through grade 3+, where handwriting is expected to be fully automatized. However, it is still a challenge for many students and can therefore tax limited working memory (Lê et al., 2021). Continuing to teach transcription to automaticity or providing scaffolds to ease the working memory demands of transcription still has ongoing value. However, here is a caveat: We should dedicate the least amount of time possible to transcription instruction to ensure we maintain greater attention to higher-order learning. Err on the side of less being more, as mentioned earlier.

In fact, this chapter included two lesson plans to emphasize the importance of dosage and minimizing the amount of time spent on transcription instruction and practice, while recognizing that it is important to teach these skills, even with older students. For example, a fuller lesson might introduce letters in a group such as *a*, *c*, and *o* and have students note what is similar and say aloud how to form each. However, if students have already learned these and are simply not remembering to close them up, you can slip in reminders as you model writing in front of them, as in the second lesson to save time. Allocate the least amount of time needed so that you save time for higher-order skills, but at the same time do not neglect these important skills either.

Leverage Working Memory to Support Motor Performance

Letter formation may appear to be primarily a physical or motor skill. However, the brain directs this (Cameron et al., 2012; Gandora et al., 2021). As a result, addressing the cognitive piece is important too. When my students struggled with handwriting, I thought about hand strength, grip position, or pressure awareness. I was not as aware of the importance of teaching students how to use verbalizations to call up and juggle information around what the letters should look like and how to form them so that students self-direct their writing at the letter-formation level as well.

In fact, researchers have found that of the four most common pencil grips, this physical level had no impact on handwriting. Instead, they recommend focusing on teaching for speed and legibility instead (Aktas, 2023; Schwellnus et al., 2012), both of which are supported by working memory (Capodieci et al., 2018; Tindle & Longstaff, 2023). Working memory enables students to hold a letter form in mind and coordinate physically forming it at the same time.

Fortunately, there are ways to teach and support this practice. Students may struggle to visualize letters and direct themselves as they form them. In the lesson just described, students had been taught to pay close attention to the salient features of well-formed letters, subvocalize how to form them, and then circle their best. These strategies tap and support working memory and lead to improvements (Berninger et al., 1997; Graham et al., 2000; Jongmans et al., 2003; Weintraub et al., 2009; Zwicker & Hadwin, 2009). This is not to diminish the importance of the physical and motor aspects of handwriting but to emphasize thinking about working memory in how we address handwriting.

Importance of Spelling Lessons and Use of Invented Spelling

Just as with letter formation, spelling must be taught, and in ways that support the working memory demands of transcription as well. Similarly to the wider benefits from explicit instruction in handwriting toward early decoding, spelling instruction supports early reading processes (Galuschka et al., 2014, 2020; Graham & Santangelo, 2014). Spelling and reading rely on the same underlying knowledge (sound–letter relationships), and nearly every spelling variation makes sense when considering these in the history of our language (Moats, 2005–2006).

For writers in the early grades, having students work at sounding out words as they compose is also important, in combination with delivering a systematic, structured spelling program. This would mean giving daily opportunities for students to compose, with adult support as needed. Having young students put their ideas on paper then work with adults to help edit spellings works to build their understanding of the alphabetic principle and facilitates early literacy learning, with concrete supports (Rowe et al., 2024; Schrodt et al., 2024). The practice of sounding out the words they would like to include in writing may better engage their attentional control and working memory than traditional spelling lessons alone would. Reflect on all that goes into sounding out and thinking about the letters needed to represent each element in the word *an-i-mal*, as you saw the child do in this lesson. Students would hold the word, its meaning, and each syllable in mind as they work out the letters to represent each chunk.

You may hesitate to have students write multiple sentences before they are proficient spellers. However, when trying to sound out the words they would like to write, they likely pay attention longer as they work to figure out each sound and corresponding letter or make use of morphological word structures (discussed next). Doing so helps them hold on to the spellings and strengthens the alphabetic principle (that letters represent sounds from spoken language) more rapidly. For example, kindergartners provided with systematic instruction to assist them with invented spelling (also called phonetic or approximated spelling) improve their word reading (Rowe et al., 2024; Sénéchal et al., 2012) and overall writing quality (Schrodt et al., 2024). This is not guessing spellings but a process that involves careful instruction in how to use their existing knowledge about letter–sound correspondences to figure out or approximate spellings until one masters conventional spelling in ways that alleviate working memory demands.

In this lesson, students drew on what they understood about the alphabetic principle and grapheme–phoneme connections to sound out words. Memorizing a disjointed spelling list is not an effective practice. Doing so overloads short-term memory, does not stick because it does not link spellings to already-known sounds in spoken words, and misses how we can better leverage working memory and logic to help writers figure out how to spell words. Instead, systematic spelling instruction should help students connect sounds to letters or graphemes and support them in becoming aware of the smallest unit of meaning, or morphemes, at the same time. The following example shows the language you could use to model for your students the kind of thinking that happens in the mind of an early writer.

Teacher Talk Example: Think-Aloud

Today, we will put our ideas on paper. When we do this, we use our memory to remember what the letters look like and how to write them. We even use a special kind of memory called working memory. This is a place in your brain that holds your ideas while you think about a few things—the name of the letter, what it looks like, how to form it, and how to use those skills. When we first learn, it can be hard to hold all this in mind. That is why it can be helpful to use little tricks like telling ourselves what to do.

We already thought about turning our notes into sentences. I want to write "An octopus can protect itself." I know I should sweep it over or indent when I begin. Now I have to remember to write a capital A *in the word* An *because this is the first word in a sentence. Let me think. I'll tell myself what to do—an* A *starts at the top and goes "over, down." Then again, the other way. Then I cross it in the middle. Then I write the* n*—"down, hook around, and down." Now I will put a little space and write "octopus." I hear three parts. The first is "oc" so I will use the letters* o *and* c*. I can also look at the text I read to see how tricky words are spelled.*

*Note: Early spellers may write "oktapus" (*k *for the /k/ sound and* a *for the "schwa" sound in the unstressed second syllable); this is not guessing at spelling. Rather, this invented spelling shows that students are hearing the sounds in speech and matching those sounds in a logical, one-to-one fashion to graphemes that represent those sounds. When students make these early efforts, it is important to give gentle, encouraging feedback such as "Yes! Those are the sounds you hear. If you saw it in a book, it would look like octopus." You can even provide them with a simple, child-friendly explanation for why. It's important that you haven't explicitly said the child was incorrect; rather, you are supporting their developing application of grapheme–phoneme knowledge and helping to enhance that knowledge in positive ways.*

This example illustrates how a student might think while putting words on paper. Share with your students that it is important to talk to oneself internally while doing this activity when first learning to transcribe. Once students automatize transcription, continuing to use such self-verbalizations (saying in their mind how to form letters) would only slow them down. However, when first practicing, directing oneself in these ways makes writing much easier. As they get better at writing, they will not need to do this anymore.

Morphology

Before moving on to analyze the lesson for sentence-level instruction and how working memory underlies these, we need a brief word about morphology (internal word structures; i.e., cats = base of cat + suffix *s*), which also plays a role in learning to read (Carlisle, 2000; Kim, 2023) and write (Kim & Graham, 2022). In English, morphology underlies word meanings as well as how we spell them (Hegland, 2021). Connections between graphemes and phonemes underpin the spellings of words. Attending to the consistent spelling of meaning cues from morphology combined with grapheme–phoneme mapping helps bind spellings to pronunciations and meanings of words to form sight words in memory (Bowers & Bowers, 2017). As students progress in acquiring reading and writing skills, morphological instruction can build on alphabetic foundational knowledge to deepen understandings about the English writing system and its use to read and spell words (Castles et al., 2018). Therefore, we discussed morphology in the vocabulary chapter and now again the transcription chapter as well.

As mentioned in Chapter 4, morphology refers to morphemes. A morpheme is the smallest unit of meaning in a word. For example, word parts such as *-ed* indicate the meaning of past tense. Simple words such as *fish* are also morphemes. The sentence "I biked" would have three morphemes—the two simple words (*I*, *bike*) and the past tense *-ed*. Understanding morphemes plays a role in learning to spell (Ardanouy et al., 2024), particularly for students with language disorders (Bowers et al., 2010; Good et al., 2015). Working memory likely supports students as they hold a word in mind and juggle the parts of the word as they pull up potential spellings and patterns they have seen in other words. For example, when a student tried to spell *intractable*, he thought about what he knows about roots (morphemes). He knew *tract* means to pull and is seen in words such as *retract* (pull back). So he figured out there should be a *t* in the middle of the word when he wanted to spell it. He had to hold the word in mind and juggle thinking about its parts, using working memory. He also had to have paid attention when learning these related words long enough to notice the pattern (*tract*) and hold on to it. As this example shows, morphology, again, is part of both basic transcription (spelling) and semantic (meaning) areas of learning to read and write. Hence, Active View of Writing includes morphology in bridging processes (Duke et al., in press; see Chapter 2 for reference to AVW).

Sentence Composing and Punctuation

Likewise, sentences cross between both realms of transcription and language. They also require the kind of mental juggling working memory supports. In the last chapter, we looked at how sentences carry meaning to readers. However, there is also a lower-order transcription piece to sentences as well. This includes spacing and punctuation. Written (punctuation) and oral language cues activate different areas of the brain (Kerkoffs et al., 2008). Punctuation relies more on visual skills, noticing and remembering how to use them. It draws on attentional control as well as working memory (Berninger et al., 2016). While handwriting and spelling are related to inhibition (Berninger & Richards, 2010; Salas & Silvente, 2020), spacing and punctuation seem more related to visual attention and motor production. Working memory underlies all of these processes (Kim et al., 2017). That is, students can draw on working memory as they reason through or remind themselves to think about which punctuation would be needed, how to spell words, and how to combine them to create meaningful sentences.

Daily Embedded Sentence Drills

In previous chapters, we talked about developing sentence skills through writing gist statements. This gist work can also provide for daily instruction and practice in punctuation. While practicing gist writing, students can include capitals, periods, and commas. Adding these differs from the language elements of producing sentences. It draws on more visual skills. Students can practice gist writing sentences and gradually extending them, always using the content they are also currently learning as the basis for what they write so that they can practice punctuation and spacing this way (Appendix I).

As students progress with daily sentence writing practice using gist frames, they can begin to fade out writing the boxes and move to practice sentence writing daily on regular lined paper, while still thinking about varied frames. They can move out of using boxes once they show mastery in grammatical accuracy in their weekly writing pieces and can speak about the different parts of speech when talking about components in their sentences. They can then self-evaluate their sentences in terms of having capitals, periods, and commas. Composing before evaluating requires working memory for students to hold the ideas in mind and juggle thinking about punctuation at the same time until automatized. Setting goals can be a helpful force in supporting their motivation to put in the effort needed to do this working memory–dependent kind of mental juggling. Students can also practice speeded sentence production drills in timed, repeated gist "sentence slams" (Anderson, 2005) as needed.

The Brain on Writing

Before moving to the teaching tips, let's look at what happens when students write. Thinking about all that happens in a child's brain can take your breath away. Figure 6.1 shows the areas of the brain that are hard at work as students write and that allow the needed connections between different areas of the brain to happen. The occipitotemporal cortex (below in back) supports the orthographic skills needed for handwriting and reviewing the words we have written. The temporoparietal area (above in back) supports the phonological processes that help students sound out words they

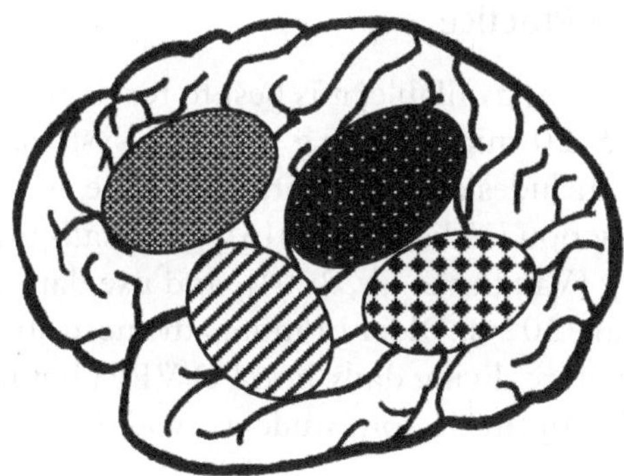

orthographic: occipitotemporal cortex (letterbox; spellings, letters)
phonological: temporoparietal cortex (sounds, phonemes)
semantic: medial and inferior temporal cortex; inferior frontal gyrus (meaning)
executive functions: prefrontal cortex and neighboring areas

FIGURE 6.1. Some major components of the reading network. (Brain regions are approximate.) From Cartwright (2023). Copyright © 2023 The Guilford Press. Reprinted by permission.

write (and read). The striped semantic area enables us to attach meaning to these sounds and visuals. Finally, above in front shows where executive functioning takes place in the prefrontal cortex and neighboring areas. Imagine only supporting three of these four areas. Think of the power we add to our instruction and their learning when we build in direct support for executive skills as well. Our executive skills, supported by these and other brain areas, provide a central regulatory role in linking and coordinating wider, varied brain regions. Together, these areas, as a primary seat of executive skills, play an important role in integrating cognitive and emotional processes that contribute to how we think and feel (Anderson & Spencer-Smith, 2013; Menon & D'Esposito, 2022).

Take It to the Classroom: Tips You Can Use Tomorrow

Returning to our big picture of Teach, Model, Score, the students are now in the "Model" phase. They are working through the writing process phases. The prior chapter addressed the language demands of moving from an organizer to writing a draft, as well as the vocabulary and sentence construction skills needed, including understanding of how writing needs to cohere to make sense to the reader. Building off of that language base, this chapter focuses on how to move that language through one's hand while transcribing. Before diving into the next sections, which provide instructional tips and explore the discrete elements to teach, you may want to look at Appendix B, which provides a big-picture, comprehensive chart of all the elements to teach with an emphasis on transcription.

Provide Short, Focused Daily Practice

Depending on grade levels and time available, it is best to teach and practice transcription skills up-front daily for 5–20 minutes using a direct, systematic, and appropriately sequenced program that includes daily deliberate practice as well, as needed. It is vital to differentiate this instruction (Valiandes, 2015), use small-group instruction for those who are not progressing (Vaughn et al., 2001), and use data to regularly monitor student progress (Choi et al., 2024). Older or more advanced students benefit from briefer "warm-up" activities before diving daily into POWER, but may not need a full dedicated block for these skills. In this lesson, students would now practice and apply these taught skills.

Teach for Transfer

The first sample lesson demonstrated explicit instruction designed to leverage the executive skills that can support this learning, such as attention and working memory through strategies such as verbalizing letter formations. The second lesson showed how to embed additional reinforcement while composing within an integrated lesson, as doing so leads to faster and greater overall gains across spelling, reading, and composing (Wolf et al., 2017).

As an example, handwriting instruction will transfer better when letter formation is reviewed, modeled, and practiced in the context of content-area writing assignments. For example, teachers can model letter formation during collaborative writes by saying, "I'm going to make a capital *T*, the first letter in *The*. What do I need to remember?" They can have students practice and rehearse how to remind themselves, "Be sure I start at the top, make my lines straight, and sit in the bottom line but don't go below." The older student in the lesson described earlier demonstrated how students can learn to do this. In this way, students see that they should apply what they learned and practiced in letter formation lessons when using the writing process to compose pieces, and how they can coordinate in working memory juggling these multiple levels of attention to skills while holding ideas in mind.

Spiral Back Regularly

Modeling application allows you to repeatedly spiral back and reteach or reinforce letter formation, spelling, or punctuation conventions already taught whenever needed. Keep in mind that introducing letters more quickly results in better overall learning and gains (Vadasy & Sanders, 2021). Therefore, err on the side of moving quickly knowing you can spiral back to reinforce skills as needed when you next model writing in front of your students. You can reteach, model, and reinforce how to form specific letters or any skill that their writing shows they are not mastering right away. Circling back and including this kind of careful skill modeling encourages transfer and integrated use in actual writing of students.

Self-Evaluate Handwriting

Keeping students engaged and attentive as they learn the shapes of the letters with activities, such as discussing what they notice about shapes, helps engage them, which is important given the importance of sustained attention to handwriting (Feder et al., 2007). Students should also be given assistance in how to self-evaluate and self-correct specific errors, using models for reference, like circling their best letters or tracing letters in extra practice as needed. They can also set goals to improve how they form certain letters or how fluently they do so. This taps into the executive skills of planning and goal setting. Also, it is important to distinguish between students who struggle to form letters neatly from those who don't know how to form them at all. Some may only need reminders to self-regulate, while others need more basic instruction (Wallis et al., 2017). They will set different goals and use different self-evaluation strategies accordingly.

Teach Keyboarding for Drafting

In addition to teaching handwriting, keyboarding instruction is important as well. Keyboarding speed predicts student writing quality (Truckenmiller, 2024). However, a note of caution about when to compose on paper versus computers. Students should primarily use keyboarding at the drafting stage, rather than during the planning and organizing phases. Students often just copy and paste quotes into outlines when they make these on technology devices. This bypasses the cognition needed to process the information and condense it. When making their outlines by hand, students select what is most important and summarize, group, and sequence the ideas they choose. They may cross out parts, make arrows, and move ideas. This is more challenging to do on computers. It also misses the opportunity that handwriting confers to deepen learning. Not only does writing by hand slow us down and thereby increase the amount of time spent processing, but it also activates areas of the brain that facilitate making deeper connections (Van der Weel et al., 2024). Students should be taught how to do these phases on paper, then alternate composing at times on paper and at times on devices.

Daily Embedded Sentence Instruction and Practice

Using daily gist sentence-expansion writing practice has been recommended all through the school year as a way to teach sentence-level writing and is supported as an evidence-based practice (Graham et al., 2012, 2016). To strengthen sentence correctness, students can generate their own tricks or mnemonics to track punctuation rules. For example, teachers can use the chart in Figure 6.2 that students call the "Swoosh" as they learn the comma rules. They can practice them in daily gists and apply them during writing time. Students can develop the habit of noticing how commas are used when they read and make systems like this chart to categorize example patterns they discover as they read.

Charts like these help students hold on to punctuation patterns, lightening the need to hold this information in working memory while writing. When these patterns around punctuation use become familiar and internalized, students can focus more on higher-order meaning-making processes. Given how punctuation is partly a visual attention skill, this kind of easy-to-recall imagery supports students in paying attention when they see these marks used in writing they read and cueing them to use these

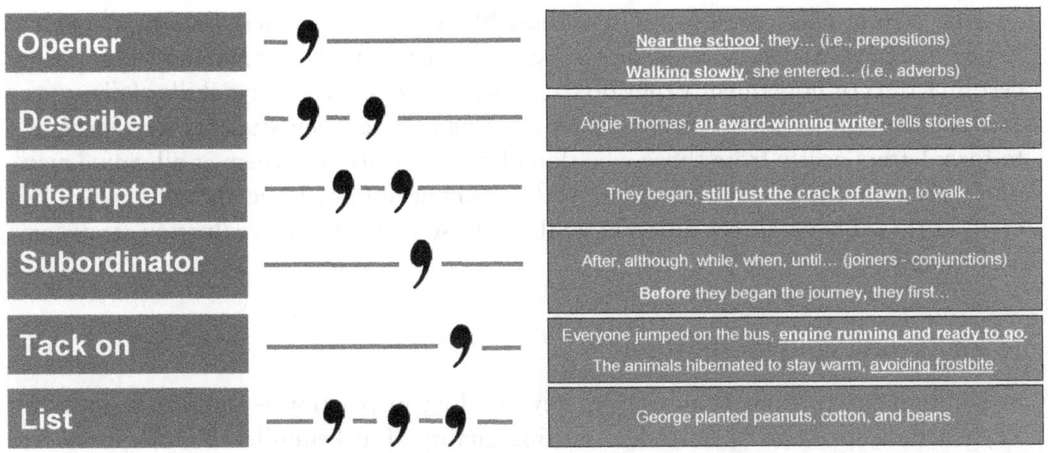

FIGURE 6.2. ODISTL varied sentence expanders.

as they write. Punctuation includes attention to meaning as we write, which requires writers to hold meanings in mind, juggle them, and think about how, where, and why they would like to place these markers, which taxes working memory and is supported by such instruction and visuals.

Sentence Fluency

The earlier chapters introduced the idea of writing gist or main idea statements daily. The format of these can vary each week to incorporate sequentially working through your grade-level grammar standards, including those for punctuation. For example, grade 1 is expected to use commas in a series. Grade 4 should use commas before a coordinating conjunction. Middle schoolers might learn semicolons. Just as you can add varied grammatical elements to teach new grammar standards each week, you can introduce and practice the punctuation standards regularly in the same way (see Figure 6.2). You can teach and add one row at a time until students show mastery of them in their writing. Recall Appendix I that lists the grammatical elements that should be taught and practiced in sequence per grade level as well. In this way, you will have a systematic way to ensure all writing components are taught, and you can regularly check your students' independent writing to ensure they are mastered.

Students who show persistent struggles with fragments, run-ons, verb tense, and other areas can also engage in timed sentence-writing fluency exercises to aid them in becoming more fluent at the sentence production level, as needed (Panos & Datchuk, 2021). Not all students, or even most, may need this extra practice, as daily quick gists sentence practice may move the majority of students to grade-level mastery, according to teachers I have worked with who shared this information with me. While more information and research are needed, daily gist practice offers a promising option, and this kind of sentence expansion is deemed an evidence-based practice by its inclusion in the What Works Teaching Elementary Students to Be Effective Writers Guide (Graham et al., 2012, 2016).

Pulling It All Together

As students move up through the grades, the amount of time needed for transcription instruction decreases. For example, for typically developing students in primary grades, transcription and working memory skills are associated with writing quality (Kim et al., 2017). Yet by third grade, transcription skills no longer contributed significantly to writing quality (Viera et al., 2023). This suggests that once transcription becomes fluent, it no longer plays the same significant role in writing quality. It becomes more effortless, as it is for us as adults, permitting students to focus more fully on constructing structure and meaning as they write. This kind of automaticity allows teachers to focus more fully on supporting higher-order executive skills such as planning or the self-monitoring needed for revision. However, it is important to note that these numbers are averages. For students who do not yet have fluent transcription, even in upper-elementary grades and beyond, their limited transcription skills would continue to impede higher-order areas needed for writing. So these students will continue to need support for transcription and working memory scaffolds so that limited transcription skills won't limit the rest of their writing processes. The sample Scope and Sequence in Appendix A reminds us of how these early skills can be faded after K–2, except for those with special needs who require additional ongoing support with them.

A final note to reiterate the importance of teaching in a way that models and offers students practice in orchestrating all the levels of language and executive skills needed when writing. As you think about how you plan your lessons, remember that these transcription skills can be directly taught and developed but can also be scaffolded and then reinforced as you support students using them in actual composing. Recall how you can model applying transcription skills when you compose in front of students, reminding yourself aloud of how to form a tricky letter, or how to spell a word, by sounding it out to listen for the phonemes, matching those to graphemes, and thinking about morphemes as well. Pulling it all together, think about instruction in layers rather than just as sequences. Each lesson will address multiple layers of instruction from supporting executive skills such as planning, revising, or goal setting, as well as word- and sentence-level language development and transcription elements, which, when unaddressed, may limit working memory capacity to do all of the important higher-order writing skills. All levels can be introduced, taught, and practiced together in close proximity within the same lessons to develop active, engaged, self-regulated writers (Berninger et al., 2017).

That's a Wrap!

Putting in the time daily to develop transcription skills yields larger benefits. It accelerates early literacy skills and frees up lower-order executive skills, including working memory. Yet, be wary not to overdo this either. It is key to dedicate the smallest amount of time needed so that your other instructional minutes can be used for the higher-order work. Research on early literacy skills suggests these skills should be taught for 30 minutes daily in early childhood, then down to 10 minutes daily by grade 1 (Siegal, 2023). The drawback to spending too much time on these skills is that doing so causes a missed opportunity since each extra minute not spent on higher-order work is lost to that work.

CHAPTER 7

Inhibition and Self-Monitoring

Goal-Driven Revision

Magic is . . . making things out of nothing.
—Frances Hodgson Burnett

Revision is where the greatest magic happens. Once students have generated ideas and drafted them, they will self-monitor what they wrote in order to revise it—and make it even better. They carefully look it over, evaluate it against a criterion, decide how to improve it, and make changes if necessary. Revision and self-monitoring draw on multiple executive skills, particularly inhibition. Specifically, inhibition contributes to the attentional control needed to revise (Altermier et al., 2008; Kim et al., 2013; Reid et al., 2023). It allows us to tune out distractions, selectively decide where to place our focus, and then sustain it (Diamond, 2013). When students learn to use scaffolds that help them to inhibit, self-monitor, and revise, writing can become so much more than words on a page. Writing, as its own form of magic, allows our students to create something out of nothing. When their writing is well revised, students can share their voice and messages with the world in beautiful and impactful ways. Even more, rather than being swayed by peers, social media, and outside forces, they learn to lead, shape, and put forward their own narratives.

Given its importance to this kind of high-quality revision, we turn our focus to the executive skill of inhibition. This is not to say that other executive skills do not also play a role in revision, or that inhibition is not also important to other areas of the writing process. (As I've noted all through this book, executive skills work in concert in most things that we do.) Inhibition plays a role throughout the writing process (Altemeier et al., 2008; Berninger et al., 2017; Cordeiro et al., 2020; Kent et al., 2014; Kim et al., 2022; Rocha et al., 2022; Ruffini et al., 2024; Soto et al., 2021). In particular, inhibition supports pausing so that one is able to reach a goal in

> *Inhibition* is the ability to pause, hold back, and control an automatic impulse, which includes resisting distractions.

better ways (Chatham et al., 2012)—in this case, improving one's writing. Therefore, the executive skill of inhibition is explored and explained through how it works during self-monitoring and revision.

Self-monitoring is essential to revision. In order to self-monitor, we must first slow down and inhibit the impulse to switch focus or end too soon. Drafting alone can drain energy, leaving writers out of steam and struggling to summon up the capacity to continue and to revise. This can make the needed inhibition even more challenging to summon up. Studies show that reading a text with the objective to revise it is more effortful than merely reading alone (Roussey & Piolat, 2008). While working on this book, I inhibited distracting thoughts by first noticing them, but I will admit this was effortful. I then directed my mind back to writing. Doing so is necessary to go the final mile when revising.

Also, keep in mind that the ability to revise effectively is developmental. When asked to revise peer writing, students in grade 2 found and revised barely a third of the needed changes, whereas students in grades 4–5 could find and repair three-quarters of these (Crawford et al., 2008). This could be connected to the fact that revision draws heavily on inhibition, which is more challenging at younger ages (Altemeier et al., 2008; Davidson et al., 2006).

You have all seen the kinds of students who struggle to inhibit their impulses. They blurt out responses before filtering whether they are appropriate. They may rush to complete a writing task, then turn it in without checking it over. They turn in work that does not reflect their true ability and they miss the rich opportunity that writing offers for furthering and deepening their learning. Fortunately, like all the other executive skills, inhibition is teachable (Kajka & Kulik, 2021; Khng, 2024).

In addition to the cognitive side of inhibition, there is an emotional dimension. This comes into play more so than with the other core executive skills discussed so far. After students have written something, they often feel proud or vulnerable. They may take feedback personally. Students must inhibit these internal feelings in order to hear the feedback and use it to revise effectively. To do this, they need to *decenter*, or step back and distance themselves, enough to identify, acknowledge, and make the needed revisions (Cameron, 1997). This decentering relies on the ability to inhibit emotional reactivity (Bernstein et al., 2019).

Students can more easily identify and revise weaknesses in their peers' writing than their own, which is likely related to the challenge of decentering. This underscores that the challenge may be distancing themselves enough from their writing to see it as clearly as they can see the writing of peers (Cameron et al., 1997). This decentering, or stepping back, is a teachable hot executive skill (Bennett et al., 2021). Given that students can see errors in others' writing, there is hope that they can find and fix their own, too, if they can decenter and reflect on their own writing as if it were someone else's.

On the other hand, writers may also be too hard on themselves (Crawford et al., 2008). Studies show that adding to writing during revisions raises the overall quality of students' writing. Yet, students do not realize this. Rather than adding, they more often remove the most effective elements and bring down the quality (Worden, 2009). This suggests they undervalue their own writing. Perhaps when they evaluate a section as weak, they remove it because they cannot inhibit the feelings of frustration or disappointment.

While planning is more of a cold, more cognitive executive skill, the inhibition that underlies revision is more of a mix of cold and hot processes because of its emotional component. Thus, it needs to be coached more extensively. In my experience, when taught, students learn to plan more easily and quickly than to revise. We find students pick up the nuts and bolts of planning within a few weeks, then the majority of the school year focuses more so on revision, perhaps suggesting that inhibition is a more complex executive skill to master than planning, at least within writing processes. Despite these challenges, teaching and scaffolding revision raises writing quality, especially when support for executive skills that include inhibition is foregrounded (Chung et al., 2021; De La Paz et al., 1998, 2013; García-Sánchez et al., 2006; Lopez et al., 2021).

This chapter continues our tour. You will watch a teacher present a clear system for self-assessing one's writing with a focus on guiding students' revisions. The subsequent sample lesson and debrief unveil how each element of the lesson relates to and supports inhibition in writing processes, then offer tips you can use tomorrow.

Back Inside Our School: What Revision Looks Like When Students Are Doing It Well

Returning to our school, it is now the end of the week. A few months have passed since our last visit. Fall's colorful maple leaves are piling up on the front stoop as you walk up the steps and enter. Students began the week by reading a new text excerpt and watching their teacher model writing. However, now that students have been through a few weeks of instruction, they know how to get started. Today students will look at exemplars on topics from previous weeks. They will put these side by side with a below-standard piece to discuss the contrasts. This guides them as they think about how to revise a piece. They will also have a scoring scale on hand. A scale is a system used to guide one's thinking while scoring, similar to a rubric. It lists the features of effective writing.

This week during collaborative writing time, students focused more on working together to revise a below-standard piece rather than composing a full piece from start to end. They read a text, picked ideas and began organizing them, then ran out of time. The next day, their teacher distributed an exemplar and a below-standard piece that responded to the topic of the week. This is where the focus shifts from learning the writing process, which happens quickly, to hone in on what makes writing effective, and draws far more so on inhibition than generative thinking and planning.

Students spend more and more time contrasting the features they see in the effective writing exemplars with what the below-standard pieces lack than they do learning how to plan. They regularly tackle bringing up below-standard pieces together in whole-class and in small-group discussions. While looking at these writing pieces, they also hold the scales they have learned to use to evaluate writing this year. They look at each element listed on the scale and reflect carefully on whether they see it in the writing, and how well done it is. The scales also give them the language to understand and talk about the features. Discussing these features helps them deepen their understanding of them, setting them up to better produce them independently.

Now students move to revise a piece they had written for homework. Listening in on one student thinking, we might hear:

> *Let's see. I need to look over this paragraph about Malala that I wrote and revise it now. I notice that I misspelled a word. Wait, we talked about holding off on edits until the end. Let me take a breath and pause myself. If I edit first, it might take forever, and I might edit parts I do not even end up using. I need to first focus on the big picture of what I wrote and see if parts should be moved, added, or removed. I might end up changing so much that I would have edited parts I will not even use. Let me pause for a minute and think about how I can revise and improve the clarity of what I want to say first.*
>
> *To do this, I'll look back at the scale and start at the top. This is rough. I'm tired, and want to take a break. Wait, I can do this. I'll do a part, then take a break. I'll evaluate my opening and how I set up to let the reader know what my piece will be about, and hint at where I'm going. Let me look over my big ideas. I listed three ways that Malala inspires others to care about her efforts to educate girls. I'll make a quick TIDE outline in reverse. I will go back in time in a way and write down what the organizer would have looked like before my piece was written. I made an organizer before I began but as I was drafting, I got a lot of new ideas and found more quotes. What I wrote now looks so different from my initial organizer. I'll write TIDE down my paper and make notes about what I included in each section so I can see the big picture of what I wrote. I want to see how my ideas link and work together to support my thesis.*
>
> *What was my goal for this week? Right, I wanted to include better detailed analysis and prove why my quotes support my thesis. Wow, remembering my goal really helps me slow down and do the careful work I need to at this point. I've been doing short writes—just one paragraph each week—for the past month and I definitely got better at analyzing quotes. I can do this. I'll take out the rubric we use to score our final pieces and look it over now to see how I did in each section, especially the analysis sections. I notice two of the body sections are strong, but my last one seems weak. Now that I look it over and rethink it, it is not that convincing. I wrote about how Malala inspires because she blogs. Anyone can blog. There are many blogs that are not inspiring. I need a better quote to really show how inspiring Malala is. I would not give it full credit at this point. I'll need to revise this. Take a breath. I've got this. Let me look back at my text and notes on the video to see if I can think of other ideas. I can also look at one of the peer exemplars we pulled apart and analyzed a few weeks ago to see how that writer analyzed the ideas. I can also see who has finished drafting and discuss my piece with that person. Revising this takes a lot of energy. I feel like I have to keep hitting the breaks and resisting the temptation to rush, but I know my pieces are always better when I push myself to revise carefully.*

Moving downstairs, we see students writing about the life cycle of frogs. One child is thinking:

> *I really like my ideas! I feel like my paragraph is one of the best I've ever written. Now I'll check it over to see that it has all the parts and that each part is good. I'll fill in my scoring sheet to note each part I have. Oh shoot! I didn't get all my points or even meet my goal for more strong vocabulary words! I feel so mad when that happens. Wait, hold on. Take a breath. I know I can still make changes and make it better. I'll look for blue words, my strong word choices, and where I used my spelling words from the week. I highlighted the blue words when I finished. I can add a few more now.*
>
> *My other goal over the past few weeks has been to have a stronger ending. This time, I did not just repeat my topic sentence, but I wrapped up my ideas in a surprising way. How are my spelling and handwriting? Hmmm, I'll circle two words I am not sure of and underline the letters that I think look the best. My edit goals were to have more words spelled correctly and more letters formed neatly.* Cycle *is hard to spell. I hear an* S, *but I know I should use a* C. *Let me look back at my text about the "i" sound. It is written with a* Y. *I'll fix that. I'll also check it over to see how well the ideas link and connect together. I use the word* they *a lot to talk about the frogs. I think I'll use a science vocabulary word,* amphibian, *instead of using* they *so much. Yes, now it is more fun to read with the varied synonyms. Okay, I'm ready to edit. I'll tap in now. I'll cover my ears, touch each word, and whisper-read each aloud so I can look for errors and listen to see if it sounds right. Hmm, "The frog starts as tadpole" does not sound right. I'll add the word* a. *This is so much better now, and I only spent a few minutes revising. A little revision and editing can go a long way!*

See It in Action: Sample Lesson

In this lesson, students move from the W (Writing a draft) phase to the ER (Edit and Revise) phase in POWER.

They will edit and revise in structured ways that promote self-monitoring and the needed underlying inhibition. The key to this structure is self-scoring. Students learn how to self-score to guide the improvements they will make. In this way, these are all connected. Self-scoring prompts and guides the ER phases in POWER.

Recalling Teach, Model, Score, self-monitoring and revision happen primarily as students "Score" at the end of each cycle. The instructional focus shifts now from modeling *how* to write to helping students understand *what* to write—by scoring for the features of effective writing so that they can revise their pieces to better reflect these features and set future goals. This helps students inhibit because they develop an internalized sense of what writing should look like. This can help them pause, compare what they know about writing to what they drafted, and self-evaluate more easily.

SAMPLE LESSON: Goal-Driven Revision

Goal: Model showing students how to do the ER (Edit and Revise) phase in POWER in a goal-driven way.

Objectives:

1. Learn how to use an analytic scoring system to self-evaluate one's writing, guide editing and revision, and set goals.
2. Learn how to self-monitor while composing a piece and afterward.
3. Practice setting goals and evaluating one's progress toward them.
4. Discover how to use exemplars to guide and support them as they revise.
5. Set goals for both process and results.

Estimated Time: 30–45 minutes

Materials: Chart paper, printed copy of large scale (or projected via a smartboard), copies of scales and scoring guidelines for each student, copies of exemplars and below-level writing samples (not yet reaching expected standards), markers, pencils, student current writing drafts, copies of a text that students will read, highlighters

Lesson Steps:

1. Introduce that this lesson will focus on how to score and self-evaluate writing, as well as set goals.
2. Review POWER. State that we will focus on the E and R in POWER now. Students can cross off the E and R in POWER at the end of the lesson (5 minutes).
3. Share that every week we write and, at the end, we always do some level of editing and revision, even if just reading it over to ensure it makes sense and for small edits before turning it in. Most weeks students will use self-scoring to guide them with the ER phase.
4. Project an exemplar written by a peer who gave permission to have the class review it. Distribute copies to all students. Have them color-code these for the parts of TIDE, and box or color-code strong words in a different color.
5. Next, pass out copies of the scoring scale (see Appendix S for grade 2 and Appendix U for grade 6).
6. First, review this strong exemplar to show students what each section should look like. Evaluate and score each section, working down each item on the scale and discussing how well each is done in the essay. At the end, note what was done well and set a goal for this writer.
7. Do the same for the below-level sample, then choose areas to revise together as a class, considering each element of TIDE, vocabulary, or other areas such as links or sentence quality. Emphasize that writers should revise before they edit and focus on the quality of their ideas more so than only on conventions such as spelling. Set a goal for this writer, together as a class.
   a. *Note:* You may not score the entire piece, if lengthy. You might only score some sections, or break it up over several days.

8. Students then use the same scale to self-score their own writing, then trade with a peer to peer-score. (The sample lesson in the next chapter dives into this more deeply.)
9. After self-scoring, set both process and product goals. Set a process goal to spend more time planning or organizing and a product goal to give more attention to writing, for example, a strong ending next time.

Wrap-Up: Summarize the lesson focusing on self-monitoring and goal setting. Have students share their goals with peers.

Lesson Analysis: How Each Component Supports the Self-Monitoring and Inhibition Needed to Self-Evaluate and Revise

A Scoring Structure Supports Executive Skills, Particularly Inhibition

To introduce how to score, this teacher presented a 20-point *analytic scale* then modeled how to use it by evaluating an exemplar response and a below-level sample with it. She then had her students use what they found to guide them as they revise and edit. This way students could see the criteria in actual writing and learn a system for scoring their own writing, which will scaffold their inhibition and revision.

A scale or rubric does more than offer a structured method for self-evaluation. It supports inhibition by putting a speed bump in place. Students will use it to self-score every time they write now. This prevents them from automatically rushing to turn in work after only drafting. When they pause and self-score, this provides a built-in mechanism to ensure they inhibit long enough to identify what to revise. Studies have shown that time is the great antidote to curbing impulsivity and allowing inhibition to kick in (Diamond, 2013). By building in self-scoring as a natural part of following the writing process, we buy the time needed to reflect and revise well.

Analytic scales make separate judgments on specific criteria such as the presence and quality of a topic sentence, evidence, or punctuation. Think of checklists with 10–20 or more points. *Holistic rubrics* respond to the work as a whole more globally and often use scales of 4–6 points (Sadler, 2009). Many assessments use a mix of these.

Pair Scales with Exemplars

In addition to introducing scoring scales, showing multiple exemplars further deepens students' understanding of the criteria for their writing. See Appendices G and H for sample exemplars. Always pair exemplars with scales so that the scoring criteria are anchored in reaching the level of writing shown in the exemplar rather than features listed on a scale. Exemplars provide more nuanced and flexible understandings of the features needed in effective writing. The scale and exemplars help students call up, hold in mind, internalize, and apply these criteria when reviewing their own writing. The better students understand the features of effective writing, the better they can sustain attention and stamina during revision, inhibiting their impulse to rush through the process. Studies have found that structuring how students self-evaluate in these ways helps them produce higher-quality writing. This is particularly the case when the steps include a structured call to action that directs them to inhibit (pause), review, and take the kind of clear actions that scoring helps them understand are needed (Chung et al., 2021; De La Paz et al., 1998), as in the mnemonic RED—Read, Evaluate, Do (Fidalgo et al., 2007).

Teacher Talk Example

Today we will talk about how we can make our writing even better. When we first turn our ideas into sentences and link them together, we create a draft. However, we are not done. We need to pause and inhibit, or hold back the feeling of wanting to be done. "Inhibit" means to be able to stop oneself from an automatic response, such as turning in work before looking it over in this case. We can look back at our last piece of writing and think about the goals we set to improve as a writer and if we met them. It is important to revise the draft before sharing it with others.

To do this, we will review our goals, look at the scoring scale, and pretend we are giving someone feedback, even though that person is yourself. I would walk down each element on the scale (or each part in TIDE-L, in younger grades) and evaluate if I have all the parts and think they are well written, paying particular attention to my goal areas. For example, maybe I wanted to write a better ending, make better word choices, and spell a higher percentage of words correctly this time. I'll also have an older exemplar on hand to help me decide whether to give points. I can pause, put on the brakes, and carefully think about whether my writing is at the same level as the exemplar when I'm unsure about giving myself a point or not. I will give myself credit (or color in a section on my rocket graph) and note where my writing can be improved. I will then revise the parts that need this. I'll save the editing for the end.

This kind of self-check is important because it makes me stop and think, and it can improve the quality of my writing a lot, and in just a little time. It does mean I have to stop and pause to do this step, but when I do, my writing is so much better.

Clear Scales and Exemplars Support Goal-Setting

Even more, when paired with exemplars, analytic scales that break out all the elements of effective writing show what each element can look like. This helps students set more specific goals. Having specific goals leads to better-quality gains than broad ("make it better") goals do (Graham et al., 2021; Patel & Laud, 2009). In general, holding goals in mind and inhibition involve overlapping areas of the brain (Berkman et al., 2012). This suggests that these are interconnected. Maintaining goals may help one inhibit, and the more specific the better.

Providing a clear scoring system helps students set goals at a granular level. When they see the list of what they need to do, they can look back specifically for these criteria in their own writing. In order to self-monitor what to improve, they need this clear understanding of what they are aiming for and a way to measure their performance against these criteria. Teachers sometimes offer students revision and editing checklists or invite students to make their own. This adds a layer of complexity that may not be needed. Too many overlapping tools can confuse and overwhelm students. Instead, if they have one scale used for multiple purposes such as to self-score, peer-score, receive feedback from adults, and guide their revision and editing, this simplifies revision. This one scale serves multiple purposes and cuts the need for learning extra tools. Students would have already learned the scale when the teacher models using it in front of the class to score peer writing, and when they used it to peer- and self-score. Now they will also use it to guide their edits and revisions. Students can customize their own scales and include points for personalized goals such as improving grammar or writing specific types of endings ("call to action" or "circle back to revisit the opening idea").

Having a goal may make inhibiting one's behavior easier. In order to be goal directed, students also need a clear vision of the goals they are working to meet. The scales and exemplars provide this direction, along with mnemonics such as TIDE, which help them understand the structure of these exemplars more deeply and reminds them to check the quality of each part of TIDE carefully. The student in this lesson could tell his D—"detailed analysis"—of how Malala used blogging to inspire was weak. Yet, he needed to see exemplars with stronger analysis to get ideas for how to strengthen his own writing. He needed to pause and inhibit to be able to come to realize this through self-scoring.

To improve this aspect (detailed analysis) of his writing, he used two strategies. First, he revisited exemplars. This helped him develop a vision of what better work could look like and helped him realize he should also revisit the earlier steps in POWER and go back to P so he could pick better ideas, too. Understanding the features of effective writing through exemplars and the phases in the writing process (in this case picking ideas) equipped him to better reach his goals. Students need goals and strategies for how to reach them. In this case, the strategies included exemplars and a deep understanding of the writing process. These kinds of strategies help students inhibit the tendency to rush and help them sustain effort. They enable students to galvanize the needed executive skills that allow them to control how they work to meet a goal (Doebel, 2020).

In this way, using scales and exemplars to help one self-score is not about judgment. It is a force that can support and ease the cognitive effort, particularly the inhibition, needed to revise. Using scoring as a way to guide revision leads to stronger outcomes (Chung et al., 2021) because it supports inhibition. This is why the full Teach, Model, Score system is essential to support the executive skills that come into play when writing.

Do All the Steps in POWER

Knowing the phases of the writing process supports inhibition indirectly as well. Students know they should follow POWER when they write. This kind of process mnemonic helps them inhibit the tendency to turn their attention elsewhere. They know to slow down after they write a draft and self-score so that they can do the ER (Edit and Revise) phases. This student rushed and did not put in the time to find the best quotes. When he self-scored and used the scale to guide him in self-evaluating and revision, he realized his analysis was weak. Students used P (Plan) when they found the gist, pulled apart the prompt, and picked ideas. They used an organizer such as TIDE to do the O (Organize their ideas). When they moved to W (Write a draft), they used sentence stems and various scaffolds.

Now at ER, they have scales and exemplars that serve as similar scaffolds that support inhibition because they equip students with what they need to recognize in order to know what needs to be edited and revised. A student once completed his draft, looked at POWER at the top of his page, and, as if a lightbulb went off in his mind, he asked aloud, "Should we do all the steps in POWER?" POWER scaffolded inhibition for this student.

Revision and Editing Draw on Inhibition Differently

Remember that the revision and editing processes differ. When editing and revising for different areas such as spelling (editing) or grammar (more meaning, or revision, focused), students recruit different kinds of language and executive skills, including those that rely on inhibition (Larigauderie et al., 2020). Students tend to focus on editing, making smaller surface changes, rather than looking at how to revise the core substance (Crawford et al., 2008). Yet meaning-based changes have more impact on raising quality (Cameron et al., 1997). It may be easier cognitively to notice needed edits than to digest and reflect on the piece as a whole. Reflecting on a piece in an integrative way that considers the whole rather than small, isolated sections is more demanding. Doing so places more intensive demands on attentional capacity and inhibition (Larigauderie et al., 2020; Piolat et al., 2005). However, smaller edits may also distract students when they revise. This can happen to the extent that writers cannot inhibit or ignore noticing these little errors. If that is the case, then encourage students to quickly address them, then return to thinking about the bigger picture and cohesion.

> *Revision* focuses on enhancing meaning. *Editing* addresses smaller fix-ups of errors.

Yet, at the same time, be careful that students do not make word-choice changes designed to improve spelling when doing so can bring down voice and richness in their writing. They might change "It was an icy day" to "It was a cold day" to avoid misspelling *icy*, losing the verbal power of such a descriptive word (Moats, 2005–2006). It is recommended that students only change their spellings if they are certain about their word choice. When revising, students in the upper-elementary grades often end up misspelling words that were initially correct (Crawford et al., 2008).

Self-Talk Can Support Inhibition

Once students begin to revise their own and their peers' work, this teacher reminds them to use positive self-talk. Inhibition requires effort. Self-talk can help students summon up the effort needed to self-score and remain motivated. Students may also experience discomfort or social tension when giving and receiving feedback on their writing (Wu & Schunn, 2021), potentially because they see their writing as an extension of themselves and feel personally criticized. This makes self-talk particularly important at this phase. Rather than succumbing to feeling overwhelmed by triggering tasks, students can learn to identify these, use their self-talk to inhibit their reactions, and more effectively manage the more hot executive skills that come into play during revision. You saw a child do this when he realized he did not meet his vocabulary goal. Yet, rather than succumb to his frustration, he talked himself out of it and got back on track.

Take It to the Classroom: Tips You Can Use Tomorrow

Identify an Analytic Scoring System

Decide on a system to use to give structured, clear feedback to students. Think of rubrics, scales, or any writing assessments you have used. Choose one that is more analytic and broken out so it can lead to goal setting in easy ways. Many structured scoring systems can work. If your school uses a rubric, you can use it but may want to adapt it to be more specific. Consider using a more specific 20-point analytic scale instead of a more holistic four-point scale as specific scales are more useful in guiding instruction (Bang, 2013; Graham et al., 2011). For examples, see Appendices S–W. An analytic scale broken down like this helps students set clear, specific goals. They also help teachers identify students' needs and monitor student progress and help students track their own growth, which sets self-regulation in motion. If your school uses a 4-point rubric, you can adapt it or put it side by side with a more broken-out, detailed scale so that students can see and use both analytic and holistic criteria. See Appendix Y for an example.

In younger grades, students can draw a rocket (Harris et al., 2008) or write the word TIDE and cross off each letter if they included each part (see Figure 7.1). Next to a rocket, they can draw a star and list the strong vocabulary or spelling words they used.

Actively Teach Students How to Score

For this lesson, you will pass out a scale, an exemplar, and a below-standard piece. Model how to score these in front of your class, having students turn and talk, score partly on their own, then share and discuss why they would or would not give full credit for each aspect. Be ready to do this multiple times before students build capacity to do this independently. Then work together as a class revising the piece. For an example, see Figure 7.2. At first, to avoid cognitive overload, avoid revising the full piece completely. They can choose one or two areas to revise. Moving forward, each week as you work through POWER, you can model revision.

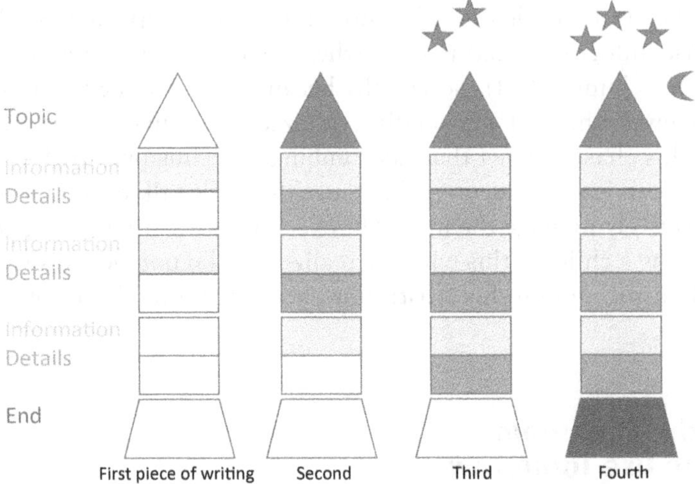

FIGURE 7.1. Rocket visual for TIDE. Rocket concept based on Harris et al. (2008).

Continue Modeling Goal Setting

When self-scoring and revising their current piece, students can set goals for future writing. See Figure 7.3 for samples from students in grades 2 and 6 who wrote their firsts pieces, later wrote again, and then celebrated their writing growth. Goals also support inhibition in how they inspire as well. By setting a goal, students become

Below-Standard Writing Sample + Revisions Below	Scores Before & After Revisions
Identify how Malala uses persuasion to convince others to care about the rights of girls and how people might respond to her efforts. Be sure to use information from both the video and the text. Malala uses persuasion to convince others to care about girls' education rights by sharing her personal story and using strong arguments.* In the video, she talks about her experience being attacked for going to school, which shows how important education is to her and why it should be a right for everyone. In the text, Malala explains that girls can't go to school, and she asks leaders to take action to change this. People might respond to her efforts by supporting her cause, like donating to her foundation. Insert revisions into above: *At merely 15 years old, Malala Yousafzai was shot by the Taliban for championing girls' education. She continues to persuade others to care about her cause through her nonviolent efforts that inspire others. By asking for help, she takes a real-world action that might spark others to do the same. After you take a step to help, you often care even more.	T 1 / 2 I 3 / 6 D 3 / 6 E 0 / 2 Link 0 / 1 Lang - vocab .5 / 1 Lang - sent .5 / 1 Conv 1 / 1 T 2 / 2 I 3 / 6 D 4 / 6 E 0 / 2 Link 0 / 1 Lang - vocab 1 / 1 Lang - sent .5 / 1 Conv 1 / 1 = 2.5 points improvement

FIGURE 7.2. Revision example from upper grades.

motivated to put in the effort that inhibition demands as they work to meet it. Students need to have deep familiarity with the scoring scales to develop this inhibition. They should score using these scales so often that the terms and ways these show up in exemplars become ingrained in their minds. Revising the key text-type terms (Appendix F) often also helps them develop the language needed to set goals and the language they can use to help themselves pause, inhibit, and direct themselves as they write.

Also, in this lesson, students scored both an exemplar and below-level pieces so they would see the features of effective writing as well as writing below the required level. The contrast helps students see the differences and understand the effective features better so that they can set clearer goals. As students give feedback on the below-level sample and work together as a group to revise it, they internalize the qualities that would make it stronger. They practice using inhibition, with social support from peers, as they pause as a class to work together to revise it. More on the power of peer feedback and how to structure this is coming up soon in Chapter 8.

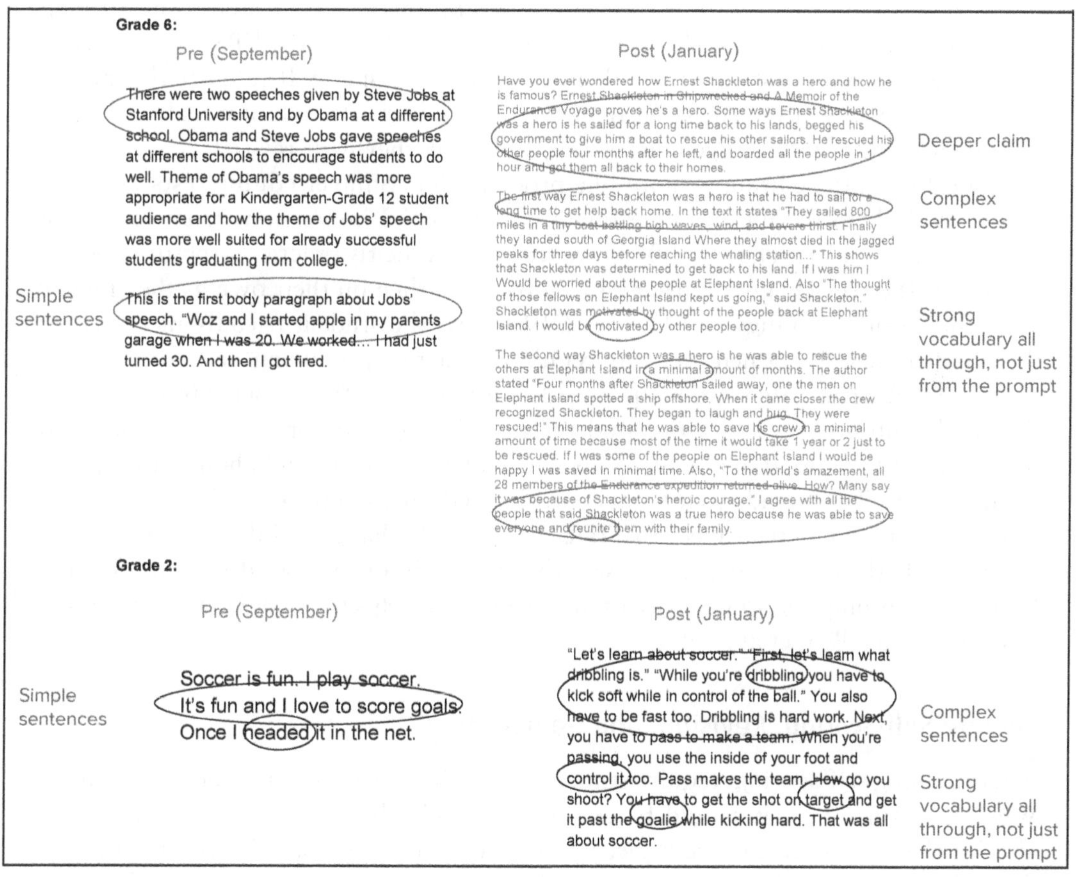

FIGURE 7.3. Pre and post gains annotated for grades 2 and 6. Post example for grade 6 is an excerpt; the student's final essay increased to six paragraphs!

Support Students in Internalizing Language

Identifying, naming, and revising each of the features in the scoring rubric gives students the language to do this independently. This language becomes part of the voice they hear in their heads when they compose and revise their own writing. As discussed earlier, developing positive self-talk along with this kind of language around the features of effective writing helps them inhibit feeling frustrated or overwhelmed and better direct their attention and behavior because they know what to do.

Teach Different Revise and Edit Strategies

As mentioned above, revision and editing draw on different cognitive processes and even activate different areas of the brain (Larigauderie et al., 2020). Revision means making the whole of the piece better, while editing is fixing the smaller clean-up issues such as spelling, punctuation, or grammar. For a catchy way to help your students understand the difference, you can use ARMS and CUPS. Remember to emphasize that writers should revise before editing. Revision will enhance the quality of the piece more so than edits (Worden, 2009). Students often do not realize there is a difference. They will change one spelling and think they have revised.

> *ARMS:* Add, Remove, Move, Substitute
> *CUPS:* Capitalize, Usage, Punctuation, Spelling

Put differently, editing is more like proofreading. Simpler editing rests on using executive skills to recruit and coordinate visual–spatial impressions from long-term memory (Larigauderie et al., 2020). Have students explicitly practice structured proofreading as they review gists during daily warm-ups, then on their own as they review what they write. Jennings and Haynes (2018) describe student-friendly methods for this kind of activity. When students regularly practice producing and editing their daily gist statements, they gradually need less attentional effort when editing because they build automaticity. As a tip, students can also "tap in" or cover their ears and read their writing aloud in a whisper (as with Tubaloos or pretend phones) to support the needed inhibition and attentional control for editing. On the other hand, to revise, students could remap their piece to TIDE if they made changes while drafting and use this to guide their revisions, as you saw the student in our school do in this chapter. Even merely prompting students to attend to meaning helps them make more meaning-based revisions (Beal et al., 1990).

Require Self-Scoring, Revision, and Goal Setting

After teaching self-scoring, require students to do this whenever they complete a draft. When they turn it in, it should be color-coded and self- and peer-scored. It should also list their goals for their next piece. In upper grades, they can also run their pieces through artificial intelligence systems such as Grammarly and add a note about the changes they made.

The goals they set can help you plan for the following week. If students mastered writing a topic sentence but are still not using irregular past tense verbs correctly, then you can move on to how to choose evidence but include past tense again in gist warm-ups. Students should set goals in order by working down the elements of TIDE (and considering features of language, or TIDE-L). You then match your lesson focus to their goals.

In the future, students should keep their goals in mind. Before drafting, students can write their goal in all caps right at the top of their papers, then monitor whether they are meeting their goals as they draft, edit, and revise. With the scales at their side and their goals clearly written, they can celebrate meeting them and set new ones. This helps them prepare for a new cycle of the writing process. In this way, revision focuses more on pursuing goals than getting the final piece to be perfect.

Revision of Short or Quick Writes

As mentioned earlier, students will write weekly, but in grade 3 and above, the majority of these will be short or *quick writes*. A quick write is usually a paragraph. It often works as a body section of a fuller essay. Instead of writing about how Malala inspires, the prompt would use the word *one*. It might ask, "Describe one way in which Malala inspires." See Appendix W for examples and for how to structure and score quick writes. You might only give four points for a quick write: stated topic, gave evidence, analyzed it or gave extra details, and included an ending. As students master these four, you can add points for areas of language. Given how challenging inhibition can be, students may be more likely to summon this up when revising shorter pieces.

Product and Process Goals

As students score and set goals, their targets will increase each week. They will set a goal to improve their topic introduction or sentence variety, as discussed. As students progress, then each week teachers will show higher and higher exemplars to stretch their writers and help them craft product goals. Within a few months, sometimes just weeks, the initial "exemplars" become "belows" that students revise as well. The scales focus on product goals—what should be included in the final piece such as a stronger opening or ending.

Both process and product goals are important. However, there is a difference. Students can set process goals that can address how they will carry out the phases in the writing process (e.g., by using POWER as a tool). They might set a goal that they will make a greater number of meaning-focused revisions. They can also set these for how they will better self-regulate as they work. For example, they can set a goal to use more self-talk as they go to stay encouraged or to take breaks every 20 minutes to make it easier to inhibit during this cognitively demanding work.

Self-Monitor for Subskills, but Stay Focused on Rich Language, Too

In addition to setting process and product goals, students can also set goals for subskills. These can include improving spelling or remembering to capitalize all sentences. You can add bonus points to the scale to give additional credit if students spell a higher percentage of words correctly than their goal, though spelling goals should always be tied to using rich language choices, too, so students do not bring down rich language to ensure spelling is accurate. Such data-based feedback helps accelerate growth in writers (Choi et al., 2024), and students can learn to track this themselves.

Note to Early Childhood Teachers

As students begin composing on paper via drawing, dictation, and writing, be sure to emphasize higher-order, language-based feedback. When managing the extra layer of teaching foundational skills in addition to composing at the paragraphs level in the early grades, teachers may tend to overemphasize code-based rather than language-focused feedback . One study found that teachers of the students who made the highest gains in both code and language areas delivered nearly four times more language-based than code-focused feedback (Farrow et al., 2024). As an example, a teacher might discuss how a chrysalis falls away as a butterfly emerges, and encourage adding detailed language about this fact rather than only focus on the lower level of spelling this word.

Time Saver! Editing and Revising Go Together

Let's return to the big picture of self-monitoring, scoring, and revision. Remember that simplicity is key. Rather than viewing editing and revision (ER in POWER) as separate from scoring, teach students that they go together. The ER in POWER happens alongside scoring. When students complete their drafts, they can turn to the final scoring scale to guide them as they edit and revise. This saves you time since students now have a regular routine that includes self- and peer-scoring. When their work makes it to you, much of the evaluation and revision is already done for you.

Scoring can be reenvisioned as part of revision and done for the purpose of setting goals. You may not be able to give individual feedback to all students as often as you would like. You may not even need to do this as often as you do. When your regular instruction includes scoring in front of the class, all students see the feedback and many have shared needs that you can emphasize. They also practice using inhibition collectively as a class, which gives them supported practice at using this executive skill.

You may worry that if you do not score everything your students write regularly, they will not receive enough feedback. Over time, students become increasingly capable at self-scoring accurately. Peer feedback correlates well with adult feedback (Sanchez et al., 2017) and is an important way to save time (Graham et al., 2011). When I first introduced scoring, I modeled it once and thought my students would be able to then score their own writing. It took more time than I expected. At first, they gave themselves and their peers all the points because they did not understand the features. I had not realized how much instruction and practice they would need to develop this deeper understanding and the inhibition needed to avoid rushing through it. In my experience working with schools, we find that it requires about 10 lessons in which a teacher leads a class in collaborative scoring before students become better able to do this independently. If students lack an understanding of expected performance, even if they pause, it is harder for them to inhibit when they do not know the features of effective writing. Repeated scoring together as a class builds this understanding.

Artificial Intelligence and Revision

Before wrapping up, here is a word on artificial intelligence (AI), inhibition, self-monitoring, and scoring. A growing number of AI programs can guide and mentor students who are learning to compose. Advances in AI offer support to writers in terms of scaffolding the planning and organizing phases in writing, but revision seems to be the place that offers the most promise at the moment. After students draft, they can be required to run it through tools such as Grammarly or others. They can make changes and document these before turning in their final work. These systems provide automated feedback that can save teachers time by recommending the lower-level kinds of corrections that technology can easily catch. Many of these systems have connected instructional elements that directly teach and offer practice in the areas identified as needing work.

Students can also create drafts in new language-generating programs such as Claude or ChatGPT. However, these drafts are often ridden with areas that need revision. Teaching students how to revise will enable them to improve what they generate through these programs as well. Teachers can also use these programs to create exemplars that show advanced thinking and that can aid students in revising their own writing, as well as for further revision practice to make them even stronger. Students can also learn prompt generation, engineering, and revision strategies. They can learn how to craft a prompt to ask AI systems questions, then how to revise their prompts until it creates what they are looking for. However, there is still an important place for knowing and being able to use the full writing process. Students must know what they are looking for and how to create it when AI cannot, or does not.

Also, a note on students with more severe executive skills challenges. If students persist in their struggle with handwriting, spelling or syntax at older ages, it can become important to think about work-arounds and focus on what will achieve a bigger impact. Teaching students to use tools such as Grammarly may help them improve their piece they are working on as well as help them learn grammar rules at the same time. However, do not throw in the towel too soon. Continue to offer time-efficient, quick reminders and practice of tips such as "Place your letters on the lines and close up circular letters," as students' handwriting is still malleable up through middle school (Lê et al., 2021). Even at this age, students can set goals and use strategies to improve their handwriting and evaluate it.

That's a Wrap!

You have now learned the three major parts in the Teach, Model, Score system. This chapter looked at the ER in POWER and how you can teach your students to "Score" as a way to help them inhibit and then self-direct the revision and editing phase of the writing process.

However, having students routinely work through the full writing process is what enables them to learn new skills, practice them, evaluate their progress, then try again with new goals each week. The full routine is what empowers students to coordinate how their executive skills can work together and results in their ability to engage their self-regulation.

Patience and perseverance are important. If you stick with it, you will watch your students transform. Over the first few weeks of the year, teachers might model the full writing process one or two times fully, walking through each phase in POWER slowly and demonstrating what to do at each step. Over time, teachers can fade how much they model as students become more independent. This will happen at different rates according to age and capability. The goal is to facilitate moving students to independence as quickly as we can. Having a system with these types of tools is important, but it is only the groundwork. Introducing the system is only the beginning. The real impact comes when you stick with it and teach it deeply. The next and final chapter, on social understandings, delves into how to take that depth to the next level.

CHAPTER 8

Social Understanding

Audience Awareness and Peer Connections

We write down words for the benefit of us,
but we revise for the benefit of others.
—Obert Skye

Coming full circle, Obert Skye reminds us of the deepest purposes of writing. We write because we have something we want to learn, to figure out, or, ultimately, to say. To communicate their messages, students must learn the features of effective writing and the processes writers use. So far, we have looked at the role of executive skills in how students learn what their more expert peers know. When we break down and teach these skills, it is as if all students get to choose from the same menu when they go to write. They can learn much of what experts know. Otherwise, only the few who have figured out how to write would know what to do. Part of this knowledge includes thinking about who their reader is and how different readers will make sense of what they write, and this is learnable.

This awareness of one's reader's perspective is also called *audience awareness*, a term that may be more familiar to you. This is the capacity to think about how our writing will be understood by our readers. Perspective taking is a higher-order cognitive skill that can be developed and that leads to better writing (Caravalho, 2002; Frank, 1992; Holliway, 2004; Littleton, 1998; Midgette et al., 2008; Wollman-Bonilla, 2001). Teaching the skills that underlie this kind of social understanding increases writing quality and strengthens empathy (Goldstein & Winner, 2012). Empathy is the foundation of positive social skills that prepare students to make the world a better place. Students can use writing to improve the world. Even more, how we teach writing, especially when we develop audience awareness and empathy, can better equip and inspire our students to care about doing this (Tamnes et al., 2018; Weimer et al., 2021).

We now unpack the executive skills that play a role in the higher-order social understandings that make audience awareness possible. These skills support our writers as they work to ensure their messages land as intended and as they take part in the interpersonal aspects of writing. Executive skills surface at this point and can be further developed through understanding and supporting the following factors:

1. Audience awareness
2. Social interactions
3. Building a writers' community

> Also known as *theory of mind* or *perspective taking*, *social understanding* relies on imagination and includes the ability to figure out or infer what others are thinking.

These are connected and build on each other. They all support the social understanding aspect of writing. Writing, in the end, is inherently a social act. Like all the previously described executive skills, social understandings are invisible yet vital to address how we teach writing. Foregrounding attention to developing this skill enables our writers to take their pieces the final mile, enjoy the company along the way, and emerge equipped to use writing for prosocial purposes.

Theory of Mind and Perspective Taking Underlie Audience Awareness

Sometimes, students write to process their feelings, to reach clarity, or to deepen their learning. When students write for an audience, their goal shifts to sharing a message. To do this, they need to consider how their ideas will be perceived and received by their readers. Essentially, they almost need to mind-read. The executive skills that come into play include all of those covered so far, as well as theory of mind, which supports perspective taking and audience awareness.

Theory of mind is a cognitive skill related to the executive skills discussed in earlier chapters (Wade et al., 2018), particularly working memory (Arslan et al., 2017). It has been studied extensively in the context of early childhood but shown to continue playing a role into the upper grades (Devine & Hughes, 2013; Lecce et al., 2017; Miller, 2022; Peskin et al., 2014; Svensson, 2018; Weimer et al., 2021). Theory of mind literally means to have an idea, or a theory, about what is happening in someone else's mind. It rests on the ability to understand that the beliefs, feelings, goals, and motivations of others differ from one's own. For a child, this initial insight involves coming to realize that another person does not think or feel the same way they do. Once they can do this, they can then get into the heads of others to try to understand how they think. I recall the first time my young toddler told me to look away, then tossed a doll down some steps. He was starting to realize that others think differently from him. This kind of social reasoning can be detected at ages as young as 4, and it activates a distinct area of the brain (Meyer et al., 2024). It is not solely based in the language or executive skills discussed in the prior chapters. While there is overlap, it is a separate skill that can be taught, supported, and developed.

This kind of understanding comes more naturally to some than others. Yet these social understanding skills play a role in writing quality for all (Cho et al., 2021; Kim, 2020; Kim & Schatschneider, 2017), and they can be taught (Trautwein et al., 2020). A significant cognitive hurdle to getting inside the minds of others is inhibiting one's own perspective (Peskin et al., 2014). Another challenge students face is mentally managing the kinds of syntactic layers in sentences they must hold in mind, such as "I think he thinks . . ." or "I think she might feel . . ." (Arslan et al., 2017), while making advanced inferences. Doing so involves cold executive skills and also taps into inferring emotions, making this a complex hot skill as well.

Audience Awareness Relies on Perspective Taking

Related to theory of mind, perspective taking is the ability to not just understand that others think differently from oneself, but to be able to figure out what they may be thinking. This understanding of others' perspectives supports writing quality (Kim, 2019) and draws on cognitive flexibility (Altemeier et al., 2008). Students must juggle thoughts, shift, and be flexible enough to see another child's side or to "see this from your point of view." Essentially, along with the closely related theory of mind, perspective taking enables students to write in a way that reflects audience awareness.

Audience awareness requires thinking about who the reader will be and how I need to adapt my writing according to my reader's perspective. Students as young as age 6 can demonstrate this key skill, learn how to imagine and anticipate readers' reactions, and even improve it (Wollman-Bonilla, 2001). Writing for external audiences, including peers in one's class, can develop it (Block & Strachan, 2019; Cohen & Riel, 1989), even if it is just an imagined audience (Midgette et al., 2008). In fact, asking students to write for an imagined audience may even help them develop theory of mind and perspective taking. Doing so causes them to activate the mentalizing areas of the brain that support inferring and interpreting what others are thinking. This kind of mentalizing is also an aspect of theory of mind, and students improve it as they age (Weimer et al., 2011). Along the same lines, students who reread their own writing but are coached to take the perspective of their reader make greater improvements (Holliway, 2009). By reminding students to consider audience awareness, we set them up to activate theory of mind and shift to think in the perspective of their imagined reader.

Social Skills Development

Beyond developing this cognitive social awareness skill, writing also offers concrete opportunities for purposeful social engagement and development. As students take part in classwide, small-group, or quick "turn and talks," they can learn, practice, and apply social skills, such as active listening, paraphrasing, and complimenting ideas they hear. When teachers introduce these kinds of prosocial norms and give students chances to practice them, students' interpersonal skills improve (Andrusyk

& Andrusyk, 2003). Learning to keep one's audience in mind when writing and while giving feedback to peers are related skills that bootstrap each other. By offering such prosocial feedback, students have tangible opportunities to regularly practice and reinforce perspective taking (Shillings et al., 2020). In turn, this has the potential to deepen audience awareness and improve peer relationships.

When going through the phases of the writing process, this peer feedback can happen as students write together or as they read each other's writing and offer constructive feedback. Doing so is shown to raise outcomes (Topping, 2009; Wu et al., 2021). Even more, when guiding students to respond to literature, teachers can highlight the social lessons learned, such as the importance of kindness, noting perspective taking and different emotional states of characters, and further strengthen the needed underlying social skill awareness (Anderson, 2000; Solow, 2018). In fact, greater exposure to stories in early grades correlates to stronger social skills (Tompkins, 2022). See Cartwright (2023) for a more in-depth discussion of this topic to see how these skills develop from early childhood through the upper grades, particularly as they relate to reading. Teaching social skills explicitly and leveraging stories as a way to strengthen them both help prepare students to participate more effectively in a writer's community.

Writer's Community

More than just a cognitive and affective task, writing occurs within a larger class community (Graham, 2018a, 2018b). This community can be a motivational and supporting force that helps propel students' writing forward. Teachers can take active steps to develop this kind of community, starting with developing perspective taking and teaching interpersonal skills. However, a community is also based on wider norms. Think of the different classes you have taught each year, how they all were unique in functioning together as a group, and how you worked to set this up. Think about how differently students act when they write on their own in isolation, perhaps at home, versus when they are working together as a class or writing in small groups. For example, they may show deeper understandings and greater synergistic creativity and stamina in a group (Kuhn, 2015). These differences speak to the impact of writing in a community and how it differs from writing by oneself. So far this book has focused on how to develop the skills individuals use when they write. This chapter hones in on how to make the most of how peers, in almost a group-think force, can support each other more broadly as well, while unveiling the underlying executive skills that make this possible.

A classroom community culture impacts how writers think, persevere, collaborate, and deepen each other's understanding of audience. It drives their goals, norms, values, and even identities as writers (Graham, 2021). According to this Writers in Community model, writers are shaped and constrained by their communities in how much they recruit and how well they use their executive skills. You may have seen actual moments when your students looked around, saw peers still hard at work, and appeared to then summon up the energy and focus to keep going based on what they observed. Essentially, seeing others recruit executive skills may inspire them to do so as well. The community around them influences the amount of effort they will put forth, their ability to maintain attention (Brandt, 2001; Russell, 1997), and how well they meet group goals (Bazerman, 2016).

So far, the preceding chapters have guided you how to establish writing activity norms that can help your students reap these benefits. For example, activities such as collaboratively picking ideas while reading, organizing these, writing together and peer scoring regularly help to build this shared community culture when these are part of regular weekly routines. Today's visit to our school will focus on how to establish this culture, see a lesson plan, and offer wrap-up tips to help you easily carry these practices to your own classroom.

Back Inside Our School: What Social Understanding Looks Like When Students Are Doing It Well

We return to our school in wintertime now. Snow has piled up on the steps. We are surrounded by students bundled up in warm coats, scarves, and gloves. As we walk back into the now familiar upper-grade classroom, we see the teacher in front of the class with a student-written paragraph being projected on the smartboard. This student has asked to have his paper shared so he could have feedback on it. All students have a copy.

Before they begin, they take out their notebooks. At this time of the year, they naturally know how to begin by jotting down some positive self-talk that they will use while writing. Students journal for a moment, then share with a peer. The teacher has all students take a few slow breaths and practice a mindfulness routine they learned in health class this term.

Next, they dive in to begin giving feedback to their peers. As they review each section, students now turn to peers near them and discuss how they would improve it. The teacher is guiding the conversation to focus on scoring and revising for audience awareness.

She is asking whether the section is clear to all readers, or if it assumes too much and should have made certain points clearer. Students debate whether the writer was intentionally setting up the statement to allow the reader to make an inference or if the writing is just unclear. Each group shares their suggestions. As the first group shares, the next group listens attentively and modifies what they were going to say.

One student contributes to the conversation around the use of quotes:

> *Building on what Sarah said, I agree that their third paragraph should include a quote from the source text. Right now, you are paraphrasing the author, Malala, but if you add a quote from her, her words will uplift your reader. The effect will be that the paragraph will read better. I'd use her quote where she talks about how her teacher taught her to use the pen to write for change: "One pen, one teacher—these can change the world." That quote reads like music and gives a message of hope. Your thesis states that Malala inspires and this quote really*

shows that. It also makes us feel like we can use our writing to make a difference too. If you add her words to your own, it makes your writing sound even better.

After working through the piece, the student who wrote it appreciates all the feedback he got and is excited to begin revising. Similarly, other students had realizations during this activity, feel reenergized, and now want to revise and continue the paragraphs they began earlier in the week. Students then move to continue writing in small groups, pairs, and some on their own as they revise what they began and continue to compose. They now give more attention to what their audience will think. Building on this momentum, their teacher posts on the board "Ask yourself: What will my reader think?"

Listening in on one conversation, we hear a student giving feedback to a peer:

I like how you opened with an interesting problem that I now want to see how you solve in your arguments. That hooked me. I want to understand how it is possible that an unknown girl in a tiny village in Pakistan could have worldwide impact on helping hundreds of thousands of girls get to go to school, especially when she was banned from attending school. Then you led into a thesis about how Malala used storytelling as a way to make people feel emotion and connection. You then gave more statistics about how many girls in the world cannot go to school. However, you didn't share a story she told in the section where it explains this more fully.

I, as a reader, might have felt more pulled in if I read even a little short story that she often tells about the teenage girl who had no way to track the oranges she was selling but to make lines in the sand. That story helps me see the practical side of why girls need to learn to read, write, and calculate. You made it seem like education is important to go to college, but this story shows how it is important in daily life, too. Also, I wasn't sure what you meant at the end. Can you explain that to me? Maybe if we talk about it, we can think of ways to make your idea clearer to readers.

Downstairs, we see students on the rug scoring and revising a peer's writing as a class. As the lesson progresses, students decide whether they would like to remain with the teacher-led group on the rug, or if they feel ready to go off and work in small groups or independently at their desks. Today the teacher is modeling the difference between writing that is a list of facts versus writing that holds together, flows, and leads the reader to new understandings about the topic. She explains how sometimes writing is merely knowledge telling (Bereiter & Scardamalia, 1987), like making a list. Other times, it involves knowledge transformation. This is where writers not only share facts but also arrange and analyze them in a new way that sparks an insight about the topic that the reader did not have before reading it. In a way, you teach your reader facts and also help build new, deeper understandings about the topic. For example, the writer might reveal a connection, an insight, a cause–effect relationship, or a contrast among the facts that the reader had not seen before but now does. Maybe you will help your reader see how clever octopuses are. They don't have big teeth, but they have nonviolent ways to stay safe by hiding or swimming fast.

The students are discussing TAP: *topic*, *audience*, *purpose*. TAP helps them remember to think about these levels while writing. Today they are reading a peer piece about octopuses. The teacher reminds them that the purpose is to do more than just tell facts but to help the reader think in new ways about how these creatures survive. The students point out how she used a hook and good word choices and helped them realize how their special abilities allow them to survive among scary predators and remain nonviolent in the meantime.

When they go off to write, they mentally call up conversations heard in class about how others will think. One child reviews her piece alone. As she reads it over, the voices she regularly hears from her peers are now running through her mind.

> *OK, we talked a few times about how to make an opening that grabs the reader's attention but is not silly. A few kids said we should open with what interests us. What interests me about octopuses? They are a pretty color. That might not interest others and may not be relevant. I know! The piece is all about how they survive. I can start off by surprising the reader. Surprises are great and grab the attention of anyone. I'll write about how dangerous the sea is for them. I'll start off by saying that most people don't know how scary the sea can be. How do I spell* most? *I'll break it into sounds and think about the letter or group of letters I use for each sound: MMM ooo sss ttt. I also need to push in since this is a new section. I think we called that indenting. Great—I have an idea I'm excited about. I think different readers will like it too. I'm getting tired. Wait, I remember we talked about how to keep ourselves going when we write. I've got this! And look, the other kids are quietly writing still too. If they can do it, I can too.*

Another child is thinking about octopuses making black ink. She reads it to her peer, "Wait, I'll say *squirt* the ink. That's a more fun word." Her peer agrees. She asks her why squirting ink matters and how it relates to the big idea of survival. Students know that they need to explain how each fact supports the main topic of the piece. She explains that when the water is dark, others can't see it. It's like a game of tag. If you hide somewhere dark, you won't get caught. They don't have to hurt the other creature, but they can still stay safe and get away. They decide to add all this information to the essay to make it more fun and interesting. Her peer keeps listening to her piece and tells her, "I like how you have a good fact that they swim fast, but you use the word *they* a lot. Is there another word you could use?" She begins with a compliment, as she has learned to do, then makes a meaningful suggestion about an area the class has talked about many times—word choice and sentence variety.

See It in Action: Sample Lesson

The previous chapter's lesson aimed to teach scoring and revision to support students with the self-monitoring and inhibition needed to do these. This chapter's lesson shows how students learn to think about audience awareness. At the same time, they learn to interact positively in ways that allow them to practice and develop social skills while they compose together and in how they give each feedback. It also demonstrates how the class works together in their writing community.

Throughout this book, each of the earlier lessons were structured to support peer social interaction during collaborative planning, writing and revision. This lesson takes an even deeper dive into further fostering social learning and development that happen throughout all phases of the writing process.

SAMPLE LESSON: Revise for TAP—Topic, Audience, and Purpose

Goal: Model and teach peer collaboration and feedback.

Objectives:

1. Teach students to collaboratively write and revise together.
2. Build a sense of audience awareness in students.
3. Learn and practice using effective social skills when writing together and giving peer feedback.

Estimated Time: 30–45 minutes

Materials: Chart paper or smartboard, markers, pencils, notebook paper (whiteboard or clipboard), copies of a text that students will read, peer writing samples

Lesson Steps:

1. Begin class with having students jot down and share positive self-talk as well as tools they will use to write today, such as POWER or strategies for how to strengthen endings. Encourage students to take a few breaths slowly or to use any mindfulness practices they have learned to help them center and get focused before the lesson begins.
2. Explain that when writers turn drafts into final pieces, they think again more carefully about TAP: the topic, audience, and purpose that they want to achieve with their writing.
3. Part I: Model giving peer feedback as a class to a sample from "another student." Include student contributions as you review each section together.
   a. Pass out this piece of writing, written by "another child."
   b. Post, review, and discuss peer feedback norms.
   c. Remind students to start with expressing what they like about a peer's writing, then to review it with a scale or checklist of features. (Students should have learned this scale and practiced using it in a prior lesson.)
   d. As students give feedback, discuss differences between what the writer might have wanted to say, but how the reader might not have understood the message.
4. Part II: Then have students work in pairs to give each other actual feedback.

5. Remind students to first share constructive feedback that is grounded in the scales.
6. Each can share positives they enjoyed in what they read and a constructive feedback tip, then look at the writing for how the writer showed audience awareness.
7. They should draw attention to how the writer seems to have considered the perspective of the reader and made their purpose for writing clear to their audience.
8. Finally, have students work together to revise their pieces to show even greater audience awareness.
9. Remind students that when discussing ideas during revision, they should use this discussion to co-construct new understandings or to learn more together.
10. If needed, a teacher and another adult can model via role playing and scaffold these kinds of discussions, or two students can be coached then model this practice in front of the class.
11. To nudge deeper thinking, encourage students to build, extend, and challenge each other's reasoning or decisions around what to include, even to suggest alternative ways of thinking.
12. Help students discover they have different understandings or points of view. They should express their ideas. The listener will first restate and paraphrase them, then add on or disagree. They should work to develop shared understandings in the meantime.
13. Remind students that these discussions help them reach their own understandings of the topic. Facts in the texts remain facts, but how they interpret facts and group them can be their choice. This is where students, as authors, make decisions when they write.
14. Have students reflect on their experiences working together, including how writing together as a class or in pairs helps them write better.
15. Finally, give students time to quietly make further revisions. Post on the board and have them copy down the question "What will my reader think?" to guide them.

Wrap-Up: Summarize that this lesson continued the self-monitoring lesson and went more deeply into practicing social skills and looking at the reader's perspective.

Note: Moving forward, have students cycle through "Teach, Model, Score" with this kind of attention to audience awareness and practicing social skills to help establish a community of writers.

Lesson Analysis: How Each Component Supports the Social Understandings Needed for Effective, Self-Regulated Writing

Theory of Mind Supports Deeper Reading Comprehension

The students in these classrooms needed to have deep comprehension in place before they could write meaningfully. Comprehension has been discussed in prior chapters but merits an important revisit in light of how it connects to social understandings.

Theory of mind, a central facet of this kind of understanding, is also essential to reading comprehension. See Cartwright (2023) for more on theory of mind and how it supports reading comprehension. Students must be able to understand more than the events or facts as they read. They must also infer characters' invisible reactions and motivations to comprehend stories more fully and write more insightfully. Similarly, in informative texts, they must learn to spot how authors angle presenting evidence in a more positive or negative light, revealing their potential biases. Is the author describing shark attacks or endangerment of these creatures? The facts writers give reveal their biases. Essentially, students need to be thinking about how the characters, or authors of texts, think.

In this lesson, the students had to understand more than what Malala said or did. For their analysis to be insightful, they needed to infer her motivations and that she cared deeply about helping girls get an education. This understanding enabled students to see that part of why she inspires others is because she cares so much herself. As students reach grade 3, they move from being expected to show a basic understanding of texts to "examining" them, or making "inferences," by grade 4 (National Governors Association Center for Best Practices [NGA] & Council of Chief State School Officers [CCSSO], 2010). This kind of inference making can be taught (Rice & Wijekumar, 2024) even at earlier ages (Elleman, 2017). For writing to have substance, students need to have the capacity for these deeper levels of insight and understanding. This is why theory of mind is important not just for writing well but also during the reading comprehension that precedes it.

Teacher Talk Example

I'm going to show you what I would say to myself in my mind if I was trying to figure out how others think. Today we looked at how readers might think while reading a piece that I wrote. We will try to imagine that we are in the head of the reader and thinking what they might think. [In younger grades, we draw a smiley face on the piece to show we are thinking about our reader, and what they will think.] We read a story about Malala and talked about what readers might think of the article. We could see how it used words like admirable *when describing her. The other article about her only stated the facts but did not describe her. I think this shows that the writer of the second piece likes her. I can see why.*

We also talked about inferring character motivations. This means we try to understand WHY people do what they do. Malala began blogging when she was only in grade 4. She could have gotten in trouble and she had nothing to gain. Her only motivation would be to help others, and even to risk her own safety. I agree with the second writer that Malala really is admirable. I'm going to work this into the piece I write now. I'll show the contrast between how she likes to buy fashionable clothes and she cares about other students. She is complicated because she is several things at once—a person who cares and a teenager who likes to shop. She is relatable and admirable. I'll use both ideas now when I go to write.

Thinking about social dynamics and understandings is important all through when we read and write, but especially when we do our final revisions. Being aware of these can help us put the final touches on our writing and be sure it has depth, surprises, and is fun to read.

Discussions Build Theory of Mind and Perspective Taking

Peer discussion can help students reach the kinds of social understandings needed to comprehend and write about why Malala acted as she did. Both hot and cold executive skills came into play during these kinds of peer exchanges, starting with theory of mind. As students read, debate, and respond to each other's writing, they regularly see how others think differently from themselves. They learn to routinely reflect on how their readers may do so. Such discussions rely on and offer the potential to continuously develop students' theory of mind (Lane & Bowmand, 2021).

These discussions offer additional value when peers challenge each other by suggesting alternative possible interpretations or ways of thinking that the writer may not have considered. The student who prompted his peer to add a little story rather than just state a statistic to the Malala essay did this. He disagreed that offering numbers would be the best way to support the point. He thought Malala was able to compel readers to care by using stories and that his peer should do this too. This challenged the writer's decision. These debates can help students think more broadly and flexibly, which can enrich their writing.

For this to happen, the writer must first recognize that their peer giving them feedback holds a different outlook. In this case, the peer thought stories were more impactful than numbers. The writer then needs to reconcile this, potentially adapting or expanding their own point of view (Brugge-Feldhake et al., 2024). The writer might think both are important but needs to decide which to give more attention to now. Teachers can also support students with shifting perspectives through prompting and modeling how to do this (Diaz-Borda et al., 2024), as well as modeling how to cope with the distress this shift can evoke.

This is where perspective shifting touches on hot skills as well. Coming to realize that my perspective may not be complete or accurate can feel uncomfortable. Students will need to self-regulate such feelings. As just suggested, seeing peers and adults talk this through and model it can help. Mindfulness practices offer additional potential support for the cognitive and affective demands around perspective shifting and can facilitate the needed self-regulation to manage these (Berti & Cigala, 2020; Thierry et al., 2022). Mindfulness has been shown to raise writing outcomes (Nunes et al., 2024), and this may partly explain why. Mindfulness is the practice of stilling the mind through bringing one's attention to a constant such as one's breath. It offers a way to ease stress, allowing students' cold and hot executive skills to work more effectively (Shields et al., 2016). Angling mindfulness as part of our regular self-talk, shown in this lesson, offers a natural way to bring this in. It may be especially helpful when reaching toward the more challenging levels of writing that involve this kind of shifting perspectives.

Over time, reading peers' writing together and providing feedback will help students see their writing through the eyes of the reader. As their theory of mind within writing gradually develops, their inner monologue changes. It begins to incorporate considering how others' perspectives may differ from those they hold. Rather than inhibiting or suppressing competing ideas that may arise, students can then better address these when they write, which raises their writing quality (Davidson et al., 2006).

Inner Language Revisited and Expanded

Earlier chapters touched on the inner monologue that guides all writers. They offered suggestions for how educators can teach students to speak to themselves in constructive ways as they write. This section now expands on self-talk to look at how social interactions and understandings can further develop it. Essentially, our inner language is built through social interaction. The more that social understandings, such as perspective taking and theory of mind, are discussed so students can learn about these from peer models, the more these transform and become part of the inner language that guides them during writing.

Broadly, there are two voices in our students' minds. One kind of inner monologue we all have leans toward mind wandering, while the other is more willfully self-directed (Perrone-Bertolotti et al., 2014). As an example, a child's mind might wander to a time when he saw an octopus at an aquarium. On the other hand, the child in this lesson engaged in purposeful, self-directed thought when she considered how to strengthen her opening. Unless taught that there are other ways to think, most students likely tend toward mind wandering when writing. Taking the bull by the horns, students can change this, but it requires realizing that their current way of thinking may not be the only way. Peer modeling, discussions, and strategies are key.

All the tools (strategies and scaffolds) introduced so far support students in doing this and culminate in making self-regulation possible. These tools help students know what to tell themselves to do when they write by providing step-by-step checklists to follow mentally. The key is to use them repeatedly until students internalize them and understand they have choices in how they can think while writing—and that experts think differently from them. This can be learned. This kind of inner self-verbalization, which includes directing oneself in how to use tools, raises learning, helps students cope with challenges, and lifts confidence (Schunk, 1986). Again, it's likely most students don't know that more expert peers struggle, too, but think differently in how they cope with these struggles.

Academic language and reasoning run through our students' minds. Because they cannot see into their peers' minds, students may not realize others have further developed these language and reasoning skills and that they can, too. Theory of mind comes into play here as well, as students may just not realize there are other ways to reason, and scaffolds such as language boxes or sentence stems that support higher-order reasoning (see Appendix R) can help them improve in these areas.

The lesson described even expanded to include a focus on developing deeper levels of reasoning as well. The kind of logic and perspective taking demonstrated in these peer exchanges and debates likewise become internalized. This helps students expand on and organize how they reason when they write independently (Kompa & Mueller, 2022). Alongside academic language, this kind of perspective taking and complex reasoning play a significant role in fostering the deep reading comprehension that drives higher writing quality (LaRusso et al., 2016). It becomes part of the inner speech students hear and use when they write.

Social Demands Intensify Executive Skill Needs

Students felt comfortable, even energized, to debate and challenge each other. The classroom norms these students follow did not happen on their own. Peers learned how to work collaboratively and offer feedback in socially skilled ways. Teachers introduced peer norms such as complimenting each other and noticing what students like, then giving feedback grounded in the scoring scale. Teachers modeled these norms, had students volunteer to model them for the class, then regularly referred to them when coaching students as they worked together. As a way to bolster this instruction, they also pointed out social lessons in texts read, such as specific ways that Malala inspired people to change their perspective and how they could use those strategies during class discussions.

This aspect of teaching writing, setting up peer norms, may be one of the most challenging to establish. These interactions call on nearly all cold and hot executive skills. They require that students coordinate using them all together, particularly the added demands that theory of mind places on understanding, managing, and adjusting to peer perspectives. For students to manage writing and do so in a social community that includes frequent peer exchanges, all hands are needed on deck, cognitively and affectively. The prior chapters set you up with the kinds of tools and structures needed to support the colder executive skills, while this one touched more so on hot skills. This is why writing instruction needs to be thought of comprehensively. Students should follow weekly cycles. These provide the chance for student writers to repeatedly practice, coordinate, and apply all they learn, including the kinds of social engagement norms that support developing theory of mind and its related perspective-taking capabilities.

How "Quality Talk" Supports Executive Skills

Another word on discussion norms before moving on. The teacher leading this lesson drew from the evidence-based practices that underlie Quality Talk, a structured approach to developing reading comprehension (Li et al., 2016) that scaffolds executive skills well. This approach similarly has students engage in a limited number of practices regularly so that they become internalized thinking norms and part of our students' inner monologue as well. The goal of Quality Talk is to facilitate helping students move beyond merely discussing textual evidence to doing something with it—to critically evaluate, synthesize, shed new light, or transform it in ways that allow for new insights. Quality Talk leverages student discussions in ways that scaffold executive skills, including perspective taking and flexibility through the back-and-forth talk. Students learn to make the kinds of inferences about information from texts or about characters' motivations, which in turn can develop their theory of mind. See Chapter 7 in Cartwright (2023) for more on how teachers can use literature to develop this skill.

In Quality Talk, students learn to practice something called "exploratory talk." They are encouraged to build shared understandings of the text through collective reasoning during discussions about it. They also learn to challenge each other's ideas or interpretations of the text and practice this regularly, as you saw. Rather than accepting a simple description of what a text might mean, they nudged one another to look for contrasts and causal relationships. For example, Malala might be a normal teenager interested in fashion, yet also deeply motivated to help others. This shows an interesting, perhaps unexpected, contrast. Students can develop a routine to regularly look for such contrasts and connections. As the number of times students engage in this kind of talk with peers rises, so do their reading and writing outcomes (Li et al., 2016). This study included writing students produced independently. This suggests that this kind of exploratory reasoning became internalized and part of the voice in their minds that guided them as they wrote.

Writer's Community

In these lessons, you observed a well-structured writer's community in action. Establishing an effective community can help make the kind of high-level writing that often seems impossible to students come into their reach. Not only can being part of these communities lift academic language and reasoning through connection and discussions, but they can also shift students' identities. Students may not view themselves as writers. They may have experienced staring at blank pages and feeling stuck.

Being part of a community, along with the instruction described all through this book, can help change this. Ernest Hemingway is credited with having said, "Sometimes I write better than I can." While Hemingway expresses a paradox, once students begin using effective tools, understand the features of the genre they write in, and critically engage in these kinds of regular peer discussions, they outgrow themselves all the time. We often find that the sky is the limit for how high students can write once they have the skills, tools, and ability to self-regulate. They constantly surprise us. Building this kind of writing community leverages social connections and drives home a deeper grasp of how applying theory of mind in writing can energize and bring our writers further than they can reach on their own.

Take It to the Classroom: Tips You Can Use Tomorrow

This chapter looks at the higher-order executive skills that play a greater role in writing as students grow, including the related areas of theory of mind, perspective taking, and reasoning that lie beneath effective writing. These can be supported through direct instruction and establishing supportive communities. Writing Workshop associated with the whole-language approach (Calkins, 1994) advocated for the importance of these communities, but may have had it out of order. The Workshop approach has students dive in and compose, in community, from day one. However, composing cannot happen unless students are first equipped with the necessary skills. The Writer's Workshop approach does not advocate for introducing, teaching, and practicing discrete cognitive and affective scaffolds first, which is essential—but *insufficient.* Once we have taught these and have well-functioning routines up and running, developing a writing community helps students continue to grow. Writer's Workshop may not have had it entirely wrong but had it backward and missed key elements (Seidenberg, 2017). The following suggestions help you take these elements to the classroom, but they should be followed and used in coordination with all the scaffolds and explicit instructional routines presented in the prior chapters.

Establish Prosocial Norms

Create and post guidelines for providing feedback on peers' writing. Include that students should warmly greet each other and face each other to show attentive body language as they listen and respond. Feedback should start with "liking," stating what we like. Students can even brainstorm and list potential compliments that they could use. Next, the person giving feedback should ask the writer what their goals are and what they would like feedback on. Suggestions on how to improve each other's writing should be anchored in the scales (see Appendices S–W). Guide students to use the exact language and phrases from the scales to ensure that the writer understands the feedback given.

Use Peer Feedback to Raise Outcomes

Peer feedback has the capacity to raise writing outcomes (Wu & Schunn, 2021) and social understandings (Patchan et al., 2016; Philippakos et al., 2016; Topping, 2009). During peer feedback, students interact in ways that call on social skills with greater intensity as they respond to each other's writing, particularly as they revise together for audience awareness. They will regularly share ideas, write pieces together, and give each other feedback and encouragement daily. This regular practice offers rich opportunities to develop perspective-taking understandings.

Teach, Model, and Practice Audience Awareness

Directly teach students to reflect on TAP (topic, audience, purpose) as they write. When you score writing together as a class, discuss how the writer addressed TAP before diving in to score the specific elements listed on the scale. Keep in mind that as you discuss these, the words your students hear during these conversations become the voice they hear in their minds later when they write independently. Have students mark up in the margins of their organizers or drafts to note the different ways that various readers may think about the ideas they presented. Doing so helps students realize that readers will not automatically think the same way.

Teach and Prompt Higher-Order Cognitive Skills

In my work with teachers, one of the most frequent questions I heard is how can they support students in reasoning better and generating more compelling insights when they write. Sentence stems can help (see Appendices O and R), as can discussions. Yet there may not be a quick fix. These invisible cognitive capacities, particularly social understandings, take time to mature, but are learned more quickly when taught. See Cartwright (2023) to learn more about developing these kinds of higher-order thinking.

As an example of a way to scaffold this, invite your students to consider asking "what if" as they analyze events and come up with hypothetical alternatives. Counterfactual reasoning is the ability to compare an actual outcome with hypothetical, or imagined, alternatives (Guajardo & Cartwright, 2016). For example, one of my students wrote that it was lucky Dorothy met the Tin Man, Lion, and Scarecrow and they helped her. Otherwise, she might have been stuck in Munchkinland forever. The child was able to imagine and consider alternative outcomes, which made his analysis richer.

For more on developing the higher-order, and often the most fun to write, aspects of essays and stories, see Appendix R. These stems help prompt students to engage in this kind of reasoning. As a rule of thumb, teachers can encourage students to be brave and take risks when they write their analyses (the D in TIDE), endings, and openings. These are the areas where we see most of the kind of higher-order reasoning described in this chapter. Students can be reminded that there is no right or wrong, but they have to "sell" their reasoning so their reader understands why, or the logic behind, why they reasoned as they did.

Increase Rigor

Earlier I mentioned the importance of raising the level of exemplars that we show students throughout the year, and from year to year. Recall that the level we show is the level they will produce. Be sure to reach high so that we do not accidentally impose ceilings. Likewise, as students move up through the grades, different factors predict writing quality outcomes. By grade 3 and above, higher-order executive skills, including perspective taking and the related area of inferencing, play a greater role (Cho et al., 2021; LaRusso et al., 2016). This suggests that the rigor of the texts, the complexity of the exemplars we provide students, and our expectations around how well they can take perspectives should be rising as well.

Gradual Release

So far, several types of stems (Appendices O and R) have been introduced as ways to help scaffold moving students along in higher-order social understandings. However, these can also become a barrier. In order for cognition to grow, students must do the thinking (Cartwright, 2023). Scaffolds such as organizers or stems need an expiration date. Overscaffolding can hold back potential. Once students use a stem a few times, these can become "banned" and they must use or even invent new stems to ensure they write flexibly.

Narrative Story Writing

Chapter 4 touched on narrative story writing structure and how CSPACE can support this. Another note on story writing. Most curricula are growing to prioritize more time on expository writing in response to texts through informative or opinion writing about what students read, particularly with the Standards shifts from 2011 (NGA & CCSSO, 2011). However, narrative writing remains important for many reasons. Writing stories draws on and activates more of the kinds of hot executive skills discussed in this chapter. Crafting stories requires students to imagine details about their characters' internal, emotional states, as well as maintain attention to the global thread that holds the events together. Students' levels of emotional regulation play a role and can hinder central coherence in stories they write (Bourke et al., 2020). Teaching, practicing, and receiving feedback seems like a promising strategy for supporting these kinds of wider hot skills.

That's a Wrap!

This chapter was my favorite to write. It's the point where writing becomes about creating possibilities and making the world better. Classrooms grow abuzz when peers begin to engage in these ways. Returning to the opening, developing social understandings has wider value beyond improving writing outcomes. This is the core of human empathy. All through time, writing has been used as a force for social uplift. When we develop our students' ability to "perspective take" and infer, we release not just their power to care but their ability to more effectively make change. As Toni Morrison says, if there's a book you want to read that hasn't been written yet, then write it. If the world we would like to live in is not there yet, prepare our students to help write it into being, and to care enough to do so.

Epilogue

The snow has cleared, and spring has arrived. As we approach our school on what is now a warm, sunny morning, the cherry blossoms that line the front stoop are in full bloom. As we walk toward the school, students who were busy playing now line up outside and head into their classes.

In the K–2 classrooms, students are abuzz. They pick up their writing from the day before and dive in and continue their work. They do so alone, in pairs, or in groups at the back table with a teacher to support them. A substitute teacher in a grade 1 classroom later shares how astonished she was to see students know just what to do before she even explained the lesson plan she had been left.

Upstairs, today is state assessment testing. Students open their text booklets. They each ask for extra scrap paper. One by one, unprompted, they start by writing personalized self-talk at the top such as "I've got this!" Or "Complex text, you're going down!" Empowered and excited, they begin to close-read the texts. They make notes on their scrap paper as they do. They capture key ideas in organized ways and note down strong vocabulary. Some add lists of conjunctions. To help them spot common themes to write about, some jot down "SPICE" (Surprise with the unexpected, Power dynamics, Inspiration/human spirit, human Connection, Evolution or character growth). SPICE is a trick their class made up. They kept track of different themes they found in what they read as a way to help them remember them and pull them up quickly. They began the year learning mnemonics such as POWER and TIDE. However, as the year went on, they began adapting these techniques, generating and then using their own class-developed tools to help them meet their increasingly sophisticated goals.

As they move to making a TIDE-L organizer, they all include language boxes. They added an L to TIDE to remind themselves to do this. As they begin writing, they hum "check it off" in their minds. They actively use not just the outline and the words in this box but the extra tips and tools they added in the margins, such as SPICE. In their minds, they pull up the many times they watched their teacher turn an outline into an essay, and all the conversations they had with classmates as they did this collaboratively. They recall talking about how to turn a jot note into a rich sentence and how to make the writing flow and hold together. Having practiced all year, the kinds of sentence stems that can help them do this easily come right to mind now as they draft.

Lunch arrives, but they are not finished yet. By the end of the day, some are still working. The stamina is remarkable. Exhausted, but proud, they head home feeling victorious. Some parents are called to pick them up because they were not even finished yet at the end of the school day. Greeted by a grinning principal at the door, both the parents and school leaders feel a moment of shared, immense pride.

The students all know they gave their best. In prior years, they often felt defeated by the assessment. Teachers had tissue boxes on hand, and students stared at a blank screen. They did not know how to begin responding to the essay questions.

This year was different. Students had what they needed to succeed. All year, they learned, practiced, and became expert at using the kinds of scaffolds that support executive skills in ways that lead to the kind of self-regulation and agency that these students, in every grade, show now.

Coming Full Circle, Literally

This book opened and now closes with the importance of using routines that support executive skills, in a regular cycle, all with the goal of us letting go and letting students chart their own learning course. Teaching students how to learn often seems like a wistful but unrealistic goal. In our field, we often see dichotomies. Either we use explicit instruction, or we set students up to learn how to learn in self-regulated ways. This may not be a dichotomy but a sequence. If we provide all of the kind of explicit instruction described throughout this book, in ways that attend to fostering self-regulation, and if we help students develop executive skills, the unexpected can happen.

With our explicit instruction, writers learn to draw from increasingly automatized handwriting and spelling transcription skills, their growing language banks, and reasoning abilities. These are tied to language, but executive skills contribute to how quickly and easily students develop in these areas as well. As this book has laid out, executive skills can be directly taught and scaffolded in the same way as the underlying literacy skills that support writing, right alongside one another in the same lessons. We can teach in ways that equip our students not only with the language but also with the reasoning needed to write well. When we explicitly focus on developing executive skills as well, we can take them even further and transform fundamentally how they self-regulate at the same time.

This is where regular cyclical routines that focus on developing skills, language, text structure, reasoning, and self-regulation are essential. Executive skills instruction and support is not a one-and-done. That may be one of the biggest misconceptions about these kinds of supports. Providing a mnemonic or organizer is only one step on a longer journey. To reveal why, this book gave you a view under the hood. It unveiled how executive skills play an important role in learning to write and offered suggestions for better understanding, teaching, and supporting these skills. Students need explicit and integrative instruction, modeling, and deliberate practice in each area of writing, including how to manage their executive skills, the unsung hero of writing instruction. They need to learn to coordinate using all these areas together. And, they can.

When they do so, the magic pixie dust of student agency kicks in, which allows them to unlock more of their immense, unrealized potential, as you saw in this final school visit. Not only can students now write better but also they have learned to self-regulate. Honoring and empowering this kind of student agency may be the most important work we do as educators, with lifelong benefits well beyond academics. Teaching, supporting, and developing executive skills offers a practical and evidence-based path for working toward this lofty goal.

Appendix of Resources and Reproducibles

Introduction to the Appendices

To pull together the threads from all the chapters, the resources in this Appendix provide a "starter kit" that will help you bring what you have learned to your classroom. While reading this book, you have learned how writing depends not only on language and reasoning skills but also on executive skills.

These appendices help you take a diagnostic-prescriptive approach that brings forward the importance of these skills. As you read each chapter, you may have seen your different students reflected in the challenges described. You can now choose from the groups of tools below that support the different executive skill needs of your students. I also encourage you to consult Cartwright's (2023) *Executive Skills and Reading Comprehension, Second Edition*, which includes an assessment tool designed to help you understand and pinpoint the specific areas of executive skills.

The appendices are organized into five main groups, with an executive skill foregrounded in each. This grouping also supports your own executive skills as a reader, making it easier for you to apply everything you have learned about supporting executive skills when teaching writing. In general, the appendices are used in the order provided as you begin to plan and carry out changes in your instruction, starting from preparing writing tasks to teaching how to plan and organize, then supporting drafting, revising, and editing.

Appendix Contents

The Big Picture

These appendices provide a big-picture scope and sequence, a list of skills to teach per grade level, then home in on specific writing tools to use over the year and across grades. These provide a bird's-eye view to assist with your planning and organization of instruction.

Getting Started

This group of appendices includes starter materials such as sample writing prompts, writing tasks, and key background knowledge vocabulary to teach. It also includes "backward design" materials such as student exemplars. These exemplars show the finish line—the outcomes we are working to support students in producing over the year.

Supporting the Executive Skills of Planning and Organizing

This group of materials is meant not only to support using the executive skills of planning and organizing but also to develop and strengthen these brain-based skills themselves. In learning to plan and organize before writing and to keep these in mind when writing, students strengthen their underlying planning and organizing executive skills as well.

Supporting the Executive Skills of Working Memory and Cognitive Flexibility

While all the support tools included in this Appendix scaffold working memory and cognitive flexibility, those included in this group play a special role in doing so.

Supporting the Executive Skills of Inhibition and Self-Monitoring

The appendices in this group provide language and tools that help students inhibit the tendency to forget to include key features of effective writing. They offer a structured way for students to guide themselves as they write and review what they have produced when their first drafts are completed.

APPENDIX A

Scope and Sequence Pacing Guide

	Fall	Winter	Spring
Grades K–2	**Introduce/Model/Practice POW+TIDE-L** **Introduce sentence skills: Daily gists** • Use noun and verb; capitalize first word/ proper nouns; use period. • Expand gists to teach pronoun, preposition, conjunction, commas in lists, adjective, adverb. **Model/practice each part of TIDE-L** • Teach in context of paragraphs. **Map stories to CSPACE**	**Model/Practice/Release use of POW+TIDE-L** **Continue daily gist/sentence lessons** • Vary openers and rearrange parts. • Use K–2 stem banks, finding stems in peer/ published writing. **Continue practicing each part of TIDE-L** • Expand use to student-created books/essays. **Teach linking words** (*first, next, last*) • Move to synonyms to link ideas. **Use CSPACE to tell and to write stories**	**Support independence with POW+TIDE-L** **Continue daily gist practice** **Continue paragraph cohesion** • Use transitions: examples (*for instance*); change in direction (*but, yet*); causal words (*because, as a result*). • Continue synonym use. **Expand use of TIDE-L books/essays** • Personal narratives **Continue mapping CSPACE**
Grades 3–5	**Introduce/Model/Practice POWER+TIDE-L** **Develop sentence skills: Daily gists** • Use noun, pronoun, verb, capitals, period, preposition, conjunction, either/or, verb tenses (modals, future, progressive), commas in lists, quote, introductory clause. **Model/practice each part of TIDE-L** • Teach in context of paragraphs. **Map stories to CSPACE**	**Model/Practice/Release use of POWER+TIDE-L** **Continue daily gist sentence lessons** • Vary gist openers, rearrange parts of speech order. • Expand stem banks by finding stems in peer/ published writing. **Continue practicing each part of TIDE-L** • Use TIDE-L for paragraphs or essays. • Improve quality of genre produced. • Use synonyms to link ideas. **Use CSPACE to tell and to write stories**	**Independently use POWER+TIDE-L** **Continue daily gist practice** **Continue paragraph cohesion** • Use transitions: sequence (*initially, next*); examples (*specifically*); change in direction (*in contrast*); cause/effect (*consequently*). **Expand and vary use of TIDE-L** • Personal narratives **Continue mapping CSPACE**
Grades 6–8+	**Introduce/Model/Practice POWER+TIDE-L** **Enhance sentence skills via gists** • Eight parts of speech, intensive pronouns/ clear antecedents • Punctuation (commas in lists, to set off clauses, appositives, parentheticals, before quotes), dash, parentheses, verbs **Teach/Practice TIDE-L (via paragraphs)** **Map stories to CSPACE**	**Model/Practice/Release use of POWER+TIDE-L** **Continue gist sentence lessons** • Vary openers, parenthetical clauses, add modifiers. • Identify complex sentence stems found in peer/ published writing. **Continue practicing each part of TIDE-L** • Improve quality of genre features produced (analysis) in paragraphs/essays now. **Use CSPACE to tell and to write stories**	**Independently use POWER+TIDE-L** **Continue gist practice** **Continue paragraph cohesion** • Transitions create cohesion and clarify relationships among ideas: *furthermore, specifically, however, instead, consequently.* **Expand use of TIDE-L essays** • Memoir, anecdotes **Continue mapping CSPACE**

Note. Teach these targets during literacy/social studies/science blocks as you write about what you read. This replaces worksheet/workbook activities.

APPENDIX B

Writing Skills Progression

Writing Skills Progression	Grades						
Gray = Introduce; Light Gray = Master; White = Tier 2/3	K	1	2	3	4	5	6+
Print letters							
Print all upper- and lowercase letters							
Spell phonetically							
Spell sounds: *b, d, f, g, h, j, k, l, m, n, p, r, s, t, v, w, y, z* Doublets *ff, ll, ss, zz* Digraphs *th, sh, ch, wh ph, ng* (*sing*), *gh* (*cough*) [*ck*, as guest) Trigraphs *-tch, -dge* Blends *s-c-r* (*scrape*), *th-r* (*thrush*), *c-l, f-t, l-k, s-t* Silent letter combinations: *kn* (*knock*), *wr* (*wrestle*), *gn* (*gnarl*), *ps* (*psych*), *rh* (*rhythm*), *-mb* (*crumb*), *-lk, -mn, -st* (*listen*)							
Segment syllables in a word and phonemes Identify initial, medial, final sounds (CVC) (not yet: /l/, /r/, or /x/)							
Distinguish long versus short vowel sounds in phonetic spelling							
Spell vowel teams (*r*-controlled, final *-e*)							
Identify vowel sound; segment syllables to spell multisyllabic words							
Spell vowel teams; common affixes; common words							
Generalize spelling patterns and use dictionaries							
Spell homonyms							
Use grammar: Use common nouns and verbs							
Plurals (i.e., *s/es*)							
Use common prepositions							
Prepositional phrases							
Accurate verb tense							
Past tense irregular verbs							
Advanced verb tenses (perfect, states)							
Common adjectives							
Adjectives and adverbs							

(continued)

Note. Based on CCSS and state literacy standards.

Writing Skills Progression *(page 2 of 2)*

Writing Skills Progression	Grades						
Gray = Introduce; Light Gray = Master; White = Tier 2/3	K	1	2	3	4	5	6+
Syntax: Expand sentences orally							
Coordinating conjunctions							
Subordinating conjunctions							
Verb tenses *(I walk; I walked*)							
Modals (e.g., *can, should*)							
Advanced grammar: Reflexive **pronouns**							
Relative pronouns (e.g., *that, which*)							
Use gerunds, participles, infinitives							
Clear pronoun referents							
Punctuate: Commas set off nonrestrictive elements, appositives							
Capitalize							
End punctuation							
Use commas in a series							
Reflexive pronouns							
Commas for items in a series or to set off introduction							
Use academic language vocabulary, grade appropriate							
Use affixes (e.g., *-ed, re-, un-, pre-, -ful, -less*)							
Produce opinion, informative, and narrative pieces with support							
Produce opinion, informative, and narrative essays							
Produce argument with counter-claim							
Use the writing process independently							
Write in response to sources, showing mastery of the reading standards (e.g., identify theme, elements, text structures, point of view, compare/contrast) as appropriate per grade level							

APPENDIX C

POWER, TIDE, and CSPACE Progressions

<table>
<tr><th>Mnemonic</th><th>Early grades</th><th colspan="2">Upper grades</th></tr>
<tr><td>POWER</td><td>P(3)
• *Preread for gist
• Pull apart prompt
• Pick ideas
Organize
Write and say more</td><td colspan="2">P(3)
• Preread for gist
• Pull apart prompt
• Pick ideas
Organize
Write and say more
edit*
Revise
*Edit is lowercased because in upper grades revision has more impact on raising overall writing quality and edits can happen last.</td></tr>
<tr><td>TIDE</td><td>Topic sentence
Information
Details (say more)
End</td><td>Topic
Important evidence
Detailed examination
End</td><td>Topic introduction
Important evidence
Detailed analysis
End</td></tr>
<tr><td>CSPACE</td><td>Characters
Setting
Problem
Actions (3+)
Conclusion
Emotion</td><td>Characters
Setting
Problem/purpose
Actions
Conclusion/climax
Emotion</td><td>Characters
Setting
Purpose (conflict)
Actions
Climax
Emotion (theme)</td></tr>
</table>

*Preread for gist is supported in K–grade 1, then done independently by grade 2.

APPENDIX D

Sample Writing Prompts

Writing Focus	Prompt Term	Definition of Term	Example Prompt
Theme or Main Idea and Summary	Identify (Use cautiously and sparingly—these writes can be less substantial)	To note or clearly indicate specifics from a wider set (toward a culminating essential question)	Lit: Identify the theme, central message, or lesson learned and show how the events convey this Info: Identify how well details support the central idea
Analyze Elements	Identify (i.e., causes and effects; problem and solution)	To note or clearly indicate specifics from a wider set of possibilities	Lit: Identify the problem faced and how one overcomes it Info: Identify causes and effects
Analyze Elements	Describe	To list, state, portray, or outline	Lit: Describe a character's traits Info: Describe the moon's phases
Analyze Elements (Opinion)	Decide, choose, or determine (argue)	To make a choice, then give supporting reasons	Lit: Decide which character is most inspiring and why Info: Decide which type of pet is best
Analyze Elements	Explain/examine	To make clear or interpret	Lit: Explain how the character overcame self-doubt Info: Examine the causes of Rome's fall
Analyze Elements	Analyze	To break down or explain each part	Lit: Describe how the author used (metaphors) to enhance meaning Info: Analyze the impact of climate on Native Americans
Text Structures	Identify: • Text structures • Point of view or bias	To observe what is not directly stated	Lit: Identify whether the text is a poem or story and how you know Info: Identify which text structure the writer used (i.e., cause/effect)
Point of View	Identify point of view or bias	To observe what is not directly stated	Lit: Identify the point of view and its impact on the reader Info: Identify biases shown in a text
Media Analysis	Evaluate	To judge or assess or make a determination	Lit: Evaluate how images enrich stories Info: Evaluate how infographics make information easier to understand
Compare and Contrast	Compare (contrast)	To tell similarities and/or differences	Lit: Compare and contrast two characters' traits Info: Compare foxes to goats
Narrative Prompts: • Tell what happens next (or next day) • Retell from a new character's perspective • Write a story with a similar theme • Tell what might have happened the day before, or earlier			

APPENDIX E

Sample Preassessment Task

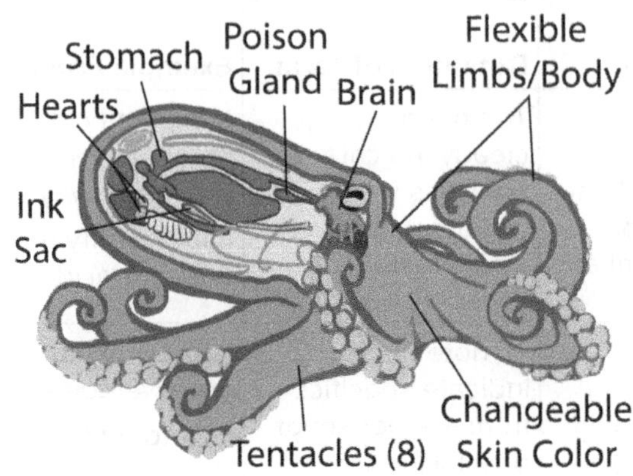

Sample Preassessment:

(It is recommended to show a 2- to 3-minute high-quality video about octopuses ahead of this task.)

Text 1: Octopuses

Octopuses live in coral reefs in the ocean. Coral reefs are brightly colored underwater structures with small holes. Octopuses move in these. Octopuses have eight arms called tentacles that are slim and bendable. If a predator grabs a tentacle, it detaches. *Detach* means "to break off." Then the octopus grows a new tentacle.

Octopuses squirt black ink. Then others cannot see it. An angry octopus turns bright colors. When afraid, it turns dark, spotted, or striped. They change colors to blend in. This is called *camouflage*. An octopus body can also change shape. It can become smaller than many large predators.

Octopuses are strong, fast swimmers. They can swim 25 miles per hour. Octopuses eat crabs and crayfish. Octopuses are smart. They have short- and long-term memory. This means they recall some information for years and some for a short while.

Text 2: Copy Cats!

The sea is filled with so many creatures who adapt to life in the big ocean. They can adapt in amazing ways. For example, an octopus can use camouflage. Animals use camouflage to change color or shape. This way they can match the area, blend in, hide, or look scary. For example, a mimic octopus can change its shape. It can look just like animals that are more dangerous. It might make itself look striped, long, and slim so that it looks just like a snake.

They can also escape by making themselves smaller. They slip through tiny spaces that would trap other creatures. For example, in a coral reef structure, they can slip through a hole almost as small as a grape!

Task: Octopuses need to protect themselves. "Protect" means to keep safe. Describe what octopuses can do to protect themselves. Support your answer with details from both texts.

APPENDIX F

Preassessment Text-Type Terms: Grades 2 and 6

Preassessment of Genre Knowledge: Grade 2

What is a topic sentence? What job does a topic sentence do?

What should a topic introduction include?

What is a fact?

What is a definition?

What does it mean to show understanding?

What should go into a concluding statement?

What are linking words?

What are simple, compound, and complex sentences?

(continued)

Preassessment of Text-Type Knowledge: Grade 6

What should be included in a topic introduction?

What is a thesis and what makes for a strong thesis?

What is a fact, definition, detail, and quote?

What is relevant evidence? What makes it relevant?

What does it mean to cite evidence?

What does it mean to examine?

What should go into a concluding statement?

What is precise language and domain-specific vocabulary?

How does one vary sentence patterns for meaning, reader interest, and style?

What is a stylistic sentence?

How do appropriate transitions clarify relationships among ideas and concepts? Give examples.

Sample Exemplar and Below Standard: Grade 2

Task: Describe what octopuses can do to protect themselves. (*Protect* means "to keep safe.") Support your answer with details from both texts.

Grade 2 Exemplar

An octopus stays safe in different ways. They live near brightly colored coral reefs in the ocean, which keep them safe from harm because they can hide and escape through small spaces in these. Next, if an enemy grabs an octopus' tentacle, it breaks off. This eight-armed sea creature just grows a new one so it can swim away. Finally, an octopus is a strong swimmer and can move fast if it is in danger. Octopuses protect themselves in such different ways. In our community, we can stand up for our members to keep everyone safe too.

Below Standard

a octopus has tentacles that can brake. Thay live in coral reefs. Thay
squrit ink Thay can be like a snak

APPENDIX H

Sample Exemplar and Below Standard: Grade 6

Grade 6 Exemplar (Post)

The article "Once Shot for Advocating For Girls' Education, Malala Is Going To Oxford" and the autobiography *I Am Malala* describe how Malala Yousafzai uses her voice to try to gain rights for girls even after she was shot by the Taliban. In both of these sources, Malala uses techniques to persuade others to use their own voices. By blogging, continuing to speak up even after being shot, and inspiring others with her words, Malala sets an effective model for how the average citizen could take actions to support their own causes.

In the article, the author describes how Malala tried to change the world through her blog. When militants took control of Malala's hometown Swat in 2007, the Taliban "banned the education of girls." That same year, Malala began blogging about "life under Taliban domination." Since blog posts can be seen by anyone, Malala was able to use this to tell people all over the world about how many girls were being robbed of their educations. According to Malala in her autobiography *I Am Malala*, " 'Let us pick up our books and our pens,' I said. 'They are our most powerful weapons. One child, one teacher, one book and one pen can change the world.' " Malala certainly did this by blogging. She used her blog as a way for others to see what was going on in Pakistan. This can certainly be used to motivate others who would like to take action in support of their own causes. Using a blog is a great way to raise awareness about things that should be changed or a way to educate people. Blogs can reach people all over the world who can be persuaded to care about your cause and may help get millions of people involved.

In 2011, Malala returned to school and also "began publicly advocating for girls' education." On her way home from school one day in 2012, Malala was shot in her head, neck, and shoulders by a masked gunman. She survived this experience and continued to speak out against what was happening to girls in her community. In her autobiography, Malala writes, "My only regret was that I hadn't had a chance to speak to them before they shot me. Now they'd never hear what I had to say." Malala did not want to be defined as "the girl who was shot by the Taliban." Instead, she wanted to be "the girl who fought for education." Malala teaches us that we should never give up when we face challenges. Standing up for something that we believe in can be difficult. We may not always feel as if we have the support we need or we may experience failure when we try. Since Malala never gave up when faced with her difficulties, her work can motivate average citizens to continue fighting for their own causes, even when things go their way. Her story can be used to remind people to never give up fighting for what they believe in.

Malala became very famous after she was shot by the Taliban for standing up for the rights of girls to go to school. She used this fame to inspire others through her autobiography and speeches. Malala gave a speech at the United Nations when she was sixteen. She said "If you want to see your future bright, you have to start working now and not wait for anyone else." In her autobiography, Malala states, "I would do everything in my power to help educate girls just like her. This was the war I was going to fight." She inspired so many people with her words and even won the Nobel Peace Prize when she was eighteen. Average people can be motivated by Malala to use their own words to inspire others. Motivating people through words is a really good way to make your point and get more people involved in your cause. It also allows you to connect with people on a personal level, which might get them to care more about your cause.

(continued)

In conclusion, Malala is an effective leader who can persuade others to do their best. She used her blog, continued to fight for a girl's right to an education after being shot, and inspired others with her autobiography and speeches. Malala is a great example of what a person should do when they are fighting for a cause.

Grade 6 Below Standard

I will write about Malala. Both of the articles showed that motivates the average citizen to take actions and support a cause.

The author of Once Shot for Advocating For Girls' Education, Malala Is Going To Oxford thinks that Malala motivates others by telling her story to other. In the quote on pg. 3, the author writes that "If you want to see your future bright, you have to start working now and not wait for anyone else," she said. The author of Primary Source Excerpts from Autobiography: *I Am Malala* thinks "Let us pick up our books and our pens. They are our most powerful weapons. One child, one teacher, one book and one pen can change the world." This is how Malala persuades others.

The author shows that Malala does not want to be just the person that got shot. It says "I don't want to be thought of as the girl who was shot by the Taliban but the girl who fought for education. This is the cause to which I want to devote my life." She wants to help others get an education. In the text it says "Malala and her father established the Malala Fund in 2013, an organization dedicated to giving all girls access to education." This is how Malala motivates people to fight for girls' education.

Malala shows how to motivate people to help many causes.

APPENDIX I

Grade-Leveled Gist Sequences to Meet State/National Standards

Main Frame

Who (noun)	Did what (verb)	When/Where (preposition)	Why/What happened (conjunction)	Who	Did What
Children	like to play	outside	because	they	can run.

Example: *Each week, expand/vary your gist frame structure to teach your grammar standards. You can call this "flex the gist" with your students.*

Who	Did what ***(past tense verb)***	When/Where	Why/What happened	Who	Did what ***(modal)***
Children	**liked** to play	outside	because	they	**could** run.

Kindergarten: Use simple sentences
- Use plural noun, verb, adjectives, and prepositions (*out*, *on*, *with*); capitalize the first word in a sentence and "I"; use end punctuation.

Grade 1: Use compound sentences
- Use common, proper, and possessive nouns, possessive and indefinite pronouns (*me*, *my*, *they*, *anyone*).
- Use adjectives, common conjunctions (*but*, *because*, *so*), determiners (*the*, *an*), and prepositions (*during*).
- Match verb tense (*hop*, *hops*) to convey time (*will walk*, *walked*); use commas in a series.

Grade 2: Expand and rearrange compound sentences
- Use collective nouns (group), irregular plurals (*feet*, *mice*), and reflective pronouns (*myself*).
- Use irregular past verbs (*sat*, *told*), adjectives, adverbs, commas in greetings, and apostrophes for contractions or possessives.
- Capitalize holidays, product names, and geographic names.

Grade 3: Complex sentences
- Use subject–verb and pronoun–antecedent agreement and subordinating conjunctions.
- Use comparative and superlative adjectives and adverbs, capitalize titles, and put commas before quotes.

Grade 4: Expand and rearrange complex sentences
- Use relative pronouns (*whose*, *that*) and adverbs (*where*, *when*); progressive tense (*I was walking*), and modals (*could*, *may*).
- Use commas before coordinating conjunctions.

(continued)

Grade-Leveled Gist Sequences *(page 2 of 2)*

Grade 5: Expand and rearrange complex sentences • Use verb tense perfect (*I had walked*; *I will have walked*) and correlative conjunctions (*neither/nor*). • Use commas in a list, with introductory element, to set off *yes/no*, to tag a question (*It's true, no?*) or when addressing (*That you, Dian?*).
Grades 6–8: Compound-complex sentences • Use clear pronoun referents; appositives; commas, dashes, and parentheses to set off nonrestrictive/parenthetical material. • Vary for reader interest and style (simple to compound-complex), verbals (gerunds, participles). • Use active/passive voice (verbs: indicative, imperative, interrogative, conditional, subjunctive mood) and ellipses.

APPENDIX J

Grades K–1 TIDE Graphic Organizer with Fullest Stems

Name: ______________________________

T	I know about		
I D	Can	Need	Have
E	These are facts about		

T ______ ID ______ ID ______ ID ______ E ______

APPENDIX K

Grades 2+ TIDE Graphic Organizer: Important Evidence and Details

T	Topic introduction	
I D	Important evidence	Details (say more)
	Important evidence	Details (say more)
	Important evidence	Details (say more)
E	Ending	

APPENDIX L

Grades 3+ TIDE Graphic Organizer: Important Evidence and Details—Scaffolded

TAG Thesis		
	I: Important evidence that supports each idea. • For example ______. • For instance ______. • The author stated ______. • According to the text ______. • From the reading I know that ______. • In paragraph ______ it said ______.	D: Details that explain how/why the evidence supports your claim. • This shows ______ because ______. • This means ______ because ______. • This proves that ______. • This is important because ______. • A reader can infer that ______.
Paragraph #1 • **F**irst • **T**o start • **T**o begin	t- i- i-	
Paragraph #2 • **A**lso • **N**ext • **P**lus • **I**n addition	t- i- i-	
Paragraph #3 • **F**inally • **L**ast	t- i- i-	
End:	**A**s you can see __________. **A**ll in all __________. **I**n conclusion __________.	

APPENDIX M

Grades 4+ TIDE Graphic Organizer: Important Evidence and Details—Scaffolded with Tips

Self-talk ______________________________ Goals/tools ____________________

Reminder: No prepositions/conjunctions/articles; yes power words, nouns, adjectives, verbs, abbreviations, and images/symbols.

<table>
<tr><td>T</td><td colspan="2">Topic introduction
Context (time/place, definition, titles/summary):
Coherent focus:
TS:</td></tr>
<tr><td rowspan="3">I
D</td><td>Important evidence
t –

i –</td><td>Detailed examination
d –</td></tr>
<tr><td>Important evidence
t –

i –</td><td>Detailed examination
d –</td></tr>
<tr><td>Important evidence
t –

i –</td><td>Detailed examination
d –</td></tr>
<tr><td>E</td><td colspan="2">Ending</td></tr>
</table>

Note. The "t" also reminds students to add their subtopics to each section.

APPENDIX N

CSPACE Graphic Organizer

Name ______________________ Date ____________

Self-talk ______________________________

Characters	Tell	Show
Setting (hint)		
Problem/Purpose		
Action: (details) *main* events	1. 2. 3. 4.	
Conclusion:		
Emotion: characters' response or lesson/theme		

APPENDIX O

TIDE Stem Banks

	K–2	Gr 3–8+
T	I know about I know facts about ______ can do so much.	-TAG: Name of source(s) . . . by . . . -The text portrays (give gist of text) -While ______, actually ______.

I
D
	Important Evidence
	Gr K–1
	• can ______
	• have ______
	• do ______
	• A first fact is that ______
	• First, next, last (K–1 only)
	
	Gr 2–8
	• A first example,
	• Another example,
	• Finally,
	• This is conveyed, shown
	• Specifically,
	• As demonstrated by
	• This can be observed/noted/seen
	• As stated in the text, ______
	• A clear example is
	• ______ states, "______"
	• According to ______, "______"
	• The article says, "______"
	• In ______'s view, "______"
	• In ______, they explain, "______"
	• In the story, ______ says, "______"
		Detailed Examination
		• Give more detail or explanation
		  o This shows that ______ because ______
		  o This supports ______
		  o The character might be thinking ______
		• Make an inference
		  o This means/implies that ______
		  o This suggests that ______
		  o It seems that ______
		  o By using ______, this suggests ______
		  o On a deeper level ______
		• Make a connection
		  o As a result, ______
		  o One might think ______
		  o One could compare this to
		  o This caused ______
		  o Due to ______
		  o Since ______
		• Evaluate: Judge, Question, Challenge
		  o This is important because ______
		  o This is fair/unfair because ______
		  o This proves that ______
		  o The author used these words to______
		  o This point of view may be challenged because ______
		  o Readers may think ______

E	Compare introduction to end to ensure they differ but relate. • In conclusion, • ______ can do so much. • ______ are terrific at ____________.	• Overall, • To sum up, • Without a doubt, • The evidence clearly shows, • All things considered,

APPENDIX P

Example of Building a Writer's Toolkit

My Writer's Notebook

	K-2	Gr 3-8+
T	I know about ____ I know facts about ____ ____ can do so much.	TAG (Title, Author, Gist) is about ____ - The main character learns / discovers ____, - The text portrays how ____ - While____, actually ____.
ID	Important Evidence Gr K-1: ____Can___, have)___, do___ A first fact is that___ (K-1 only) Gr 2-8: An example is ___ This is conveyed / shown when Specifically, As demonstrated by This can be observed/noted/seen As stated in the text, ____ ____ states, ____ In ___'s view, ____ ___ agrees when she/he writes ___ In___, they explain, ___ In the story, they say, ___ By using ___, this suggests ___	Detailed Examination Give more detail or explanation: This shows that ____ because ____ This supports ____ Make an inference: This suggests / implies / means that ____ It seems that____ / Readers may think ____ By using ____, the suggests ____ On a deeper level ____ Make a connection: As a result ____/ This caused ____ One could compare this to ____ Due to / Since ____ Evaluate: Judge, Question, Challenge: This is important or fair/unfair because This proves that / The point of view is that
E	Compare intro to end (differ, but relate) In conclusion, ____ ____ can do so much. ____ are terrific at ____.	Overall, To sum up, Without a doubt, All things considered,

POWeR

Plan

Pre-read for gist

Pull apart task

- Do what?

Pick Ideas (from text)

Organize ideas

Topic Introduction

Important Evidence

Detailed Examination

End

(L – Language box)

Write (draft),

and say more

edit

Revise

Ways to Link Ideas and Create Cohesion in Writing: A Maturity Continuum

Type of Link / Cohesive Tie	Age Range	Example	Description
Temporal Links	Gr K-1	first, next, last, finally, later	Move beyond these quickly, as they can stunt quality
Connectors that emphasize relationships	Gr 3 +	for, and, nor, but, or, yet, so	FANBOYS (coordinating conjunctions)
		after, before, until, when	Show more complex relationships than do coordinating conjunctions. Cue words to reveal text structures such as cause/effect or compare/contrast as well. They not only create cohesion but show relationships.
		where, wherever	
		For example, for instance	
		Although, because, since, yet, unless, as a result, despite, in order to	
		However, instead of, rather, despite	
Semantic repetition	All	Birds can soar. They soar (or fly) to the sky. (synonyms, repeated words etc)	Synonyms or exact words repeated
Anaphoric	All	Sue is a cook. She makes food.	Refer back to idea from prior sentence (pronoun referent)
Global	Gr 3 +	Now I will describe, In the prior section, Another way in which	Linking phrases or sentences leading to or linking back to next or prior content globally

(continued)

Example of Building a Writer's Toolkit *(page 2 of 2)*

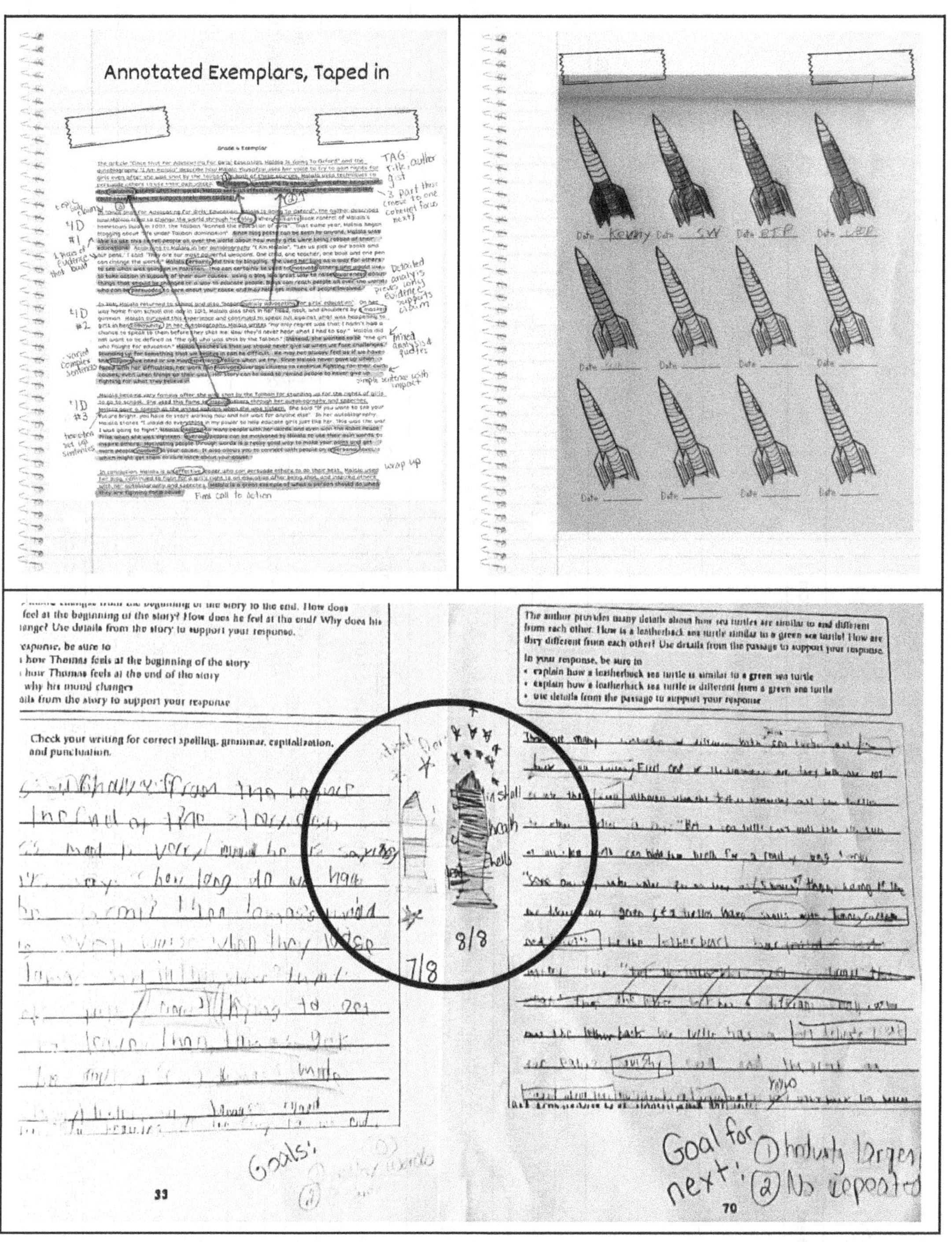

APPENDIX Q

K–8 Composition Development Phases

	Context	Topic	Information	Details/Examination	End
K–1 Early Knowledge Telling		Octopuses	An octopus swims (2–3 sets of facts)	in the ocean. (2–3 partial or full details)	This is what . . .
		Octopuses can do so much.	They swim fast. (3+ sets of facts)	They can go 50 miles per hour. (3+ fuller details or sentences per fact)	Octopuses survive in special ways.
Gr 2–3 Knowledge Telling	Octopuses can protect themselves. An octopus can swim up to 25 miles per hour so they can escape from predators. In coral reefs, they can hide because they do not want to be seen. (3+ body chunks.) These sea creatures are so good at protecting themselves. (Show connections. Add inference or show connections in second sentence or via conjunctions such as *and, so, but, because*.)				
	Ants are tiny insects with amazing jobs. The soldier ant uses its gigantic head to block the entrance from dangerous invaders who might kill them or take their food. (Three sets of these types of sentences.) Small bugs have big jobs!				
Gr 4–5 Knowledge Transforming	Time/place Definition Gist, Titles		2–3 quality, representative (not exhaustive) facts, or explained quote	State connections: explain meaning of information or why it was given	
	GW Carver, a famous Southern peanut farmer in the 1800s, helped farmers better use soil and crops they grew. . . . After helping farmers plant peanuts, they now had too many. To solve this problem, George taught farmers to use science to innovate and make peanut milk, peanut paper, and peanut soap. . . . George kept coming up on his own with good ideas that worked as solutions.				
	Time/place Definition Gist, Titles	Coherent focus	Well-chosen, representative fact or well-explained quote	Nongeneric examination begins to make new meaning/gain new insights that prove why evidence presented was best choice to support topic statement claim	Wrap up and extend with new thought
	Both the effects and rescue efforts made something already tragic even worse at every step. A first effect was that just moving their bodies through the water became difficult because the penguins would "wobble and roll in the dense oil," unable to move freely. Not only did the oil ruin their nearby food, but it also must have threatened their ability to catch even distant, untouched food they need in the water.				

	Context	Topic	Information	Details/Examination	End
Middle School/High School Knowledge Transforming to Knowledge Crafting			2–3 fact details or well-explained quotes that are representative (not exhaustive)	Insightful analysis/inference that notices beyond what is obviously stated and proves why evidence given was best choice to give	Wrap up and extend with some new insight
	Unless they fully geared their talks to their audiences, this suggests Jobs values finding what you love more so than Obama, who puts more importance on working hard all the time no matter what you do.				
				Make deeper connections and more layers of insight/multiple perspectives	
	Given that Jobs puts far less stress to hard work than Obama, he likely had to overcome fewer hurdles with dogged determination all through his life than Obama may have, or he was thinking about his audience and how these competitive college graduates had proven they are already hard working.				
				Infer motives, make a broader connection, evaluate, question/challenge text, consider alternatives, keener perception	Wrap up and extend with new insight or connection
	Some might argue Obama's advice is more likely to lead to success for most students, which may be true. However, Obama's advice is limiting in that he does not encourage students to find what they enjoy at all, whereas Jobs' advice suggests that everyone can find happiness along with success. While it could be dangerous to only pursue what you love, it is discriminating to tell public school students to work hard with no regard for their happiness.				

Note. Though grade leveled, we typically see writing progression bands of at least **five grades** within one classroom. Some students may include more or fewer body sections within a paragraph.

APPENDIX R

Detailed Examination Stems

Features of Detailed Examination Students May Notice and Name

In detailed examination, justify how or why the important evidence proves the topic statement (claim or thesis). Use these not just to <u>*link to*</u> *evidence, but also* <u>*link back*</u> *to strengthen the piece's opening central focus.*

Expand evidence with more detail or explanation.

- Add relevant details/evidence that make the overall piece's main idea stronger/clearer.
  - Upper grades: Identify and weave in additional evidence to bolster examination section.
- Explain how your chosen evidence supports the topic.
  - This shows that . . . because . . . Or link back to big idea with *and, so, but, because*.

Add inferences (Levels 1–3).

- 1: Restate the obvious, almost word for word or in an overly general or surface way.
- 2a: Expand: Explain easily implied, but not directly stated, more specific inference.
  - This means that . . . This suggests that . . . It seems that . . . This implies . . . This reveals . . .
- 2b: Label/classify evidence with one word (or short phrase) that captures core meaning (e.g., *brave*).
- 3. Reveal a new insight or meaning (may be surprising, but reasonable).
  - Note what is interesting, surprising, strange, revealing, and connect this back to big idea.

Make connections.

- Connect two or more ideas in text(s) to create a new idea or show their relationship.
- Deepen meanings made by relating evidence to own experiences/connections.
  - Build on personal, *specific* connections to make *general* observations (shed use of *I*).
- Recall own related background knowledge; carefully use this to enrich meaning of evidence.
- Cause/effect or contrast: This caused . . . Due to . . . Since . . . As a result . . . Led to . . . While . . . , actually . . .
- Invent hypothetical alternative or multiple meanings.
- If it were otherwise (Instead of) . . . then . . .
- It could/would/might; On a deeper level . . . ; By ____________, the author ________________
- It might seem that . . . , but actually (compare/contrast)
- This might mean . . . or . . . , but the better interpretation is . . . because . . .
- Evaluate: judge, question, or challenge.
- Analyze significance:
  - This matters/is important because . . .
  - The author used these words (or this technique) because . . .
  - Identify signposts (Probst/Beers) and analyze their significance.
  - First versus third person makes reader feel . . . (involved, emotional vs. like observer).
- Judge by implicit, external criteria, often moral judgment (good/bad).
- Synthesize: use metaphor or analogy.
- Without wandering too far from text, offer tightly connected comparison or even metaphor.

APPENDIX S

Goal-Setting Menu for Grade 2: Informative/Opinion

Author: ______________________________ Date: ______________

Topic: ______________________ ☐ Informative/Explanatory ☐ Opinion
☐ Used Graphic Organizer

	Pts	Self	Peer	Adult
Topic Introduction 1 pt = almost full topic, 2 pts = full topic stated				
Full topic sentence/State opinion	2			
Important **D**etails/**R**easons & **E**laborations (Information and details relate to topic) 1 pt = adds more, 2 pts = strengthens fact/reason's support of topic/opinion				
Information from text: Fact/Reason	1			
Details explain how: facts develop topic/reason support opinion	2			
Information from text: Fact/Reason	1			
Details explain how: facts develop topic/reason support opinion	2			
Information from text: Fact/Reason	1			
Details explain how: facts develop topic/reason support opinion	2			
Ending				
Conclusion	1			
Links				
Use links	1			
Language				
Strong vocabulary	2			
Varied sentences (long, short, compound)	1			
Conventions				
Neat handwriting	1			
Grammar: nouns, verbs, prepositions, adjectives/adverbs, and conjunctions	1			
Punctuation: Every sentence has capitals and end marks	1			
Spelling	1			
Total	20			

Done Well:

Goals:

APPENDIX T

Scoring Guidelines for Grade 2: Informative/Opinion

Introduce Topic (W.2.1 and W.2.2)

- Topic introduction states full topic in a complete sentence:
  - **2 pts:** *An octopus can protect itself in many ways./I would like to be an octopus for a day (if opinion).*
  - **1 pt:** *Octopuses are busy every day.* (Does not respond to prompt fully.)
- If one fact follows "because," it is not a topic sentence (unless gives overarching category):
  - **Yes:** *An octopus can protect itself because it has good defenses.* (Then all facts show defenses.)
  - **No:** *An octopus can protect itself because it has tentacles. They also blend in.*
- If opinion piece, should convey consistent opinion in topic sentence or via reasons to get full 2 points.

Important Details/Reasons and Elaborations (W.2.1 and W.2.2)

Important Information/Reasons

- Relevant and on par with complexity of texts read (precise verbs, specific adjectives . . .). States more than barebone facts. Needs detail and specificity in presentation of information. Copied facts must be relevant.
- When more than three different sets of information/reasons are given, evaluate first three (or any representative three).
- Each new information/idea grouped in its own clear sentence or section (group of sentences) on that idea.

Details/Elaborations

- Make clearer ***how*** facts "develop points" or ***how*** reasons "support opinion." Can include (a) an explanation of fact or (b) simply additional detail but strengthens the point (not just adds info). I & D can be one or two or more sentences.
- Following this first fact sentence: "They can break off tentacles and grow new ones."
  - **2 pts** = *Without arms, they could not swim away from danger and would die.* (Explains fact's importance.)
  - **2 pts** = *They detach them when enemies attack them.* (Fact serves to further explain self-protection.)
  - **1 pt** = *This helps them survive. This must hurt.* (Not specific enough.)
  - **1 pt** = *They do this daily. They have eight tentacles.* (True, but don't develop central idea of protection.)

Ending (W.2.1 and W.2.2)

- Wraps up main idea in novel way, referring back to overall topic. Does not repeat topic sentence, word for word:
  - *An octopus can protect itself in many ways.*
- Give 0.5 for formulaic endings that, for example, repeat topic sentence word for word or "This is how . . ."

(continued)

Note. References are to Common Core State Standards for English Language Arts, Grade 2.

Scoring Guidelines for Grade 2: Informative/Opinion *(page 2 of 2)*

Links (W.2.2.C)

- Words and phrases connect similar ideas within a group of information or link to the topic. Look for two or more carefully repeated phrases/ideas that link ideas throughout (*and*, *also*, *because*). Or use cohesive devices to link: pronouns that refer back to key idea, key word repeated (0.5 for robotic links).

Language (L.2.1.F)

- Vocabulary: **Skim 50 body words**. Count strong words. (Exclude fully copied quotes, but do count integrated words lifted from text.) Deduct "banned" words (*stuff, things*). 5 words (10%) = 1 pt, 8 words (15%) = 2 pts.
  - (In class: students circle all strong words and write # at top; teachers set 1–2 pt criteria for each piece.)
- Varied sentences: **Skim five body sentences** for CCSS L's—mix of compound sentences, openers, closers, adjectives, or adverbial or prepositional phrases or clauses. (*Down the road lived a green toad* or *Walking slowly, she smiled*)

Conventions (L.2.1–L.2.2)

- Handwriting: legible
- Grammar correct in 60% of N + V + P + adj/adv + C sentence(s). Don't award point if no sentences meet this criterion.
- Punctuation: All sentences have capitals and period, commas within lists.
- Spelling: Award point if 94% of words spelled correctly; up to 3 per 50 words misspelled, acceptable.

APPENDIX U

Goal-Setting Menu for Grade 6: Informative/Argument

Author: ______________________________ Date: ________________

Topic: ________________________

☐ Used Graphic Organizer
☐ Informative/Explanatory Argument

	Pts	Adult	Peer	Self
Topic Introduction				
Introduce engaging context clearly	1			
Focused thesis statement/claim	1			
Important evidence (knowledge)/**R**eason **D**etailed examination (understanding)/**E**laboration (all link to central idea)				
Information: Evidence/Reason 1 pt = topic stated and well set up + 1 pt = well chosen	2			
Detailed examination and analysis: develops topic/supports claim 1 pt = explains (own words), 2 pts = examines significance/importance	2			
Information: Evidence/Reason 1 pt = topic stated and well set up + 1 pt = well chosen	2			
Detailed examination and analysis: develops topic/supports claim 1 pt = explains (own words), 2 pts = examines significance/importance	2			
Information: Evidence/Reason 1 pt = topic stated and well set up + 1 pt = well chosen	2			
Detailed examination and analysis: develops topic/supports claim 1 pt = explains (own words), 2 pts = examines significance/importance	2			
Ending				
Concluding section follows from central information or examination 1 pt = relates, 2 pts = relates and extends	2			
Links				
Appropriate transitions clarify the relationships among ideas and concepts	1			
Language				
Uses formal style, precise language, domain-specific vocabulary	1			
Vary sentences for reader interest, style, and meaning	1			
Conventions				
CCSS grade level: grammar, punctuation for effect and spelling	1			
Total	20			
Done Well:				
Goals:				

APPENDIX V

Scoring Guidelines for Grade 6: Informative/Argument

Topic Introduction (W.6.1/2)

Context: who/what, did what. Include time/place, definition or title, and brief gist.

- In essay, at least 1 sentence gives context. In (low tide) paragraph, topic statement includes context.
- (For full essay, context more developed but still not a "retell." If context is overdone, subtract ½ point.)

Focused Thesis/Claim

- State topic/claim + (**respond to prompt**) central idea(s) about topic/claim.
  - *The sources use examples and imagery and offer a vision to show how social media can further good causes.*
  - *The video, blog, and text use different methods to convey this message, but all inspire action.*
- If "because" is used in topic statement, it leads to an overview of ideas or reasons, not diving into one idea.

Important Evidence/Reasons and Detailed Examination/Elaboration (W.6.1/2)

Important Evidence/Reason: relevant facts, definitions, details, or quotes inform

- 1pt = *Set up:* To be reader friendly, group related information in a clearly named category (mini-claim/subtopic/point—often 1–2 words), and clearly introduce evidence (1–2 sentences—paragraph; own paragraph—essay).
- 1pt = *Relevance:* quote(s) or 2–3 rich details on par with complexity of text read, clearly develop/support points.
- Include 3 body sections to develop/support points. If only 2 sections, be clear why.
  - If more than three sections, evaluate first 3 (or any representative 3).
  - Information represents, but not necessarily exhausts, each idea.

Detailed Examination helps reader make new meanings about central idea. (High tide = more detail)

- 2 pts = synthesizes different parts of text or conveys new insights beyond stating the obvious.
- 1 pt = may use stem (e.g., "This shows that . . .") or predictable explanation but does not offer a strong inference.

Ending (W.6.1/2)

- 1 pt = wraps up central idea in novel way; does not repeat topic statement, but synthesizes (low tide = 2 pts).
- 2 pts = extends to bigger picture; addresses "so what?"
  - *Together these approaches are more likely to inspire action than one alone might.*

(continued)

Note. References are to Common Core State Standards for English Language Arts, Grade 6.

Scoring Guidelines for Grade 6: Informative/Argument *(page 2 of 2)*

Links (W.6.1.c)

- Words and phrases connect similar ideas within a group of information or link to the topic. Give partial credit for formulaic such as *first, next, last*, but begin here if no links, and move ahead soon to repeating central idea.
- In essay, each paragraph begins with a topic sentence or phrase that serves as a link to central idea.

Language (L.6.2.b and L.6.3.a)

- Vocabulary: **Skim 50 body words**. Count strong words. (Exclude fully copied quotes, but do count integrated words lifted from text.) Deduct "banned" words (*stuff, things*). 8+ words (15%).
  - (In class: Students circle all strong words and write # at top; teachers set 1–2 pt criteria for each piece.)
- Varied sentences: **Skim 5 body sentences** for complexity, pronouns, openers, closers, adjectives, adverbial or prepositional phrases or clauses. 3/5+ or more (some still simple) well constructed.
  - (In class: Teach mini-lessons/reinforce CCSS L standards, then require each after taught.)

Conventions (L.6.1-L6.2)

- Sentences complete—no fragments or run-ons. See CCSS (i.e., no vague pronouns, use commas, dashes to set off parenthetical elements). 90%+ grammar correct. 98% spelled correctly; up to 1 word misspelled per 50.

APPENDIX W

Scale for Quick Writes: Grades 3+

Name: ______________________________ Date: ______________

TtIDtID Rubric (T = Topic, t = subtopic, I = Important evidence, D = Detailed analysis)	Possible Points	Teacher	Self	Peer
Topic 1 point = topic restated and well set up	1			
Information from text: facts, definitions, details/reason 1 point = well-chosen information	1			
Detailed examination: develops and supports the topic 1 point = adds more 2 pts = strengthens fact/reasons support of topic	2			
Content Points	**4**			
Language—Bonus points				
Links with synonyms/pronouns Phrases connect ideas	1			
Strong words and powerful phrases	1			
Varied sentences—uses conjunctions, prepositional phrases	1			
Grammar, punctuation, and spelling	1			
Links and Language Points	**4**			
Grand Total Points	**8**			

APPENDIX X

Explain Your Scores

After scoring, color-coding, and annotating your writing or after peer-scoring, complete this sheet to explain why you gave the scores you did. Refer to the Scoring Guidelines to support your reasoning for each area.

Summarize the opening context—the topic, author, time/place, or big idea.

Summarize the topic sentence or thesis.

What is the coherent focus or list?

Summarize each I (Important evidence), followed by each D (Detailed examination) here:

1st I: (Explain how it is relevant and compelling)

1st D:

2nd I:

2nd D:

3rd I (if needed):

3rd D (if needed):

(continued)

Explain Your Scores *(page 2 of 2)*

Summarize the ending, including extension.

How did the writer link or cohere the writing? Write transition words or repeated ideas/ phrases that link.

Write strong vocabulary here.

Select 2–3 sentences. Write conjunctions, prepositional phrases, and so on, that make sentences strong here.

APPENDIX Y

TIDE Writing Rubric: Adjusted Holistic and Analytic Scale

TIDE Writing Rubric for Expository/Informational Writing (Essay)

To use this single-point rubric, check off the "meeting expectations" elements if they met the standard. If not, jot a short note about why in the column on the left, or why it was exceeded on the right. Teachers often target one area (rather than the full list) for the class to score for and comment on when using this tool.

Category	Beginning/ Approaching	Meeting Expectations	Well Developed
Ideas (Content and Development) **Focus:** The presence and quality of a main idea; the extent to which the main idea is developed through details; the quality of the details used to support the main idea.		*A main idea is clear and is developed through relevant details.* • **Thesis Statement:** Clearly states a thesis with three well-developed and insightful ideas. • **Important Evidence:** Includes two specific, relevant, and thoughtfully selected pieces of evidence for each idea from the thesis. • **Detailed Examination:** Examines and analyzes each piece of important evidence with depth and ties it to the thesis through meaningful connections.	
Organization (Structure and Transitions) **Focus:** The extent to which the writing is organized as a whole (externally); the extent to which the ideas are logically sequenced (internally) with a beginning, middle, and ending; the quality of transitional words/phrases. The writing is organized with effective use of varied transitions.		*The writing is organized with effective use of varied transitions.* • **Introduction:** Clearly introduces the topic with background information and a focused thesis. • **Paragraph Structure:** Each paragraph builds on one idea from the thesis and develops it logically. • **Clarity and Flow:** Ideas are logically and cohesively sequenced. • **Ending:** Summarizes the thesis and extends ideas thoughtfully to broader implications (e.g., connections to real-world applications). • **Links:** Transitions are varied, purposeful, and enhance overall coherence between sections.	

(continued)

Note. Used by permission of Tanya Veinotte Frowd.

TIDE Writing Rubric *(page 2 of 2)*

Category	Beginning/ Approaching	Meeting Expectations	Well Developed
Language Use (Sentence Fluency, Word Choice, Voice) **Focus:** The quality of stylistic choices (voice, word choice, variety of sentence lengths and types/ syntax) and their impact on the writing. Sentence structure is considered in terms of style, not grammatical correctness.		*Language use contributes to clear and fluid writing.* • **Fluency:** Sentences are varied in length, structure, and style, enhancing fluency and engagement. • **Word Choice:** Precise, vivid, and expressive, with topic-specific vocabulary that enhances clarity and precision. • **Voice (Tone and Style):** Engaging, purposeful, and distinct while maintaining a formal tone appropriate for expository writing.	
Conventions (Mechanics and Grammar) **Focus:** The extent to which the writing demonstrates control over expected grade-level conventions and their impact on communication.		*A variety of generally correct conventions contribute to effective communication.* • **Error Control:** Few or no errors in grammar, punctuation, spelling, or capitalization. • **Impact:** Conventions enhance readability, clarity, and polish.	

References

Aktaş, N. (2023). Does primary students' writing ergonomics affect their handwriting legibility? *Language Teaching and Educational Research, 6*(1), 24–38.

Alamargot, D., & Chanquoy, L. (2001). *Through the models of writing.* Kluwer Academic.

Alarcón-Rubio, D., Sánchez-Medina, J. & Prieto-García, J. (2014). Executive function and verbal self-regulation in childhood: Developmental linkages between partially internalized private speech and cognitive flexibility. *Early Childhood Research Quarterly, 29*(2) 95–105.

Allyn, P. (n.d.). https://pamallyn.com/quotes.

Altemeier, L., Abbott, R., & Berninger V. W. (2007). Executive functions for reading and writing in typical literacy development and dyslexia. *Journal of Clinical and Experimental Neuropsychology, 30*(5), 588–606.

Altemeier L. E., Abbott R. D., & Berninger V. W. (2008). Executive functions for reading and writing in typical literacy development and dyslexia. *Journal of Clinical and Experimental Neuropsychology, 30*(5), 588–606.

Altemeier L., Jones J., Abbott R. D., & Berninger V. W. (2006). Executive functions in becoming writing readers and reading writers: Note taking and report writing in third and fifth graders. *Developmental Neuropsychology, 29*(1), 161–173.

Alves, R. A., & Limpo, T. (2015). Progress in written language bursts, pauses, transcription, and written composition across schooling. *Scientific Studies of Reading, 19*(5), 374–391.

Anderson, J. (2005). *Mechanically inclined.* Routledge.

Anderson, P. L. (2000). Using literature to teach social skills to adolescents with LD. *Intervention in School and Clinic, 35*(5), 271–279.

Anderson, V., & Spencer-Smith, M. M. (2013). Children's frontal lobes: no longer silent. In D. Stuss & R. Knight (Eds.), *Principles of frontal lobe function* (2nd ed., pp. 18–134). Oxford University Press.

Andrusyk, D., & Andrusyk, S. (2003). *Improving student social skills through the use of cooperative learning strategies* (master's research project). Saint Xavier University and SkyLight Field-Based Master's Program.

Arán Filippetti, V., & Richaud M. C. (2015). Do executive functions predict written composition?: Effects beyond age, verbal intelligence and reading comprehension. *Acta Neuropsychologica, 13*(4), 331–349.

Ardanouy, E., Zesiger, P., & Delage, H. (2024). Intensive and explicit derivational morphology training in school-aged children: An effective way to improve morphological awareness, spelling, and reading? *Reading and Writing, 37*(10), 2049–2073.

Arrimada, M., Torrance, M., & Fidalgo, R. (2018). Effects of teaching planning strategies to first-grade writers. *British Journal of Educational Psychology, 89*(4), 670–688.

Arslan, B., Taatgen, N. A., & Verbrugge, R. (2017). Five-year-olds' systematic errors in second-order false belief tasks are due to first-order theory of mind strategy selection: A computational modeling study. *Frontiers in Psychology, 8*, 275.

Bang, H. J. (2013). Reliability of National Writing Project's Analytic Writing Continuum Assessment System. *Journal of Writing Assessment, 6*(1). https://escholarship.org/uc/item/03g148gh.

Baron, L. S., & Arbel, Y. (2022). Inner speech and executive function in children with developmental language disorder: Implications for assessment and intervention. *Perspectives of the ASHA Special Interest Groups, 7*(6), 1645–1659.

Beal, C. R., Garrod, A. C., & Bonitatibus, G. J. (1990). Fostering children's revision skills through training in comprehension monitoring. *Journal of Educational Psychology, 82*(2), 275–280.

Beck, I. L., McKeown, M. G., & Kucan, L. (2013). *Bringing words to life: Robust vocabulary instruction* (2nd ed.). Guilford Press.

Benedek-Wood, E., Mason, L. H., Wood, P. H., Hoffman, K. E., & McGuire, A. (2014). An experimental examination of quick writing in the middle school science classroom. *Learning Disabilities: A Contemporary Journal, 12*(1), 69–92.

Bennett, M. P., Knight, R., Patel, S., So, T., Dunning, D., Barnhofer, T., et al. (2021). Decentering as a core component in the psychological treatment and prevention of youth anxiety and depression: a narrative review and insight report. *Translational Psychiatry, 11*(1), 288.

Berkman E. T., Falk, E. B., & Lieberman, M. D. (2012). Interactive effects of three core goal pursuit processes on brain control systems: Goal maintenance, performance monitoring, and response inhibition. *PLOS ONE, 7*(6), e40334.

Berninger, V. W. (1999). Coordinating transcription and text generation in working memory during composing: Automatic and constructive processes. *Learning Disability Quarterly, 22*(2), 99–112.

Berninger, V. W., & Abbott, S. (2020). *Revised PAL research-based reading and writing lessons and reproducible instructional materials.* Pearson.

Berninger, V., Abbott, R., Cook, C. R., & Nagy, W. (2017). Relationships of attention and executive functions to oral language, reading, and writing skills and systems in middle childhood and early adolescence. *Journal of Learning Disabilities, 50*(4), 434–449.

Berninger, V. W., Abbott, R. D., Swanson, H. L., Lovitt, D., Trivedi, P., Lin, S. J., et al. (2010). Relationship of word- and sentence-level working memory to reading and writing in second, fourth, and sixth grade. *Language, Speech, and Hearing Services in Schools, 41*(2), 179–193.

Berninger, V. W., Nagy, W., Tanimoto, S., Thompson, R., & Abbott, R. D. (2015). Computer instruction in handwriting, spelling, and composing for students with specific learning disabilities in grades 4 to 9. *Computers and Education, 81*(C), 154–168.

Berninger, V. W., Vaughan, K. B., Abbott, R. D., Abbott, S. P., Rogan, L. W., Brooks, A., et al. (1997). Treatment of handwriting problems in beginning writers: Transfer from handwriting to composition. *Journal of Educational Psychology, 89*(4), 652–666.

Berninger, V. W., Vaughan, K., Abbott, R. D., Begay, K., Coleman, K. B., Curtin, G., et al.

(2002). Teaching spelling and composition alone and together: Implications for the simple view of writing. *Journal of Educational Psychology, 94*(2), 291–304.

Berninger V. W., & Winn, W. D. (2006). Implications of advancements in brain research and technology for writing development, writing instruction, and educational evolution. In C. A. MacArthur, S. Graham, & J. Fitzgerald (Eds.), *Handbook of writing research* (pp. 96–114). Guilford Press.

Bernstein, A., Hadash, Y., & Fresco, D. M. (2019). Metacognitive processes model of decentering: Emerging methods and insights. *Current Opinion in Psychology, 28,* 245–251.

Berti, S., & Cigala, A. (2020). Mindfulness for preschoolers: Effects on prosocial behavior, self-regulation and perspective taking. *Early Education and Development, 33*(1), 38–57.

Best, J. R., & Miller, P. H. (2010). A developmental perspective on executive function. *Child Development, 81*(6), 1641–1660.

Block, M. K., & Strachan, S. L. (2019). The impact of external audience on second graders' writing quality. *Reading Horizons: A Journal of Literacy and Language Arts, 58*(2). https://scholarworks.wmich.edu/reading_horizons/vol58/iss2/5.

Boardman, A. G., Klingner, J. K., Buckley, P., Annamma, S., & Lasser, C. J. (2015). The efficacy of collaborative strategic reading in middle school science and social studies classes. *Reading and Writing, 28*(9), 1257–1283.

Bodrova, E., Leong, D. J., & Akhutina, T. V. (2011). When everything new is well-forgotten old: Vygotsky/Luria insights in the development of executive functions. *New Ideas in Psychology, 29*(2), 228–242.

Bogaerds-Hazenberg, S. T. M., Evers-Vermeul, J., & van den Bergh, H. (2021). A meta-analysis on the effects of text structure instruction on reading comprehension in the upper elementary grades. *Reading Research Quarterly, 56*(3), 435–462.

Borne, A., Lemaitre, C., Bulteau, C., Baciu, M., & Perrone-Bertolotti, M. (2024). Unveiling the cognitive network organization through cognitive performance. *Scientific Reports, 14(*1), 11645.

Bourke, L., & Adams, A.-M. (2003). The relationship between working memory and early writing assessed at the word, sentence and text level. *Educational and Child Psychology, 20*(3), 19–36.

Bourke, L., Marriott-Fellows, M., Jones, A., Humphreys, L., Davies, S. J., Zuffiano, A., & López-Pérez, B. (2020). Writing with imagination: The influence of hot and cold executive functions in children with autism characteristics and typically developing peers. *Reading and Writing, 33*(5), 935–961.

Bowers, J. S., & Bowers, P. N. (2017). Beyond phonics: the case for teaching children the logic of the English spelling system. *Educational Psychologist, 2,* 124–141.

Bowers, P. N., Kirby, J. R., & Deacon, S. H. (2010). The effects of morphological instruction on literacy skills: A systematic review of the literature. *Review of Educational Research, 80*(2), 144–179.

Brimo, D., Apel, K., & Fountain, T. (2017). Examining the contributions of syntactic awareness and syntactic knowledge to reading comprehension. *Journal of Research in Reading, 40*(1), 57–74.

Britton, J. (1970). *Language and learning.* University of Miami Press.

Bruce, M., & Bell, M. (2022). Vocabulary and executive functioning: A scoping review of the unidirectional and bidirectional associations across early childhood. *Human Development, 66*(3), 167–187.

Brügge-Feldhake, M., Riegel, U., & Zimmermann, M. (2024). Didactical model to promote perspective taking. *British Journal of Religious Education, 46*(4), 436–446.

Butterfuss, R., & Kendeou, P. (2018). The role of executive functions in reading comprehension. *Educational Psychology Review, 30*(3), 801–826.

Calkins, L. (1994). *The art of teaching writing.* Heinemann.

Cameron, C. E., Brock, L. L., Hatfield, B. H., Cottone, E. A., Rubinstein, E., LoCasale-Crouch, J., et al. (2015). Visuomotor integration and inhibitory control compensate for each other in school readiness. *Developmental Psychology, 51*(11), 1529–1543.

Cameron, C. E., Brock, L. L., Murrah, W. M., Bell, L. H., Worzalla, S. L., Grissmer, D., & Morrison, F. J. (2012). Fine motor skills and executive function both contribute to kindergarten achievement. *Child Development, 83*(4), 1229–1244.

Cameron, C. A., Edmunds, G., Wigmore, B., Hunt, A. K., & Linton, M. J. (1997). Children's revision of textual flaws. *International Journal of Behavioral Development, 20*(4), 667–680.

Capodieci, A., Lachina, S., & Cornoldi, C. (2018). Handwriting difficulties in children with attention deficit hyperactivity disorder (ADHD). *Research in Developmental Disabilities, 74*, 41–49.

Carlisle, J. F. (2000). Awareness of the structure and meaning of morphologically complex words: Impact on reading. *Reading and Writing, 12(*3), 169–190.

Cartwright, K. B. (2023). *Executive skills and reading comprehension: A guide for educators* (2nd ed.). Guilford Press.

Cartwright, K. B., Barber, A. T., Zumbrunn, S. K., & Duke, N. K. (2023). Self-regulation and executive function in language arts learning. In D. Lapp, D. Fisher, & N. K. Duke (Eds.), *Handbook of research on teaching the English language arts* (5th ed., pp. 312–332). Routledge.

Carvalhais, L., Limpo, T., & Pereira, L. Á. (2021). The contribution of word-, sentence-, and discourse-level abilities on writing performance: A 3-year longitudinal study. *Frontiers in Psychology, 3*(12), 668139.

Carvalho, J. B. (2002). *Developing audience awareness in writing. Journal of Research in Reading, 25*(3), 271–282.

Castles, A., Rastle, K., & Nation, K. (2018). Ending the reading wars: Reading acquisition from novice to expert. *Psychological Science in the Public Interest, 19*(1), 5–51.

Chai, C. (2006). Writing plan quality: Relevance to writing scores. *Assessing Writing, 11*(3), 198–223.

Chandler, M., Gerde, H., Bowles, R., McRoy, K., Pontifex, M., & Bingham, G. (2021). Self-regulation moderates the relationship between fine motor skills and writing in early childhood. *Early Childhood Research Quarterly, 57*, 239–250.

Chatham, C. H., Claus, E. D., Kim, A., Curran, T., Banich, M. T., & Munakata, Y. (2012). Cognitive control reflects context monitoring, not motoric stopping, in response inhibition. *PLOS ONE, 7*(2), e31546.

Chien H. Y. (2020). Effects of two teaching strategies on preschoolers' oral language skills: Repeated read-aloud with question and answer teaching embedded and repeated read-aloud with executive function activities embedded. *Frontiers in Psychology, 10*, 2932.

Chilton, M. W., & Ehri, L. C. (2015). Vocabulary learning: Sentence contexts linked by events in scenarios facilitate third graders' memory for verb meanings. *Reading Research Quarterly, 50*(4), 439–458.

Cho, K., & MacArthur, C. (2010). Student revision with peer and expert reviewing. *Learning and Instruction, 20*(4), 328–338.

Cho, M., Kim, Y. S. G., & Olson, C. B. (2021). Does perspective taking matter for writing?: Perspective taking in source-based analytical writing of secondary students. *Reading and Writing, 34*(8), 2081–2101.

Choi, S., McMaster, K. L., Kohli, N., Shanahan, E., Birinci, S., An, J., et al. (2024). Longitudinal effects of data-based instructional changes for students with intensive learning needs: A piecewise linear–linear mixed-effects modeling approach. *Journal of Educational Psychology, 116*(4), 608–628

Chung, H. Q., Chen, V., & Olson, C. B. (2021). The impact of self-assessment, planning and goal setting, and reflection before and after revision on student self-efficacy and writing performance. *Reading and Writing, 34*, 1885–1913.

Cohen, M., & Riel, M. (1989). The effect of distant audiences on students' writing. *American Educational Research Journal, 26*(2), 143–159.

Collins, A. A., Ciullo, S., Graham, S., Sigafoos, L. L., Guerra, S., David, M., & Judd, L. (2021). Writing expository essays from social studies texts: A self-regulated strategy development study. *Reading and Writing, 34*(7), 1623–1651.

Connelly, V., Gee, D., & Walsh, E. (2007). A comparison of keyboarded and handwritten compositions and the relationship with transcription speed. *British Journal of Educational Psychology, 77*(Pt. 2), 479–492.

Cordeiro, C., Limpo T., Olive T., & Castro S. L. (2020). Do executive functions contribute to writing quality in beginning writers?: A longitudinal study with second graders. *Reading and Writing, 33*(4), 813–833.

Cordeiro, C., Magalhães, S., Nunes, A., Olive, T., Castro, S. T. & Limpo, T. (2022). Mindful acceptance predicts writing achievement in 6th-graders. *Journal of Research in Childhood Education, 36*(2), 346–362.

Cordeiro, C., Magalhães, S., Rocha, R., Mesquita, A., Olive, T., Castro, S. L., & Limpo, T. (2021). Promoting third graders' executive functions and literacy: A pilot study examining the benefits of mindfulness vs. relaxation training. *Frontiers in Psychology, 12*, 643794.

Costa, L. C., Spencer, S. V., & Hooper, S. R. (2022). Emergent neuroimaging findings for written expression in children: A scoping review. *Brain Sciences 12*(3), 406.

Costa, L. J., Green, M., Sideris, J., & Hooper, S. R. (2018). First-grade cognitive predictors of writing disabilities in grades 2 through 4 elementary school students. *Journal of Learning Disabilities, 51*(4), 351–362.

Covey, S. (2004). *Seven habits of highly effective people.* Free Press.

Cragg, L., & Nation, K. (2010). Language and the development of cognitive control. *Topics in Cognitive Science, 2*(4), 631–642.

Cramer, A. M., & Mason, L. H. (2014). The effects of strategy instruction for writing and revising persuasive quick writes for middle school students with emotional and behavioral disorders. *Behavioral Disorders, 40*(1), 37–51.

Crawford, L., Lloyd, S., & Knoth, K. (2008). Analysis of student revisions on a state writing test. *Assessment for Effective Intervention, 33*(2), 108–119.

Crossley, S. A., & McNamara, D. S. (2010). Cohesion, coherence, and expert evaluations of writing proficiency. In S. Ohlsson & R. Catrambone (Eds.), *Proceedings of the 32nd Annual Conference of the Cognitive Science Society* (pp. 984–989). Cognitive Science Society.

Crossley, S. A., & McNamara, D. S. (2016). Say more and be more coherent: How text elaboration and cohesion can increase writing quality. *Journal of Writing Research, 7*(3), 351–370.

Dajani, D. R., & Uddin, L. Q. (2015). Demystifying cognitive flexibility: Implications for clinical and developmental neuroscience. *Trends in Neurosciences, 38*(9), 571–578.

Davidson M. C., Amso D., Anderson L. C., & Diamond A. (2006). Development of cognitive control and executive functions from 4–13 years: Evidence from manipulations of memory, inhibition, and task switching. *Neuropsychologia, 44*(11), 2037–2078.

De La Paz, S., Malkus, N., Monte-Sano, C., & Montanaro, E. (2011). Evaluating American history teachers' professional development: Effects on student learning. *Theory and Research in Social Education, 39*(4), 494–540.

De La Paz, S., & Sherman, C. K. (2013). Revising strategy instruction in inclusive settings: Effects for English learners and novice writers. *Learning Disabilities Research and Practice, 28*(3), 129–141.

De La Paz, S., Swanson, P. N., & Graham, S. (1998). The contribution of executive control to the revising of students with writing and learning difficulties. *Journal of Educational Psychology, 90*(3), 448–460.

Deshler, D. D., Alley, G. R., Warner, M. M., & Schumaker, J. B. (1981). Instructional practices for promoting skill acquisition and generalization in severely learning disabled adolescents. *Learning Disability Quarterly, 4*(4), 415–421.

Devine, R. T., & Hughes, C. (2013). Silent films and strange stories: theory of mind, gender, and social experiences in middle childhood. *Child Development, 84*(3), 989–1003.

Diamond, A. (2013). Executive functions. *Annual Review of Psychology, 64*(1), 135–168.

Diamond, A., & Lee, K. (2011). Interventions shown to aid executive function development in children 4 to 12 years old. *Science, 333*, 959–964.

Diaz-Borda, G. A., Garcia-Zambrano, S., & Pfeiffer Flores, E. (2024). Behavioral interventions for teaching perspective-taking skills: A scoping review. *Journal of Contextual Behavioral Science, 34*(3), 100816.

Dockrell, J. E., & Connelly, V. (2021). Capturing the challenges in assessing writing: Development and writing dimensions. In T. Limpo & T. Olive (Eds.), *Executive functions and writing* (pp. 103–135). Oxford University Press.

Doebel, S. (2020). Rethinking executive function and its development. *Perspectives on Psychological Science, 1*(1), 1–15.

Drijbooms, E., Groen, M. A., & Verhoeven, L. (2017). How executive functions predict development in syntactic complexity of narrative writing in the upper elementary grades. *Reading and Writing, 30*(1), 209–231

Duke, N. K., & Cartwright, K. B. (2021). The science of reading progresses: Communicating advances beyond the Simple View of Reading. *Reading Research Quarterly, 56*(Suppl. 1), S25–S44.

Duke, N. K., Graham, S., & Cartwright, K. B. (2025). *The Active View of Writing*. Unpublished document.

Duke, N. K., Pearson, P. D., Strachan, S. L., & Billman, A. K. (2011). Essential elements of fostering and teaching reading comprehension. In S. J. Samuels & A. E. Farstrup (Eds.), *What research has to say about reading instruction* (4th ed., pp. 51–93). International Reading Association.

Elleman, A. M. (2017). Examining the impact of inference instruction on the literal and inferential comprehension of skilled and less skilled readers: A meta-analytic review. *Journal of Educational Psychology, 109*(6), 761–781.

Englert, C. S., Raphael, T. E., Anderson, L. M., Anthony, H. M., & Stevens, D. D. (1991). Making strategies and self-talk visible: Writing instruction in regular and special education classrooms. *American Educational Research Journal, 28*(2), 337–372.

Fancher, L. A., Priestley-Hopkins, D. A., & Jeffries, L. M. (2018). Handwriting acquisition and intervention: A systematic review. *Journal of Occupational Therapy, Schools, & Early Intervention, 11*(4), 454–473.

Farrow, J., Hindman, A. H., & Wasik, B. A. (2024). Exploring relations between teachers' language- and code-based writing supports to early literacy and vocabulary learning in children with language vulnerabilities. *Reading and Writing Quarterly,* 40(6), 1–22.

Fayol, M., Alamargot, D., & Berninger, V. W. (Eds.). (2012). *Translation of thought to written text while composing: Advancing theory, knowledge, research methods, tools, and applications*. Psychology Press.

Feder, K. P., & Majnemer, A. (2007). Handwriting development, competency, and intervention. *Developmental Medicine and Child Neurology, 49(*4), 312–317.

Feng, X., Perceval, G. J., Feng, W., & Feng, C. (2020). High cognitive flexibility learners perform better in probabilistic rule learning. *Frontiers in Psychology, 11,* Article 415.

Fidalgo, R., Torrance, M., & García, J.-N. (2008). The long-term effects of strategy-focused writing instruction for grade six students. *Contemporary Educational Psychology, 33*(4), 672–693.

Filipe, M., Veloso, A. & Frota, S. (2023). Executive functions and language skills in preschool children: The unique contribution of verbal working memory and cognitive flexibility. *Brain Sciences, 13*(3), 470.

Fiorella, L. (2023). Making sense of generative learning. *Educational Psychology Review, 35*(2), 50.

Flook, L., Smalley, S. L., Kitil, M. J., Galla, B. M., Kaiser-Greenland, S., Locke, J., et al. (2010). Effects of mindful awareness practices on executive functions in elementary school children. *Journal of Applied School Psychology, 26*(1), 70–95.

Flower L. & Hayes J. (1981). A cognitive process theory of writing. *College Composition and Communication, 32*(4), 365–387.

Foorman, B. R., & Torgesen, J. (2001). Critical elements of classroom and small-group instruction promote reading success in all children. *Learning Disabilities Research and Practice, 16*(4), 203–212.

Frank, L. A. (1992). Writing to be read: Young writers' ability to demonstrate audience awareness when evaluated by their readers. *Research in the Teaching of English, 26*(3), 277–298.

Frayer, D., Frederick, W. C., & Klausmeier, H. J. (1969). *A schema for testing the level of cognitive mastery.* Wisconsin Center for Education Research.

Friedman, N. P., & Miyake, A. (2017). Unity and diversity of executive functions: Individual differences as a window on cognitive structure. *Cortex, 86*, 186–204.

Friedman, N. P., & Robbins, T. W. (2022). The role of prefrontal cortex in cognitive control and executive function. *Neuropsychopharmacology, 47*(1), 72–89

Galbraith, D., Torrance, M., & Hallam, J. (2006). Effects of writing on conceptual coherence. *Proceedings of the 28th Annual Conference of the Cognitive Science Society*, pp. 1340–1345.

Galuschka, K., Görgen, R., Kalmar, J., Haberstroh, S., Schmalz, X., & Schulte-Körne, G. (2020). Effectiveness of spelling interventions for learners with dyslexia: A meta-analysis and systematic review. *Educational Psychologist, 55*(1), 1–20.

Galuschka, K., Ise, E., Krick, K., & Schulte-Körne, G. (2014). Effectiveness of treatment approaches for children and adolescents with reading disabilities: A meta-analysis of randomized controlled trials. *PLOS ONE, 9*(2), e89900.

Gandotra, A., Csaba, S., Sattar, Y., Cserényi, V., Bizonics, R., Cserjesi, R., & Kotyuk, E. (2021). A Meta-analysis of the relationship between motor skills and executive functions in typically-developing children. *Journal of Cognition and Development, 23*(1), 83–110.

García-Sánchez, J.-N., & Fidalgo-Redondo, R. (2006). Effects of two types of self-regulatory instruction programs on students with learning disabilities in writing products, processes, and self-efficacy. *Learning Disability Quarterly, 29*(3), 181–211.

Gioia, A. R., Ahmed, Y., Woods, S. P., & Cirino, P. T. (2023). Properties of a combined measure of reading and writing: The assessment of writing, self-monitoring, and reading (AWSM reader). *Reading and Writing, 36*(3), 723–744.

Goldstein, T. R., & Winner, E. (2012). Enhancing empathy and theory of mind. *Journal of Cognition and Development, 13*(1), 19–37.

Gooch, D., Thompson, P., Nash, H. M., Snowling, M. J., & Hulme, C. (2016). The development of executive function and language skills in the early school years. *Journal of Child Psychology and Psychiatry, 57*(2), 180–187.

Good, J. E., Lance, D. M., & Rainey, J. (2015). The effects of morphological awareness training on reading, spelling, and vocabulary skills. *Communication Disorders Quarterly, 36*(3), 142–151.

Gough, P. B., & Tunmer, W. E. (1986). Decoding, reading, and reading disability. *Remedial and Special Education, 7*(1), 6–10.

Graham, S. (2018a). A revised writer(s)-within-community model of writing. *Educational Psychologist, 53*(4), 258–279.

Graham, S. (2018b). A writer(s) within community model of writing. In C. Bazerman, V. Berninger, D. Brandt, S. Graham, J. Langer, S. Murphy, et al. (Eds.), *The lifespan development of writing* (Vol. 53, pp. 258–279). National Council of Teachers of English.

Graham, S. (2019). Changing how writing is taught. *Review of Research in Education, 43*(1), 277–303.

Graham, S. (2021). Executive control and the writer(s)-within-community model. In T. Limpo & T. Olive (Eds.), *Executive functions and writing* (pp. 38–76). Oxford University Press.

Graham, S., Bollinger, A., Booth Olson, C., D'Aoust, C., MacArthur, C., McCutchen, D., & Olinghouse, N. (2012, revised 2018). *Teaching elementary school students to be effective writers* (NCEE 2012- 4058). National Center for Education Evaluation and Regional Assistance, Institute of Education Sciences, U.S. Department of Education.

Graham, S., Bruch, J., Fitzgerald, J., Friedrich, L., Furgeson, J., Greene, K., et al. (2016, revised 2019). *Teaching secondary students to write effectively* (NCEE 2017-4002). National Center for Education Evaluation and Regional Assistance, Institute of Education Sciences, U.S. Department of Education.

Graham, S., & Harris, K. R. (2017). Reading and writing connections: How writing can build better readers (and vice versa). In C. Ng & B. Bartlett (Eds.), *Improving reading and reading engagement in the 21st century* (pp. 175–194). Springer.

Graham, S., Harris, K. R., Adkins, M., & Camping, A. (2021). Do content revising goals change the revising behavior and story writing of fourth grade students at-risk for writing difficulties? *Reading and Writing, 34*(7), 1915–1941.

Graham, S., Harris, K. R., & Fink, B. (2000). Is handwriting causally related to learning to write?: Treatment of handwriting problems in beginning writers. *Journal of Educational Psychology, 92*(4), 620–633.

Graham, S., Harris, K., & Hebert, M. A. (2011). *Informing writing: The benefits of formative assessment. A Carnegie Corporation Time to Act report.* Alliance for Excellent Education.

Graham, S., Kiuhara, S. A., & MacKay, M. (2020). The effects of writing on learning in science, social studies, and mathematics: A meta-analysis. *Review of Educational Research, 90*(2), 179–226.

Graham, S., & Perin, D. (2007). *Writing Next.* Carnegie Foundation.

Graham, S., & Santangelo, T. (2014). Does spelling instruction make students better spellers, readers, and writers? *Reading and Writing, 27*(9), 1703–1743.

Gray, S. I., Levy, R., Alt, M., Hogan, T. P., & Cowan, N. (2022). Working memory predicts new word learning over and above existing vocabulary and nonverbal IQ. *Journal of Speech, Language, and Hearing Research, 65*(3), 1044–1069.

Guajardo, N. R., & Cartwright, K. B. (2016). The contribution of theory of mind, counterfactual reasoning, and executive function to pre-readers' language comprehension and later reading awareness and comprehension in elementary school. *Journal of Experimental Child Psychology, 144*, 27–45.

Hammond, Z. (2014). *Culturally responsive teaching and the brain.* Corwin Press.

Hand, E. D., Lonigan, C. J., & Puranik, C. S. (2024). Prediction of kindergarten and first-grade reading skills: Unique contributions of preschool writing and early-literacy skills. *Reading and Writing, 37*(1), 25–48.

Hanford, E. (2022). *Sold a story: How teaching kids to read went so wrong* [Podcast]. APM Reports, American Public Media. https://features.apmreports.org/sold-a-story/.

Hansford, N., Reenstra, E., & Laud, L. (2024). *ThinkSRSD: A secondary analysis cohort investigation.* Manuscript submitted for publication. https://osf.io/vkc8f.

Harris, K. R., Graham, S., & Adkins, M. (2015). Practice-based professional development and self-regulated strategy development for Tier 2, at-risk writers in second grade. *Contemporary Educational Psychology, 40*, 5–16.

Harris, K. R., Graham, S., & Mason, L. H. (2006). Improving the writing, knowledge, and motivation of struggling young writers: Effects of self-regulated strategy development with and without peer support. *American Educational Research Journal, 43*(2), 295–340.

Harris, K. R., Graham, S., & Mason, L., & Friedlander, B. (2008). *Powerful writing strategies for all students.* Brookes.

Harris, K. R., Graham, S., Mason, L., McKeown, D., & Olinghouse, N. G. (2018). Self-regulated strategy development in writing: A classroom example of developing executive function processes and future directions. In L. Meltzer (Ed.), *Executive function in education:From theory to practice* (2nd ed., pp. 326–356). Guilford Press.

Harris, K., Kim, Y., Yim, S., Camping, A. & Graham, S. (2023). Yes, they can: Developing transcription skills and oral language in tandem with SRSD instruction on close reading of science text to write informative essays at grades 1 and 2. *Contemporary Educational Psychology, 73*, 102150.

Hayes, J. R., Flower, L., Schriver, K. A., Stratman, J. F., & Carey, L. (1987). Cognitive processes in revision. In S. Rosenberg (Ed.), *Advances in applied psycholinguistics: Vol. 1. Disorders of first-language development; Vol. 2. Reading, writing, and language learning* (pp. 176–240). Cambridge University Press.

Haynes, C., Smith, S. L., & Laud, L. (2019). Structured literacy approaches to teaching written expression. *Perspectives on Language and Literacy, 45*(3), 22–28.

Hebert, M., Bohaty, J. J., Nelson, J. R., & Brown, J. (2016). The effects of text structure instruction on expository reading comprehension: A meta-analysis. *Journal of Educational Psychology, 108*(5), 609–629.

Hegland, S. S. (2021). *Beneath the surface of words: What English spelling reveals and why it matters.* Learning About Spelling.

Holliway, D. R. (2004). Through the eyes of my reader: A strategy for improving audience perspective in children's descriptive writing. *Journal of Research in Childhood Education, 18*(4), 334–349.

Hooper, S. R., Costa, L. J., McBee, M., & Anderson, K. L. (2011). Concurrent and longitudinal neuropsychological contributors to written language expression in first and second grade students. *Reading and Writing, 24*(2), 221–252.

Hooper, S. R., Swartz, C. W., Wakely, M. B., de Kruif, R. E., & Montgomery, J. W. (2002). Executive functions in elementary school children with and without problems in written expression. *Journal of Learning Disabilities, 35*(1), 57–68.

Hooper, S. R., Wakely, M. B., de Kruif, R. E., & Swartz, C. W. (2006). Aptitude-treatment interactions revisited: effect of metacognitive intervention on subtypes of written expression in elementary school students. *Developmental Neuropsychology, 29*(1), 217–241.

Ibbotson, P., & Kearvell-White, J. (2015). Inhibitory control predicts grammatical ability. *PLOS ONE, 10*(12), e0145030.

Ihara, A. S., Nakajima, K., Kake, A., Ishimaru, K., Osugi, K., & Naruse, Y. (2021). Advantage of handwriting over typing on learning words: Evidence from an N400 event-related potential index. *Frontiers in Human Neuroscience, 15*, 679191.

James, K. H. (2017). The importance of handwriting experience on the development of the literate brain. *Current Directions in Psychological Science, 26*(6), 502–508.

James, K. H., & Engelhardt, L. (2012). The effects of handwriting experience on functional brain development in pre-literate children. *Trends in Neuroscience and Education, 1*(1), 32–42.

Jennings, T., & Haynes, C. (2018). *From talking to writing* (2nd ed.). Landmark-Outreach.

Johnson, J. A., Bardos, A. N., & Tayebi, K. A. (2003). Discriminant validity of the Cognitive Assessment System for Students with Written Expression Disabilities. *Journal of Psychoeducational Assessment, 21*(2), 180–195.

Jongmans, M. J., Linthorst-Bakker, E., Westenberg, Y., & Smits-Engelsman, B. C. (2003). Use of a task-oriented self-instruction method to support children in primary school with poor handwriting quality and speed. *Human Movement Science, 22*(4–5), 549–566.

Kajka, N., & Kulik, A. (2021). The influence of metacognitive strategies on the improvement of reaction inhibition processes in children with ADHD. *International Journal of Environmental Research and Public Health, 18*(3), 878.

Kalliontzi, E., Ralli, A. M., Palikara, O., & Roussos, P. (2022). Examining the relationship between oral language skills and executive functions: Evidence from Greek-speaking 4–5-year-old children with and without developmental language disorder. *Research in Developmental Disabilities, 124*, 104215.

Kellogg, R. T. (1990). Effectiveness of prewriting strategies as a function of task demands. *American Journal of Psychology, 103*(3), 327–342.

Kent, S., Wanzek, J., Petscher, Y., Al Otaiba, S., & Kim, Y. S. (2014). Writing fluency and quality in kindergarten and first grade: The role of attention, reading, transcription, and oral language. *Reading and Writing, 27*(7), 1163–1188.

Kerkhofs, R., Vonk, W., Schriefers, H., & Chwilla, D. J. (2008). Sentence processing in the visual and auditory modality: Do comma and prosodic break have parallel functions? *Brain Research, 1224*, 102–118.

Khng, K. H. (2024). Cognitive inhibition in the classroom. In W. L. D. Hung, A. Jamaludin, & A. A. Rahman (Eds.), *Applying the science of learning to education* (pp. 243–266). Springer Nature.

Kidd, E. (2012). Implicit statistical learning is directly associated with the acquisition of syntax. *Developmental Psychology, 48*(1), 171–184.

Kiefer, M., Schuler, S., Mayer, C., Trumpp, N. N., Hille, K., & Sachse, S. (2015). Handwriting or typewriting?: The influence of pen or keyboard-based writing training on reading and writing performance of preschool children. *Advances in Cognitive Science, 11*(4), 136–146.

Kim, J. S., & Burkhauser, M. A. (2022). Teaching for transfer can help young children read for understanding. *Phi Delta Kappan, 103*(8), 20–24.

Kim, J. S., Gilbert, J. B., Relyea, J. E., Rich, P., Scherer, E., Burkhauser, M. A., & Tvedt, J. N. (2024). Time to transfer: Long-term effects of a sustained and spiraled content literacy intervention in the elementary grades. *Developmental Psychology, 60*(7), 1279–1297.

Kim, Y.-S. G. (2020). Structural relations of language, cognitive skills, and topic knowledge to written composition: A test of the direct and indirect effects model of writing (DIEW). *British Journal of Educational Psychology, 90*(4), 910–932.

Kim, Y.-S. G. (2022). Do written language bursts mediate the relations of language, cognitive, and transcription skills to writing quality? *Written Communication, 39*(2), 200–227.

Kim, Y- S. G. (2023). Executive functions and morphological awareness explain the shared variance between word reading and listening comprehension. *Scientific Studies of Reading, 27*(5), 451–474.

Kim, Y.-S. G. (2024a, February 6). Using the science of writing to support literacy instruction (Season 2, Episode 3) [Podcast episode]. In *All For Literacy.* Lexia Webinar. https://www.lexialearning.com/resources/all-for-literacy-podcasts/using-the-science-of-writing-to-support-literacy-instruction-with-dr-young-suk-kim.

Kim, Y.-S. G. (2024b). Writing fluency: Its relations with language, cognitive, and transcription skills, and writing quality using longitudinal data from kindergarten to grade 2. *Journal of Educational Psychology, 116*(4), 590–607.

Kim, Y.-S. G., & Graham, S. (2022). Expanding the Direct and Indirect Effects Model of Writing (DIEW): Reading–writing relations, and dynamic relations as a function of measurement/dimensions of written composition, *Journal of Educational Psychology, 114(*2), 215–238.

Kim, Y.-S. G., Harris, K. R., Goldstone, R., Camping, A., & Graham, S. (2024). The science of teaching reading is incomplete without the science of writing: A randomized control trial of integrated teaching of reading and writing. *Scientific Studies of Reading, 29*(1), 32–54.

Kim, Y.-S. G., Otaiba, S. A., Sidler, J. F., & Gruelich, L. (2013). Language, literacy, attentional behaviors, and instructional quality predictors of written composition for first graders. *Early Childhood Research Quarterly, 28*(3), 461–469.

Kim, Y.-S. G., & Park S.-H. (2019). Unpacking pathways using the direct and indirect effects model of writing (DIEW) and the contributions of higher order cognitive skills to writing. *Reading and Writing, 32*(5), 1319–1343.

Kim, Y.-S. G., & Schatschneider, C. (2017). Expanding the developmental models of writing: A direct and indirect effects model of developmental writing (DIEW). *Journal of Educational Psychology, 109*(1), 35–50.

Kim, Y.-S. G., Yang, D., Reyes, M., & Connor, C. (2021). Writing instruction improves students' writing skills differentially depending on focal instruction and children: A meta-analysis for primary grade students. *Educational Research Review, 34*, 100408.

Kim, Y.-S. G., & Zagata, E. (2024). Enhancing reading and writing skills through systematically integrated instruction. *Reading Teacher, 77*(6), 787–799.

Kirby, M. S., Spencer, T. D., & Chen, Y. J. I. (2021). Oral narrative instruction improves kindergarten writing. *Reading and Writing Quarterly, 37*(6), 574–591.

Klein, P. D., Casola, M., Dombroski, J., Shaw, K. W. Y., & Thompson, S. (2024). Online intervention to prevent summer learning loss for struggling first grade writers. *Reading and Writing Quarterly, 41*(4), 1–25.

Klein, S., Guiltner, V., Sollereder, P., & Cui, Y. (2010). Relationships between fine-motor, visual-motor, and visual perception scores and handwriting legibility and speed. *Physical & Occupational Therapy in Pediatrics, 31*(1), 103–114.

Kompa, N. A., & Mueller, J. L. (2022). Inner speech as a cognitive tool—or what is the point of talking to oneself? *Philosophical Psychology, 37(*8), 1971–1994.

Kuhn, D. (2015). Thinking together and alone. *Educational Researcher, 44*(1), 46–53.

Lane, J. D., & Bowman, L. C. (2021). How children's social tendencies can shape their theory of mind development: Access and attention to social information. *Developmental Review, 61,* 100977.

LaRusso, M., Kim, H. Y., Selman, R., Uccelli, P., Dawson, T., Jones, S., et al. (2016). Contributions of academic language, perspective taking, and complex reasoning to deep reading comprehension. *Journal of Research on Educational Effectiveness, 9(*2), 201–222.

Larigauderie, P., Guignouard, C., & Olive, T. (2020). Proofreading by students: Implications of executive and non-executive components of working memory in the detection of phonological, orthographical, and grammatical errors. *Reading and Writing, 33*(5), 1015–1036.

Laud, L. E., & Patel, P. (2008). Teach struggling writers to unite their paragraphs. *Teaching Exceptional Children Plus, 5*(1), Article 4.

Laud, L., & Zampitella, T. (2025, May). *The genre shuffle: How writing instructional planning has evolved—and why interleaving is winning.* Think SRSD. https://www.thinksrsd.com/planning-genre-sequences.

Lê, M., Quémart P., Potocki A., Gimenes M., Chesnet D., & Lambert E. (2021). Modeling the influence of motor skills on literacy in third grade: Contributions of executive functions and handwriting. *PLOS ONE, 16*(11), e0259016.

Lecce, S., Bianco, F., Devine, R. T., & Hughes, C. (2017). Relations between theory of mind and executive function in middle childhood: A short-term longitudinal study. *Journal of Experimental Child Psychology, 163*, 69–86.

Levine, S. (2019). Using everyday language to support students in constructing thematic interpretations. *Journal of the Learning Sciences, 28*(1), 1–31.

Li, M., Murphy, P. K., Wang, J., Mason, L. H., Firetto, C. M., Wei, L., & Chung, K. S. (2016). Promoting reading comprehension and critical–analytic thinking: A comparison of three approaches with fourth and fifth graders. *Contemporary Educational Psychology, 46,* 101–115.

Limpo, T., & Alves, R. A. (2013a). Modeling writing development: Contribution of transcription and self-regulation to Portuguese students' text generation quality. *Journal of Educational Psychology, 105(*2), 401–413.

Limpo, T., & Alves, R. A. (2013b). Teaching planning or sentence-combining strategies: Effective SRSD interventions at different levels of written composition. *Contemporary Educational Psychology, 38(*4), 328–341.

Limpo, T., Alves, R., & Connelly, V. (2017). Examining the transcription-writing link: Effects of handwriting fluency and spelling accuracy on writing performance via planning and translating in middle grades. *Learning and Individual Differences, 53,* 26–36.

Limpo, T., Alves, R. A., & Fidalgo, R. (2014). Children's high-level writing skills: development of planning and revising and their contribution to writing quality. *British Journal of Educational Psychology, 84*(Pt. 2), 177–193.

Limpo, T., Vieira, A. I., Magalhães, S., Rocha, R., Cordeiro, C., Rodrigues, R., et al. (2023). Examining the impact and moderating effects of an 8-week mindfulness-based program in grade 4. *Mindfulness, 14*(8), 2026–2043.

Limpo, T., Vigário, V., Rocha, R., & Graham, S. (2020). Promoting transcription in third-grade classrooms: Effects on handwriting and spelling skills, composing, and motivation. *Contemporary Educational Psychology, 61,* 101856.

Littleton, E. B. (1998). Emerging cognitive skills for writing: Sensitivity to audience presence in five- through nine-year-olds' speech. *Cognition and Instruction, 16*(4), 399–430.

Llaurado, A., & Dockrell, J. E. (2019). Children's plans for writing: Characteristics and impact on writing performance. *Journal of Literacy Research, 51*(3), 336–356.

Longcamp, M., Zerbato-Poudou, M. T., & Velay, J. L. (2005). The influence of writing practice on letter recognition in preschool children: A comparison between handwriting and typing. *Acta Psychologia, 119*(1), 67–79.

López, P., Torrance, M., Rijlaarsdam, G. & Fidalgo, R. (2021). Evaluating effects of different forms of revision instruction in upper-primary students. *Reading and Writing, 34*(7), 1741–1767.

Lubin, A., Regrin, E., Boulc'h, L., Pacton, S., & Lanoë, C. (2016). Executive functions differentially contribute to fourth graders' mathematics, reading, and spelling skills. *Journal of Cognitive Education and Psychology, 15*(3), 444–463.

MacArthur, C. A., Jennings, A., & Philippakos, Z. A. (2019). Which linguistic features predict quality of argumentative writing for college basic writers, and how do those features change with instruction? *Reading and Writing, 32*(6), 1553–1574.

MacArthur, C. A., Schwartz, S. S., & Graham, S. (1991). A model for writing instruction: Integrating word processing and strategy instruction into a process approach to writing. *Learning Disabilities Research and Practice, 6*(4), 230–236.

Mason, L., & Brady, S. (2022). Promoting executive functions during the writing process. In T. Limpo & T. Olive (Eds.), *Executive functions and writing.* Oxford University Press.

Mason, L. H., Harris, K. R., Graham, S., & Friedlander, B. (2017). Efficacy of self-regulated strategy development instruction for developing writers with and without disabilities in rural schools: A randomized controlled trial. *Rural Special Education Quarterly, 36*(4), 168–179.

Mason, L. H., Reid, R., & Hagaman, J. L. (2012). *Building comprehension in adolescents: Powerful strategies for improving reading and writing in content areas.* Brookes.

McClelland, M. & Cameron, C. (2019). Developing together: The role of executive function and motor skills in children's early academic lives. *Early Childhood Research Quarterly, 46*(1), 142–151.

McCloskey, G., Perkins, L. A., & Van Divner, B. (2009). *Assessment and intervention for executive function difficulties.* Routledge.

McKeown, D., Wijekumar, K., Owens, J., Harris, K., Graham, S., Lei, P., & FitzPatrick, E. (2023). Professional development for evidence-based SRSD writing instruction: Elevating fourth grade outcomes. *Contemporary Educational Psychology, 73*(1), 102152.

McNamara, D., Crossley, S. A., & McCarthy, P. M. (2010). Linguistic features of writing quality. *Written Communication, 27*(1), 57–86.

Meichenbaum, D. (1976). Cognitive-functional approach to cognitive factors as determinants of learning disabilities. In R. M. Knights & D. J. Bakker (Eds.), *The neuropsychology of learning disorders: Theoretical approaches* (pp. 423–442). University Park Press.

Meichenbaum, D. H., & Goodman, J. (1971). Training impulsive children to talk to themselves: A means of developing self-control. *Journal of Abnormal Psychology, 77*(2), 115–126.

Menon, V., & D'Esposito, M. (2022). The role of PFC networks in cognitive control and executive function. *Neuropsychopharmacology, 47*(1), 90–103.

Meyer, M., Brezack, N., & Woodward, A. L. (2024). Neural correlates involved in perspective-taking in early childhood. *Developmental Cognitive Neuroscience, 66*, 101366.

Midgette, E., Haria, P., & MacArthur, C. (2008). The effects of content and audience awareness goals for revision on the persuasive essays of fifth- and eighth-grade students. *Reading and Writing, 21*(2), 131–151.

Miller, C. M., Patel, S. W., & Ndebele, D. H. (2023). The acquisition of language by children: How do children learn language so quickly and effortlessly? *Literature and Linguistics Journal, 2*(1), 60–68.

Miller, E. K., & Wallis, J. D. (2009). Executive function and higher-order cognition: Definition and neural substrates. In L. R. Squire (Ed.), *Encyclopedia of neuroscience* (Vol. 4, pp. 99–104). Academic Press.

Miller, S. A. (2022). *Advanced theory of mind.* Oxford University Press.

Moats, L. C. (2005–2006, Winter). How spelling supports reading: And why it is more regular and predictable than you may think. *American Educator.*

Moats, L. C. (2020). *Speech to print: Language essentials for teachers* (3rd ed.). Brookes.

Montgomery, J. W., Gillam, R. B., & Plante, E. (2024). Enhancing syntactic knowledge in school-age children with developmental language disorder: The promise of syntactic priming. *American Journal of Speech-Language Pathology, 33*(2), 580–597.

Mueller, P. A., & Oppenheimer, D. M. (2014). The pen is mightier than the keyboard: Advantages of longhand over laptop note taking. *Psychological Science, 25*(6), 1159–1168.

Murray, D. (2003). *A writer teaches writing.* Cengage Learning.

Myhill, D., Jones, S., & Lines, H. (2018). Supporting less proficient writers through linguistically aware teaching. *Language and Education, 32*(4), 333–349.

National Center for Education Statistics. (2011). *The Nation's Report Card: Writing 2011* (NCES 2012-470). Institute of Education Sciences, U.S. Department of Education.

National Governors Association Center for Best Practices & Council of Chief State School Officers. (2010). *Common Core State Standards.* Authors.

Niedo, J., Abbott, R. D., & Berninger, V. W. (2014). Predicting levels of reading and writing achievement in typically developing, English-speaking 2nd and 5th graders. *Learning and Individual Differences, 32,* 54–68.

Nunes, A., Cordeiro, C., Rocha, R., Limpo, T., & Castro, S. L. (2024). "Breathe, plan, write, and evaluate": The effects of an SRSD intervention and instructional feedback on 4th graders' writing and motivation. *Frontiers in Education, 9,* 1–11.

Olinghouse, N. G., & Wilson, J. (2013). The relationship between vocabulary and writing quality in three genres. *Reading and Writing, 26*(1), 45–65.

Olive, T. (2011). Working memory in writing. In T. Oliver (Ed.), *Past, present, and future contributions of cognitive writing research to cognitive psychology* (pp. 485–503). Psychology Press.

Olive, T. (2014). Toward a parallel and cascading model of the writing system: A review of research on writing processes coordination. *Journal of Writing Research, 6*(2), 173–194.

Olive, T., & Kellogg, R. T. (2002). Concurrent activation of high- and low-level production processes in written composition. *Memory & Cognition, 30*(4), 594–600.

Olive, T., Kellogg, R. T., & Piolat, A. (2008). Verbal, visual and spatial working memory demands during text composition. *Applied Psycholinguistics, 29,* 669–687.

Olson, C., Matuchniak, T., Chung, H., Stumpf, R., & Farkas, G. (2017). Reducing achievement gaps in academic writing for Latinos and English learners in grades 7–12. *Journal of Educational Psychology, 109*(1), 1–21.

Oshchepkova, E. S., Shatskaya, A. N., & Kovyazina, M. S. (2023). The longitudinal influence of the level of executive function development on children's transcriptional skills: a modern view of A. Luria's ideas. *Frontiers in Psychology, 14,* 1199683.

Otero, T. M. & Barker, L. A. (2014). The frontal lobes and executive functioning. In S. Goldstein & J. Naglieri (Eds.), *Handbook of executive functioning* (pp. 29–94). Springer.

Panos, K. L., & Datchuk, S. M. (2021). Constructing simple sentences: Effects of a writing fluency intervention for middle school students with disabilities. *Remedial and Special Education, 42*(2), 107–117.

Patchan, M. M., Schunn, C. D., & Correnti, R. J. (2016). The nature of feedback: How peer feedback features affect students' implementation rate and quality of revisions. *Journal of Educational Psychology, 108*(8), 1098–1120.

Patel, P., & Laud, L. E. (2009). Using goal-setting in "P(paw)LANS" to improve writing. *Teaching Exceptional Children Plus, 5*(4), Article 3.

Pearson, P. D., & Gallagher, M. C. (1983). The instruction of reading comprehension. *Contemporary Educational Psychology, 8*(3), 317–344.

Peng, P., Wang, W., Filderman, M. J., Zhang, W., & Lin, L. (2024). The active ingredient in reading comprehension strategy intervention for struggling readers: A Bayesian network meta-analysis. *Review of Educational Research, 94*(2), 228–267.

Perone, S., Simmering, V. R., & Buss, A. T. (2021). A dynamical reconceptualization of executive-function development. *Perspectives on Psychological Science, 16*(6), 1198–1208.

Perrone-Bertolotti, M., Rapin, L., Lachaux, J.-P., Baciu, M., & Lœvenbruck, H. (2014). What is that little voice inside my head?: Inner speech phenomenology, its role in cognitive performance, and its relation to self-monitoring. *Behavioural Brain Research, 261,* 220–239.

Peskin, J., Prusky, C., & Comay, J. (2014). Keeping the reader's mind in mind: Development of perspective-taking in children's dictations. *Journal of Applied Developmental Psychology, 35*(1), 35–43.

Pfeiffer, B., Moskowitz, B., Paoletti, A., Brusilovskiy, E., Zylstra, S. E., & Murray, T. (2015). (2015). Brief report—Developmental Test of Visual–Motor Integration (VMI): An effective outcome measure for handwriting interventions for kindergarten, first-grade, and second-grade students? *American Journal of Occupational Therapy, 69*(4), 6904350010p1–6904350010p7.

Pinker, S. (2007). *The language instinct.* Harper. (Original work published 1994)

Pinto, G., Bigozzi, L., Gamannossi, B. A., Vezzani, C. (2009). Emergent literacy and learning to write: A predictive model for Italian language. *European Journal of Psychology and Education, 24,* 61–78.

Piolat, A. (2007). Effects of note-taking and working-memory span on cognitive effort and recall performance. In M. Torrance, L. v. Waes, & D. Galbraith (Eds.), *Writing and cognition: Research and applications* (pp. 109–124). Brill.

Piolat, A., Olive, T., & Kellogg, R. T. (2005). Cognitive effort during note taking. *Applied Cognitive Psychology, 19*(3), 291–312.

Planton, S., Jucla, M., Roux, F.-E., & Démonet, J.-F. (2013). The "handwriting brain": A meta-analysis of neuroimaging studies of motor versus orthographic processes. *Cortex, 49*(10), 2772–2787.

Planton, S., Longcamp, M., Péran, P., Démonet, J.-F., & Jucla, M. (2017). How specialized are writing-specific brain regions?: An fMRI study of writing, drawing and oral spelling. *Cortex, 88,* 66–80.

Poch, A. L., & Lembke, E. S. (2017). A not-so-simple view of adolescent writing. *International Journal for Research in Learning Disabilities, 3*(2), 27–44.

Premack, D., & Woodruff, G. (1978). Does the chimpanzee have a theory of mind? *Behavioral and Brain Sciences, 1*(4), 515–526.

Puranik, C. S., Boss, E., & Wanless, S. (2019). Relations between self-regulation and early writing: Domain specific or task dependent? *Early Childhood Research Quarterly, 46,* 228–239.

Quinlan, T., Loncke, M., Leijten, M., & Van Waes, L. (2012). Coordinating the cognitive processes of writing: The role of the monitor. *Written Communication, 29*(3), 345–68

Quitadamo, I., & Kurtz, M. (2007). Learning to improve: Using writing to increase critical thinking performance in general education biology. *CBE Life Science Education,* 6(2),140–154.

Rapp, B., & Lipka, K. (2011). The literate brain: The relationship between spelling and reading. *Journal of Cognitive Neuroscience, 23*(5), 1180–1197.

Rau, P. S., & Sebrechts, M. M. (1996). How initial plans mediate the expansion and resolution of options in writing. *Quarterly Journal of Experimental Psychology, Section A, 49*(3), 616–638.

Ray, K., Dally, K., Colyvas, K., & Lane, A. E. (2021). The effects of a whole-class kindergarten handwriting intervention on early reading skills. *Reading Research Quarterly, 56*(Suppl. 1), S193–S207.

The Reading League. (2022). *Science of reading: Defining guide*. Author.

Reid, E. K., Ahmed, Y., & Keller-Margulis, M. A. (2023). Contributions of attentional control, hyperactivity-impulsivity, and reading skills to performance on a fourth-grade state writing test. *Journal of School Psychology, 99*(3), 101220.

Ren, J., Wang, M., & Conway, C. M. (2024). Can explicit instruction boost statistical learning?: A meta-analytical review. *Journal of Educational Psychology, 116*(7), 1215–1237.

Rice, M., & Wijekumar, K. K. (2024). Inference skills for reading: A meta-analysis of instructional practices. *Journal of Educational Psychology, 116*(4), 569–589.

Rocha, R. S., Castro S. L., Limpo T. (2022). The role of transcription and executive functions in writing: A longitudinal study in the transition from primary to intermediate grades. *Reading and Writing, 35,* 1911–1932.

Rocha, R. S., Soeiro, I., Magalhães, S., Castro, S. & Limpo, T. (2024). Effects of SRSD writing interventions in grade 3: examining the added value of attention vs. transcription training components. *Reading and Writing, 37,* 1457–1487.

Rodríguez, C., Jiménez, J. E., & Balade, J. (2024). The impact of oral language and transcription skills on early writing production in kindergarteners: Productivity and quality. *Early Childhood Education Journal, 53*(4), 1–11.

Romberg, A. R., & Saffran, J. R. (2010). Statistical learning and language acquisition. Wiley Interdisciplinary Reviews. *Cognitive Science, 1*(6), 906–914.

Roussey, J.-Y., & Piolat, A. (2008). Critical reading effort during text revision. *European Journal of Cognitive Psychology, 20*(4), 765–792.

Rowe, D. W., Piestrzynski, L., Hadd, A. R., & Reiter, J. W. (2024). Writing as a path to the alphabetic principle: How preschoolers learn that their own writing represents speech. *Reading Research Quarterly, 59*(1), 32–56.

Ruffini, C., Osmani F., Martini, C., Giera, W., & Pecini, C. (2024). The relationship between executive functions and writing in children: a systematic review. *Child Neuropsychology, 30*(1), 105–163.

Saddler, B., & Graham, S. (2005). The effects of peer-assisted sentence-combining instruction on the writing performance of more and less skilled young writers. *Journal of Educational Psychology, 97*(1), 43–54.

Sadler, D. R. (2009). Transforming holistic assessment and grading into a vehicle for complex learning. In G. Joughin (Ed.), *Assessment, learning and judgement in higher education* (pp. 45–63). Springer Science+Business Media.

Salas, N., & Silvente, S. (2019). The role of executive functions and transcription skills in writing: a cross-sectional study across 7 years of schooling. *Reading and Writing 33,* 877–905.

Sanchez, C. E., Atkinson, K. M., Koenka, A. C., Moshontz, H., & Cooper, H. (2017). Self-grading and peer-grading for formative and summative assessments in 3rd through 12th grade classrooms: A meta-analysis. *Journal of Educational Psychology, 109*(8), 1049–1066.

Sanders, E. A., Berninger, V. W., & Abbott, R. D. (2018). Sequential prediction of literacy achievement for specific learning disabilities contrasting in impaired levels of language in grades 4 to 9. *Journal of Learning Disabilities, 51*(2), 137–157.

Santangelo, T., & Graham, S. (2016). A comprehensive meta-analysis of handwriting instruction. *Educational Psychology Review, 28*(2), 225–265.

Sarmiento, C. M., Truckenmiller, A. J., Cho, E., & Wang, H. (2024). Academic language use in middle school informational writing. *British Journal of Educational Psychology.*

Scardamalia, M., & Bereiter, C. (1987). Knowledge telling and knowledge transforming in written composition. In S. Rosenberg (Ed.), *Advances in applied psycholinguistics: Reading, writing, and language learning* (Vol. 2, pp. 142–175). Cambridge University Press.

Schillings, M., Roebertsen, H., Savelberg, H., Whittingham, J., & Dolmans, D. (2019). Peer-to-peer dialogue about teachers' written feedback enhances students' understanding on how to improve writing skills. *Educational Studies, 46*(6), 693–707.

Schrodt, K., FitzPatrick, E., Lee, S., McKeown, D., McColloch, A., & Evert, K. (2024). The effects of invented spelling instruction on literacy achievement and writing motivation. *Education Sciences, 14*(9), 1020.

Schunk, D. H. (1986). Verbalization and children's self-regulated learning. *Contemporary Educational Psychology, 11*(4), 347–369.

Schunk, D. H. (1987). Peer models and children's behavioral change. *Review of Educational Research, 57*(2), 149–174.

Schunk, D. H., & Swartz, C. W. (1993). Goals and progress feedback: Effects on self-efficacy and writing achievement. *Contemporary Educational Psychology, 18*(3), 337–354.

Schwartz, S. (2024, November 5). Which states have passed 'Science of Reading' laws?: What's in them? *Education Week.* https://www.edweek.org/teaching-learning/which-states-have-passed-science-of-reading-laws-whats-in-them/2022/07.

Scruggs, T. E., & Mastropieri, M. A. (2000). The effectiveness of mnemonic instruction for students with learning and behavior problems: An update and research synthesis. *Journal of Behavioral Education, 10*(2–3), 163–173.

Sedova, K., Sedlacek, M., Svaricek, R., Majcik, M., Navratilova, J., Drexlerova, A., et al. (2019). Do those who talk more learn more?: The relationship between student classroom talk and student achievement. *Learning and Instruction, 63,* 101217.

Seidenberg, M. (2017). *Language at the speed of sight: How we read, why so many can't, and what can be done about it.* Basic Books.

Sénéchal, M., Ouellette, G., Pagan, S., & Lever, R. (2012). The role of invented spelling on learning to read in low-phoneme awareness kindergartners: A randomized-control-trial study. *Reading and Writing, 25*(4), 917–934.

Shanahan, E., Reno, E., Chandler, B., Novelli, C., An, J., Choi S. & McMaster, K. (2024). Effects of writing instruction on the reading outcomes of students with literacy difficulties in pre-kindergarten to fifth grade: a meta-analysis. *Reading and Writing, 38*(3), 627–650.

Shen, M. & Troia, G. A. (2017). Relationship between reading motivation, reading activity, oral language, and reading achievement in children with attention-deficit/hyperactivity disorder. *International Journal of Special Education, 32*(1), 134–179.

Shields, G. S., Sazma, M. A., & Yonelinas, A. P. (2016). The effects of acute stress on core executive functions: A meta-analysis and comparison with cortisol. *Neuroscience and Biobehavioral Reviews, 68,* 651–668.

Siegal, S. (2023, November 3). Dr. Carol Connor's research legacy (or, How I learned the importance of individualized literacy instruction) [Podcast episode]. In *Lunch & Lit.* Right to Read Project. https://righttoreadproject.com/lunch-lit.

Snow, C. (1983). Literacy and language: Relationships during the preschool years. *Harvard Educational Review, 53(*2), 165–189.

Solow, K. (2018). Using children's books to build empathy in children [Master's thesis]. *Expressive Therapies Capstone Theses, 28.*

Soto, E. F., Irwin, L. N., Chan, E. S. M., Spiegel, J. A., & Kofler, M. J. (2021). Executive functions and writing skills in children with and without ADHD. *Neuropsychology, 35*(8), 792–808.

Spiegel, J. A., Goodrich, J. M., Morris, B. M., Osborne, C. M., & Lonigan, C. J. (2021). Relations between executive functions and academic outcomes in elementary school children: A meta-analysis. *Psychological Bulletin, 147(*4), 329–351.

St Clair-Thompson, H. L., & Gathercole, S. E. (2006). Executive functions and achievements in school: Shifting, updating, inhibition, and working memory. *Quarterly Journal of Experimental Psychology, 59*(4), 745–759.

Stievano, P., Michetti, S., McClintock, S. M., Levi, G., & Scalisi, M. G. (2016). Handwriting fluency and visuospatial generativity at primary school. *Reading and Writing, 29*(7), 1497–1510.

Strong, J. Z. (2020). Investigating a text structure intervention for reading and writing in grades 4 and 5. *Reading Research Quarterly, 55*(4), 545–551.

Svensson, B. (2018). Theory of mind development and narrative writing: A longitudinal study. *Australian Journal of Applied Linguistics, 1*(3), 118–134.

Swain, N. (2024). *Harnessing the science of learning.* Routledge.

Swanson H. L., & Berninger V. W. (1996). Individual differences in children's working memory and writing skill. *Journal of Experimental Child Psychology, 63*(2), 358–385.

Tamnes, C. K., Overbye, K., Ferschmann, L., Fjell, A. M., Walhovd, K. B., Blakemore, S. J., & Dumontheil, I. (2018). Social perspective taking is associated with self-reported prosocial behavior and regional cortical thickness across adolescence. *Developmental Psychology, 54*(9), 1745–1757.

Thierry, K., Vincent, R., & Norris, K. (2022). A mindfulness-based curriculum improves young children's relationship skills and social awareness. *Mindfulness, 13*(3), 730–741.

Tindle, R., & Longstaff, M. G. (2015). Writing, reading, and listening differentially overload working memory performance across the serial position curve. *Advances in Cognitive Psychology, 11*(4), 147–155.

Tindle, R., & Longstaff, M. G. (2023). Working memory and handwriting share a common resource: An investigation of shared attention. *Current Psychology, 42*(6), 3945–3956.

Tomasello, M. (2003). *Constructing a language: A usage-based theory of language acquisition.* Harvard University Press.

Tompkins, V. (2022). Relations between the home literacy environment and young children's theory of mind. *Cognitive Development, 62*, 1–18.

Topping, K. J. (2009). Peer assessment. *Theory Into Practice, 48*(1), 20–27.

Traga Philippakos, Z. A. (2021). Think aloud modeling: Expert and coping models in writing instruction and literacy pedagogy. *Language and Literacy Spectrum, 31*(1), Article 1.

Trautwein, F.-M., Kanske, P., Böckler, A., & Singer, T. (2020). Differential benefits of mental training types for attention, compassion, and theory of mind. *Cognition, 194,* 104039.

Troia, G. A., Brehmer, J. S., Glause, K., Reichmuth, H. L., & Lawrence, F. (2020). Direct and indirect effects of literacy skills and writing fluency on writing quality across three genres. *Education Sciences, 10*(11), 297.

Truckenmiller, A. J. (2024, March). *Innovations in CBM-WE: The writing architect.* Session presented at the annual conference of the Council for Exceptional Children.

Truckenmiller, A., & Chandler, B. (2023). Writing to read: Parallel and independent contributions of writing research to the science of reading. *Reading League Journal, 4*(1), 5–11.

Truckenmiller, A. J., Cho, E., & Troia, G. A. (2022). Expanding assessment to instructionally relevant writing components in middle school. *Journal of School Psychology, 94*(1), 28–48.

Vadasy, P. F., & Sanders, E. A. (2021). Introducing grapheme-phoneme correspondences (GPCs): Exploring rate and complexity in phonics instruction for kindergarteners with limited literacy skills. *Reading and Writing, 34*(1), 109–138.

Vadasy, P. F., Sanders. E. A., & Cartwright, K. B. (2022). Cognitive flexibility in beginning decoding and encoding. *Journal of Education for Students Placed at Risk, 28*(4), 412–438.

Valcan, D., Malpique, A., Pino-Pasternak, D., Asil, M., & Teo, T. (2024). The contributions of executive functioning to handwritten and keyboarded compositions in year 2 children. *Contemporary Educational Psychology, 77*,102272.

Valiandes, S. (2015). Evaluating the impact of differentiated instruction on literacy and reading in mixed ability classrooms: Quality and equity dimensions of education effectiveness. *Studies in Educational Evaluation, 45,* 17–26.

Vander Hart, N., & Power, M. (2021). Teaching writing strategies with tiered supports for middle school students with and without special needs: a case study. *Preventing School Failure: Alternative Education for Children and Youth, 66*(2), 167–174.

Van der Weel, F. R., & Van der Meer, A. L. H. (2024). Handwriting but not typewriting leads to widespread brain connectivity: A high-density EEG study with implications for the classroom. *Frontiers in Psychology, 14*, 1219945.

Vanderberg, R., & Swanson, H. L. (2007). Which components of working memory are important in the writing process? *Reading and Writing, 20*(7), 721–752.

Vaughn, S., Gersten, R., Dimino, J., Taylor, M. J., Newman-Gonchar, R., Krowka, S., et al. (2022). *Providing reading interventions for students in grades 4–9* (WWC 2022007). National Center for Education Evaluation and Regional Assistance, Institute of Education Sciences, U.S. Department of Education. https://files.eric.ed.gov/fulltext/ED617876.pdf.

Vaughn, S., Hughes, M. T., Moody, S. W., & Elbaum, B. (2001). Instructional grouping for reading for students with LD: Implications for practice. *Intervention in School and Clinic, 36*(3), 131–137.

Vieira, A. I., Magalhães, S., & Limpo, T. (2023). Relating transcription, executive functions and text quality in Grades 2–3: A cross-lagged panel analysis. *British Journal of Educational Psychology, 93*(2), 482–499.

Wade, M., Prime, H., Jenkins, J. M., Yeates, K. O., Williams, T., & Lee, K. (2018). On the relation between theory of mind and executive functioning: A developmental cognitive neuroscience perspective. *Psychonomic Bulletin and Review, 25*(6), 2119–2140.

Wagner, R., Puranik, C., Foorman, B., Foster, E., Gehron Wilson, L., Tschinkel, E., & Thatcher Kantor, P. (2011). Modeling the development of written language. *Reading and Writing, 24*(2), 203–220.

Wallis, P., Richards, T., Boord, P., Abbott, R., & Berninger, V. (2017). Relationships between translation and transcription processes during fMRI connectivity scanning and coded translation and transcription in writing products after scanning in children with and without transcription disabilities. *Creative Education, 8*(5), 716–748.

Wanzek, J., Gatlin, B., Al Otaiba, S., & Kim, Y.-S.-G. (2017). The impact of transcription writing interventions for first grade students. *Reading and Writing Quarterly: Overcoming Learning Difficulties, 33*(5), 484–499.

Weimer, A. A., Warnell, K. R., Ettekal, I., Cartwright, K. B., Guajardo, N. R., & Liew, J. (2021). Correlates and antecedents of theory of mind development during middle childhood and adolescence: An integrated model. *Developmental Review, 59*, 100945.

Weintraub, N., Yinon, M., Hirsch, I. B.-E., & Parush, S. (2009). Effectiveness of sensorimotor and task-oriented handwriting intervention in elementary school-aged students with handwriting difficulties. *Occupational Therapy Journal of Research, 29*(3), 125–134.

White, K. M. (2013). Associations between teacher–child relationships and children's writing in kindergarten and first grade. *Early Childhood Research Quarterly, 28*(1), 166–176.

Wijekumar, K., Meyer, B. J. F., & Lei, P. (2017). Web-based text structure strategy instruction improves seventh graders' content area reading comprehension. *Journal of Educational Psychology, 109*(6), 741–760.

Wineburg, S. S. (1991). Historical problem solving: A study of the cognitive processes used in the evaluation of documentary and pictorial evidence. *Journal of Educational Psychology, 83*(1), 73–87.

Wissinger, D. R., De La Paz, S., & Jackson, C. (2021). The effects of historical reading and writing strategy instruction with fourth-through sixth-grade students. *Journal of Educational Psychology, 113(*1), 49–67.

Wolf, B., Abbott, R. D., & Berninger, V. W. (2017). Effective beginning handwriting instruction: Multi-modal, consistent format for two years, and linked to spelling and composing. *Reading and Writing, 30*(2), 299–317.

Wollman-Bonilla, J. E. (2001). Can first-grade writers demonstrate audience awareness? *Reading Research Quarterly, 36*(2), 184–201.

Worden, D. L. (2009). Finding process in product: Prewriting and revision in timed essay responses. *Assessing Writing, 14*(3), 157–177.

Wu, Y., & Schunn, C. D. (2021). The effects of providing and receiving peer feedback on writing performance and learning of secondary school students. *American Educational Research Journal, 58*(3), 492–526.

Zelazo, P., & Carlson, S. (2012). Hot and cool executive function in childhood and adolescence: Development and plasticity. *Child Development Perspectives, 6*(4), 354–360.

Zhou, Q., Chen, S. H., & Main, A. (2012). Commonalities and differences in the research on children's effortful control and executive function: A call for an integrated model of self-regulation. *Child Development Perspectives, 6*(2), 112–121.

Zimmerman, B. J., & Risemberg, R. (1997). Becoming a self-regulated writer: A social cognitive perspective. *Contemporary Educational Psychology, 22*(1), 73–101.

Zwicker, J. G., & Hadwin, A. F. (2009). Cognitive versus multisensory approaches to handwriting intervention: A randomized controlled trial. *Occupational Therapy Journal of Research, 29*(1), 40–48.

Index

Note. *f* or *t* following a page number indicates a figure or a table